A GUIDE TO OLD ENGLISH

A GUIDE
TO OLD ENGLISH

by Bruce Mitchell
Fellow of St. Edmund Hall, Oxford
(sometime Scholar of the Australian National University)

OXFORD
BASIL BLACKWELL
1968

Printed in Great Britain by
Robert Cunningham and Sons Ltd.
Alva, Scotland

FOREWORD

The Guide aims at making easier the initial steps in the learning of Old English. It is intended for beginners and will, it is hoped, prove especially useful to those wishing to acquire a reading knowledge of the language. But potential specialists in philology should find it a help in their preliminary studies of the essential grammar. The Guide contains no texts, but can be used with any existing primer or reader by students working with or without a teacher; for the latter, a section on 'How to Use this Guide' has been provided.

In general, the Guide devotes more space than is usual to the simple explanation of difficult points and to ways of reducing rote learning and of solving problems which arise for the reader of Old English texts. It is divided into seven sections—Preliminary Remarks on the Language, a simple treatment of Orthography and Pronunciation, Inflexions, Word Formation, Syntax (where stress is laid on the important differences between Old and Modern English), a brief Introduction to Anglo-Saxon Studies in which language and literature, history, and archaeology, are discussed, and a highly selective Bibliography for the beginner. There is no section on Phonology. But important sound-changes are treated briefly when they provide the accepted explanation of apparent irregularities in inflexion. Those who want a full treatment of sound-changes and accidence are recommended to A. Campbell's *Old English Grammar*; see §254 of this book. But the Guide aims at being self-contained, as far as it goes.

Acknowledgements are due—and are made gratefully—to Vera Jennings, Dorothy Coldicutt, and T. P. Dobson, all of Melbourne, who 'first taught my tottering feet to lisp Anglo-Saxon'; to Professor A. D. Hope of Canberra; to my teachers at Oxford, especially Professor J. R. R. Tolkien, Professor C. L. Wrenn, Professor A. Campbell, and Professor G. V. Smithers (now of the University of Durham); to my colleagues at St. Edmund Hall, especially R. E. Alton, the Rev. H. E. J. Cowdrey, and the Rev. E. G. Midgley; to Professor Grahame Johnston of Melbourne; to Professor T. P. Dunning, C.M., of University College, Dublin, for advice and valued encouragement; to Professor Simeon Potter of Liverpool, who read the first draft and suggested the addition of Chapter VI; to A. J. Bliss of University College, Dublin, for invaluable criticism of the drafts and for most generous help with the proofs; to Douglas Gray of Pembroke College, Oxford; to Dr. R. Harris of Magdalen College,

Oxford; to H. L. Schollick of Basil Blackwell, Publisher, Oxford; to the printers; to those of my pupils who acted as guinea-pigs while the Guide was taking shape; and to my wife.

Thanks are also gratefully extended to the authors of books from which I have quoted or to which I have referred. The diagrams in §§29 and 31 are based on those in *The Principles of the International Phonetic Association*. The sections on archaeology, in particular, make no claim to originality, and I hope that my avowed purpose of providing an introductory guide for the beginner will serve to excuse the liberties I have taken with the work of others. A section of this Guide has been reprinted in *The Batile of Maldon and Other Old English Poems* translated by Kevin Crossley-Holland, edited by Bruce Mitchell, and published by Macmillan and Co., Ltd.; thanks are due to both publishers for permission to do this.

Those familiar with three Oxford books—Henry Sweet's *Anglo-Saxon Primer* revised by Norman Davis, Henry Sweet's *Anglo-Saxon Reader* revised by C. T. Onions, and A. Campbell's *Old English Grammar*—will perceive perhaps even more readily than I do the enormity of my debt to them. They have been my almost daily companions in the class-room and study, and it is not too much to say that without them this book would probably never have appeared. They have so influenced my teaching and my thinking that echoes of them cannot fail to appear in my work. While hoping that the echoes are not so strong that they deafen my own voice completely, I acknowledge my debt to them humbly, gratefully, and sincerely.

I shall welcome any criticisms, corrections, or suggestions, on fact or lay-out, which any reader cares to send me.

BRUCE MITCHELL

Michaelmas 1964

FOREWORD TO SECOND EDITION

I warmly thank reviewers, colleagues, and pupils, for suggestions and criticisms. I have incorporated many—and so improved the book. Limitations of space forbade the inclusion of some. Others I could not accept. I am especially grateful to Professors Dorothy Whitelock of Cambridge, G. W. K. Johnston of the Royal Military College, Duntroon, F. C. Robinson of Stanford University, and G. H. Russell of the Australian National University, and to Messrs. T. P. Dobson of the University of Melbourne and E. P. Wilson of St. Edmund Hall.

One reviewer observed that the book seemed to be 'written for someone rather slow of understanding'. I am desperately sorry if **anyone trying to learn Old English from it** has felt that. I can only say that the *Guide* is (as far as I could make it) the book I should like to have had when I started Old English.

BRUCE MITCHELL

St. Valentine's Day 1968

P.S. Just as this second edition was going to press, I received by courtesy of Dr. Elisabeth Okasha and her pupils at King's College, University of Aberdeen, some very valuable suggestions based on practical experience with, and tutorial discussion of, the *Guide*. The publisher and printer have kindly allowed me to make some late alterations which attempt to incorporate these suggestions. I am immensely grateful to all concerned, and offer my sincere thanks.

BRUCE MITCHELL

4 July 1968

CONTENTS

FOREWORD   vii

ABBREVIATIONS AND SYMBOLS   xvi

HOW TO USE THIS GUIDE   1

I PRELIMINARY REMARKS ON THE LANGUAGE (§§1-4)   9

II ORTHOGRAPHY AND PRONUNCIATION (§§5-9)   11

    i Orthography (§5)   11
    ii Stress (§6)   11
    iii Vowels (§7)   11
    iv Diphthongs (§8)   12
    v Consonants (§9)   13

III INFLEXIONS (§§10-135)   14

    Introduction (§§10-14)   14

    i Pronouns (§§15-21)   15
    ii Nouns and Sound-Changes relevant to them (§§22-62)   16
      Weak Nouns (§§22-25)   16
      Some Technical Terms (§§26-32)   17
      Strong Nouns like *stān* (masc.) and *scip* (neut.) (§§33-44)   19
      Masculine and Neuter Nouns in -*e* (§§45-46)   23
      Strong Feminine Nouns (§§47-51)   24
      i-Mutation (§§52-57)   25
      Nouns affected by *i*-Mutation (§§58-60)   26
      u-Nouns (§§61-62)   27

    iii Adjectives (§§63-76)   28
      Introduction (§§63-64)   28
      Weak Declension (§65)   28
      Strong Declension (§§66-67)   28
      Stem Changes in Adjectives (§§68-73)   29
      Comparison of Adjectives (§§74-76)   30

    iv Observations on Noun, Adjective, and Pronoun Declensions (§§77-81)   31

    v Numerals (§§82-86)   31

    vi Strong Verbs and Sound-Changes relevant to them (§§87-114)   32
      Introduction (§§87-89)   32
      Principal Parts of the Strong Verbs (§§90-95)   33

Breaking (§§96-99)   35
Influence of initial ġ, sc, ċ (§100)   36
Influence of Nasals (§101)   37
Summary of the Strong Verbs of Class III (§102)   37
The Effects of Sound-Changes on other Strong Verbs
  (§103)   37
Strong Verbs of Class VII (§104)   38
Grimm's Law and Verner's Law (§§105-109)   38
Conjugation of the Strong Verb (§§110-114)   40

vii Weak Verbs and Sound-Changes relevant to them
  (§§115-126)   43
Introduction (§115)   43
Class 1 (§§116-123)   43
Class 2 (§§124-125)   47
Class 3 (§126)   47

viii Other Verbs (§§127-130)   48
Bēon (§127)   48
Dōn and gān (§128)   48
Willan (§129)   49
Preterite-Present Verbs (§130)   49

ix Is a verb strong or weak? To which class does it
  belong? (§§131-134)   49

x Adverbs (§135)   51
Formation (§135)   51
Comparison (§135)   51

IV WORD FORMATION (§§136-138)   52
Introduction (§136)   52
Compounding (§137)   53
The Addition of Affixes (§138)   54

V SYNTAX (§§139-214)   58
Introduction (§§139-142)   58
i Word-Order (§§143-147)   60
ii Sentence Structure (§§148-153)   63
Recapitulation and Anticipation (§148)   63
The Splitting of Heavy Groups (§149)   64
Correlation (§§150-153)   65

iii Noun Clauses (§§154-161)   68
Introduction (§154)   68
Dependent Statements and Desires (§§155-156)   68
Dependent Questions (§§157-160)   70
The Accusative and Infinitive (§161)   73

Contents

iv Adjective Clauses (§§162-165) 73
Definite Adjective Clauses (§§162-163) 73
Indefinite Adjective Clauses (§164) 77
Mood (§165) 78

v Adverb Clauses (§§166-181) 79
Introduction (§§166-167) 79
Non-Prepositional Conjunctions (§168) 82
Prepositional Conjunctions (§§169-171) 87
An Exercise in Analysis (§172) 90
Clauses of Place (§173) 91
Clauses of Time (§174) 92
Clauses of Purpose and Result (§175) 93
Causal Clauses (§176) 94
Clauses of Comparison (§177) 95
Clauses of Concession (§178) 95
Clauses of Condition (§179) 96
Adverb Clauses Expressing Other Relationships (§180) 98
Other Ways of Expressing Adverbial Relationships
(§181) 98

vi Parataxis (§§182-186) 99
Introduction (§§182-183) 99
List of Conjunctions and Adverbs commonly used
(§184) 100
Parataxis without Conjunctions (§185) 101
Some Special Idioms (§186) 102

vii Concord (§187) 102

viii The Uses of the Cases (§§188-192) 104
Nominative (§188) 104
Accusative (§189) 104
Genitive (§190) 104
Dative (§191) 105
Instrumental (§192) 105

ix Articles, Pronouns, and Numerals (§§193-194) 105
Articles and Pronouns (§193) 105
Numerals (§194) 107

x Verbs (§§195-212) 107
The Uses of the Present and Preterite Tenses (§§195-
198) 107
The Resolved Tenses (§§199-204) 109
Introduction (§199) 109
The Verb 'to have' as an Auxiliary (§200) 109
The Verb 'to be' as an Auxiliary of Tense (§201) 110
The Passive (§§202-203) 110
Other Uses of the Present and Past Participles
(§204) 111

The Uses of the Infinitives (§205)   111
The 'Modal' Auxiliaries (§§206-211)   112
    Introduction (§206)   112
    Magan (§207)   113
    Mōtan (§208)   114
    Cunnan (§209)   114
    Sculan (§210)   114
    Willan (§211)   115
Impersonal Verbs (§212)   115

  xi Prepositions (§§213-214)   115

VI AN INTRODUCTION TO ANGLO-SAXON STUDIES (§§215-
    251)   118

    i Some Significant Dates (§§215-216)   118
    ii History (§§217-218)   118
    iii Archaeology (§§219-230)   124
        Introduction (§219)   124
        List of Abbreviated Titles (§220)   125
        Weapons and Warfare (§221)   126
        Life and Dress (§222)   127
        Architecture and Buildings (§§223-224)   127
        Sculpture and Carving (§225)   129
        Jewellery and Metal-Work (§226)   129
        Embroidery (§227)   130
        Coins (§228)   130
        Manuscripts and Runic Inscriptions (§229)   130
        The Sutton Hoo Ship-Burial (§230)   130

    iv Language (§§231-235)   131
        Changes in English (§231)   131
        The Danish Invasions (§232)   132
        The Norman Conquest (§233)   132
        Vocabulary (§234)   133
        Some Questions (§235)   134

    v Literature (§§236-251)   134
        Introduction (§§236-246)   134
        Poetry (§§247-249)   140
        Prose (§§250-251)   141

VII SELECT BIBLIOGRAPHY (§§252-268)   143
    General (§252)   143
    I Preliminary Remarks on the Language (§253)   143
    II Orthography and Pronunciation and III Inflexions
       (§254)   144
    IV Word Formation (§255)   144

V Syntax (§256)   144

VI Introduction to Anglo-Saxon Studies (§§257-268)   145
   History (§257)   145
   Archaeology (§258)   145
   Language (§§259-261)   145
      History of English Prose (§259)   145
      Vocabulary (§§260-261)   146
         Changes of Meaning (§260)   146
         Borrowings (§261)   146
   Literature (§§262-268)   146
      Topics raised in §§236-246 (§262) 146
      General Criticism (§263)   146
      Poetry Texts (§264)   147
      Appreciation of the Poetry (§265) 147
      The Use of Oral Formulae (§266)   148
      Metre (§267)   148
      Prose Texts (§268)   149

APPENDIX A   Strong Verbs   150
APPENDIX B   Christian Influence in Old English Litera-
        ture: A Supplementary Note   157

INDEX OF SUBJECTS   159

INDEX OF WORDS   163

ABBREVIATIONS AND SYMBOLS

LANGUAGES AND DIALECTS

Gmc.	Germanic	nWS	non-West-Saxon
IE	Indo-European	OE	Old English
Lat.	Latin	OHG	Old High German
ME	Middle English	WS	West-Saxon
MnE	Modern English		

Before the name of a language or dialect

e = Early   l = Late   Pr = Primitive

GRAMMATICAL TERMS

acc.	accusative	nom.	nominative
adj.	adjective	pass.	passive
adv.	adverb	p.d.	see § 100
conj.	conjunction	pers.	person
cons.	consonant	pl.	plural
dat.	dative	poss.	possessive
dem.	demonstrative	prep.	preposition
fem.	feminine	pres.	present
gen.	genitive	pret.	preterite
imp.	imperative	pret.-pres.	preterite-present
ind.	indicative	pron.	pronoun
inf.	infinitive	ptc.	participle
infl.	inflected	sg.	singular
inst.	instrumental	st.	strong
masc.	masculine	subj.	subjunctive
neut.	neuter	wk.	weak

's' may be added where appropriate to form a plural.

SYMBOLS

>   became

<   came from

*   This precedes a form which is not recorded. Usually it is a form which probably once existed and which scholars reconstruct to explain the stages in sound-changes; see § 103.3.

     Sometimes it is a form which certainly never existed but which is invented to show that one sound-change preceded another. An example is *ċierfan* in § 100, note.

—   over a letter denotes a long vowel or diphthong.

˘   over a letter denotes a short vowel or diphthong.

e̮   as for example in § 100 means 'short and long e'.

— ˘   in § 41 denote a long and short syllable respectively.

´ ˴ ×   denote respectively a syllable carrying full, secondary, or no, stress.

xvi

HOW TO USE THIS GUIDE

This section is particularly addressed to those of you who are working without a teacher. I hope that when you have finished with this book you will not disagree too strongly—as far as elementary Old English grammar is concerned, at any rate—with the pithy observations made by Dr. Johnson to Boswell in 1766:

> People have now-a-days, said he, got a strange opinion that everything should be taught by lectures. Now, I cannot see that lectures can do so much good as reading the books from which the lectures are taken. I know nothing that can be best taught by lectures, except where experiments are to be shown. You may teach chemistry by lectures.—You might teach making of shoes by lectures!

THE IMPORTANCE OF READING AND PARSING

Those working by themselves will have to choose one or more of the primers or readers mentioned below, for reading of texts and learning of grammar must go hand-in-hand. The ability to recognize forms in the texts you are reading and an awareness of the basic structure of Old English are far more important than a parrot knowledge of the paradigms. Hence, from the beginning, you must get into the habit of analysing and thoroughly understanding each form you meet in your texts. Here you will find 'parsing' a great help. Since this word is taboo in many places, it had better be explained if it is to be used here.

All it means, of course, is recognizing what part of speech the word is—noun, pronoun, adjective, verb, and so on—and what particular form the word has in your sentence. The information needed is

Noun: Meaning, gender, number, case, and the reason for the case, e.g. accusative because it is object, genitive denoting possession, or dative of the indirect object.

Pronoun: As for noun. Here you need to know the noun to which the pronoun refers. (If it is a relative pronoun, see §162.)

Adjective: As for noun. Sometimes, of course, an adjective is used with a noun, sometimes it is used alone, either as a complement or where a noun is more usual, e.g. 'The good often die before their time'.

Verb: If you have the infinitive, you merely need the meaning. Otherwise you need to work out the person, number,

tense, and mood, and then deduce the infinitive. Unless
you are familiar with the verb, you will have to do all
this before you can find its meaning. For hints on how
to do it, see §134.

Adverbs and interjections (a name given to words like 'Oh!' 'Alas!'
and 'Lo!') will give little trouble. It is important to notice the case
of a word governed by a preposition, for a difference in case sometimes indicates a difference in meaning; see §§213-214. Conjunctions
are a greater source of difficulty. Lists of them are given in §§168,
171, and 184, and references to discussions on them are set out in
'Understanding the Syntax' below.

Note
    The importance of gender varies. Sometimes it is obvious, some-
times it is of no real importance. But at times it provides a vital
clue. Thus in *Hē ġehīerþ þās word and þā wyrcð, þās* and *þā* could
be acc. sg. fem. or acc. pl. Only the fact that *word* is neuter will tell
us that we must translate 'He hears these words and does them'.

LENGTH MARKS

Long vowels have been marked (‾) throughout, with the exception
noted below. A knowledge of the length of vowels (or 'quantity', as
it is called) is essential for the understanding of OE metre and for
the serious study of phonology. Hence, when you learn the inflexions,
you will need to remember both the form of the word and the length
of its vowels. You will almost certainly find that your reader will
mark the long vowels and you should take advantage of this by
noting carefully those which occur in both familiar and unfamiliar
words.

But since the length-marks are not shown in the Old English
MSS, many editions of prose and verse texts do not show them.
Examples are the standard editions of the Anglo-Saxon Chronicle
and of the Homilies of Ælfric and Wulfstan, the texts published by
Methuen (in their Old English Library) and by the Early English
Text Society, and *The Anglo-Saxon Poetic Records* (published by
Columbia University Press) which contain all the extant poetry.
You will have to use one or more of these works fairly early in your
career. In the hope that you will find the transition to such texts
easier if you have already seen short passages in the form in which
they appear in these works, I have not regularized the spelling (see
§3) or marked vowel-length in the illustrative quotations in chapters
V and VI. Most of the passages quoted are taken from texts which
appear in nearly all readers. You can use these passages by writing
them out, marking in the length-marks yourself, and then comparing

them with the correct version in your reader. You can check individual words in the glossary. But you will find it more interesting if you track down the context of the longer prose passages and those in verse with the help of the references in your glossary. By so doing, you will improve your knowledge of vowel quantity and widen your acquaintance with OE literature.

LEARNING THE INFLEXIONS

Those who want to test their knowledge of the paradigms and to try their hand at translating into Old English (a very useful way of learning the language, especially important since no-one speaks it today) will find A. S. Cook *Exercises in Old English* (Ginn, 1895) a useful book. There are second-hand copies about. *An English— Anglo-Saxon Vocabulary*, compiled by W. W. Skeat and printed for private distribution only by the Cambridge University Press in 1879, is a difficult book to find. But there may be a copy in your university or college library.

I suggest that those coming to this book without any knowledge of Old English learn the inflexions in the order set out below. But remember that texts must be read and an understanding of the syntax acquired at the same time. Hints on how to do this are given later in this section.

1. Read §§1-4.
2. Now work through §§5-9. Make sure that you can recognize the new letters æ þ and ð, and practise reading aloud one of the simple texts referred to below, following generally the natural stress of MnE.
3. Now read §§10-12.
4. The next step is to learn the paradigms in A below, in the order in which they are set out there.
5. (a) When you have learnt the pronouns, nouns, and adjectives, in A, you can see whether §§77-81 help or hinder you. Experience on this point differs.
   (b) When you have learnt the verbs in A, you should read §§131-134.
6. You can now turn to the paradigms referred to in B below. B contains what may be called the 'derived paradigms', i.e. those which can be derived from the paradigms set out in A when certain sound-changes are understood. The sound-changes are presented in the hope that they will make your work easier, not as an end in themselves. Thus, if you meet a word *hwatum* in your reading, you will not be able to find out its meaning

unless you know that it comes from an adjective *hwæt* 'active, bold'. You will know this only if you have read §70.

7. The paradigms in C are important ones of fairly frequent occurrence which need not be learnt all at once. When you come across one of them in your reading, you can consult the relevant section. In this way, you will absorb them as need arises.

A Key Paradigms

These paradigms must be known thoroughly. At this stage, concentrate on them alone; disregard anything else in these sections.

1. The pronouns set out in §§15-21. Note particularly §19. (The dual forms in §21 may be passed over at first.)
2. *Nama* (§22) and, after reading §§63-64, *tila* (§65).
3. Now read §§26-32.
4. *Stān* (§33), *scip/word* (§34), and *giefu/lār* (§§47-48).
5. The strong declension of the adjectives (§§66-67).
6. Now read §§14, 87-89, and 115.
7. *Fremman* (§§116-117) and *lufian* (§§124-125).
8. *Habban* (§126) and *bēon* (§127).
9. The principal parts of the strong verbs (§§90-95).
10. The conjugation of strong verbs (§§110-113).

B Derived Paradigms

The paradigms in this group may be derived from those in A as follows:

1. From *nama*, those in §§23-25.
2. From *stān*, *scip*, or *giefu*, those in §§35-44, 48-51, and 52-60. See now §13.
3. From *tila* and *til*, those in §§68-73.
4. From *fremman*, those in §§116-123.
5. From *lufian*, those in §§124-125.
6. From §§90-95, those in §§96-109.
7. From §§110-113, those in §114.

Note

Some nouns which often go like *stān*, *scip*, or *giefu*, once belonged to other declensions. As a result, they sometimes have unusual forms which may cause you difficulty in your reading. It might be just as well if you learnt to recognize these fairly early in your career. They include: *ćild* (§34), *hæleþ* and *mōnaþ* (§44), some nouns in *-e* (§§45-46), the feminine nouns discussed in §§49 and 51, the relationship nouns (§60), and the *u*-nouns (§§61-62).

C Other Paradigms

1. Other Strong Nouns (§§45-46 and 61-62).
2. Comparison of Adjectives (§§74-76).
3. Numerals (§§82-86).
4. Verbs
   (a) Class 3 weak verbs (§126).
   (b) *Dōn* and *gān* (§128).
   (c) *Willan* (§§129 and 211).
   (d) Preterite-present verbs (§§130 and 206-210).
5. Adverbs (§135).

LEARNING THE VOCABULARY

Many OE words are easily recognizable from their MnE counterparts, though sometimes the meaning may be different; see §4 and look up the word 'lewd' in the Oxford English Dictionary.

Other words differ in spelling and pronunciation as a result of changes in ME and MnE. The short vowels *e, i, o, u,* have remained relatively constant (see §7). But the long vowels and the diphthongs have sometimes changed considerably. Words with a long vowel in OE sometimes appear in MnE with the vowel doubled, e.g. *fēt* (masc. pl.) 'feet' and *dōm* (masc.) 'doom'. Sometimes, they have *-e* at the end, e.g. *līf* (neut.) 'life' and (with, in addition, one of the differences discussed below) *hām* (masc.) 'home' and *hūs* (neut.) 'house'.

Correspondences like the last two are more difficult to spot. Yet a knowledge of them is easily acquired and will save you much hard work. Thus, if you know that OE *ā* often appears in MnE as *oa*, you will not need to use your glossary to discover that *bār* (masc.) means 'boar', *bāt* (fem. or masc.) 'boat', *brād* 'broad', and *hār* 'hoar(y)'. Words like *āc* (fem.) 'oak', *hlāf* (masc.) 'loaf', and *hlāfas* (masc. pl.) 'loaves', will not present much more difficulty.

The table which follows will help you to recognize more of these correspondences. But it is not complete and the correspondences do not always apply. Thus OE *hāt* is MnE 'hot' and you may find it interesting to look up in a glossary or dictionary the four OE words spelt *ār* and see what has happened to them.

OE spelling	MnE spelling	Vowels	Consonants
fæt (neut.)	vat	æ = a	f = v
rǣdan	read	ǣ = ea	
dǣd (fem.)	deed	ǣ = ee	
hālig	holy	ā = o	
hām (masc.)	home	ā = o.e	
āc (fem.)	oak	ā = oa	c = k

OE spelling	MnE spelling	Vowels	Consonants
hlāf (masc.)	loaf		hl = l
ecg (fem.)	edge		cg = dge
dēman	deem	ē = ee	
frēosan	freeze		s = z
ċild (neut.)	child		ċ = ch
miht (fem.)	might		h = gh
scip (neut.)	ship		sc = sh
līf (neut.)	life	ī = i.e	
ġiellan	yell	ie = e	ġ = y
ġiefan	give	ie = i	ġ = g
dōm (masc.)	doom	ō = oo	
hūs (neut.)	house	ū = ou.e	
nū	now	ū = ow	
synn (fem.)	sin	y = i	

See §253 for a book which may help you to learn the vocabulary. The principles on which words were formed in OE are set out in §§136-138. Once you understand these, you will be able to deduce the meaning of some new words by their similarity to words you already know; see §136. For correspondences in endings, see §138.

UNDERSTANDING THE SYNTAX

The fundamental differences between the syntax of Old English and that of Modern English are set out in §§139-153. These, and §§182-183, should be studied as soon as you can read simple sentences with some degree of fluency and before you pass on to the connected passages of Old English recommended below. Other sections which should be read fairly soon are §§154-155, 157-158, and 160 (noun clauses and their conjunctions), §162 (relative pronouns), §§166-167 and §§169-170 (conjunctions introducing adverb clauses), §189 note, and §§195-199 (the uses of the tenses and the syntax of the resolved verb forms).

The remaining parts of the syntax should be used for reference when the need arises; note especially the topics mentioned in §§141-142 and the lists of conjunctions in §§168, 171, and 184. When you begin to feel some confidence, you can try the exercise in §172.

If at first you find these sections too long and complicated, you are advised to use one of the books cited in §256.

TEXTS TO READ

There is a lot to be said for starting with sentences such as those in Henry Sweet *First Steps in Anglo-Saxon* (Oxford, 1897) or in Henry Sweet *An Anglo-Saxon Primer* (Oxford, 8th edition or earlier).

Failing this, or after it, you could read portions of the Bible. The books by N. Davis and G. L. Brook cited in §256 contain selections, as do

A. S. Cook *First Book in Old English* (Ginn, 1894)
G. T. Flom *Introductory Old English Grammar and Reader*
(Heath, 1930)
M. Anderson and B. C. Williams *Old English Handbook*
(Cambridge, U.S.A., 1935).

It would now be appropriate to read §§215-218, 231-235, and 250-251, of this Guide, before moving on to some or all of the following prose texts:

Ælfric's *Colloquy*.
Selections from the Anglo-Saxon Chronicle, especially the annals
for 755, 871, and 893-897.
The story of the voyages of Ohthere and Wulfstan.
Selections from *Apollonius of Tyre*.
One of Ælfric's *Catholic Homilies* or *Lives of the Saints*.

The first two of these are available in separate editions in Methuen's Old English Library, by G. N. Garmonsway and A. H. Smith respectively. Readers which may prove useful include:

Henry Sweet *Anglo-Saxon Reader* revised by Dorothy Whitelock
(Oxford, 15th edition)
A. J. Wyatt *An Anglo-Saxon Reader* (Cambridge, 1919)
W. F. Bolton *An Old English Anthology* (Edward Arnold, 1963).

But most Old English readers, including some of those mentioned above, contain at least some of these texts.

After this, you could read §§236-249 and §267 of the Guide. Then tackle *The Battle of Maldon*, which appears in most readers and in an edition by E. V. Gordon in Methuen's Old English Library. Try reading parts of it aloud—not too quickly. From here, you can take your own path through the poetry, reading some of the shorter poems such as *The Battle of Finnsburh*, *The Battle of Brunanburh*, *Deor*, *The Ruin*, *The Wife's Lament*, *The Husband's Message*, *Genesis B*, and *The Dream of the Rood*. Finally, you could move to *Beowulf*.

The sections on archaeology (§§219-230) and the Select Bibliography (§§252-268) should be consulted when occasion arises. If you have difficulty in deciding which of the poems to read first, or if you want a translation or literary notes on them, you may find useful:

The Battle of Maldon and Other Old English Poems, translated by
Kevin Crossley-Holland, introduced by Bruce
Mitchell (Macmillan (London), St. Martin's Press
(New York), 1965).

It now remains for me to wish you success—and pleasure—in your studies. In 991, before the battle of Maldon, Byrhtnoth called across the cold waters of the river to his Danish foes:

> Nu eow is gerymed;   gað ricene to us,
> guman to guþe;   god ana wat
> hwa þære wælstowe   wealdan mote.
>
>   (*The Battle of Maldon*, ll. 93-95)

This can be paraphrased

> 'Now the way is clear for you; O warriors,
> hasten to the battle; God alone knows
> how things will turn out'.

It is my hope and wish that *your* efforts will prosper—*Wel þe þæs geweorces!*

I PRELIMINARY REMARKS
ON THE LANGUAGE

§1 Professor Campbell defines Old English as 'the vernacular Germanic language of Great Britain as it is recorded in manuscripts and inscriptions dating from before about 1100'. It is one of the Germanic group of the Indo-European family of languages. Those who are unfamiliar with this concept should read about it in one of the histories of the English language cited in the Bibliography.

§2 There are four dialects distinguishable in the extant monuments—Northumbrian, Mercian, Kentish, West-Saxon. The differences are apparent in the spelling; otherwise, of course, we should not know about them. After 900 West-Saxon was increasingly used as a standard written language. It is for this reason that, initially at any rate, you learn West-Saxon. But even here the spelling conventions were never as rigidly observed as they are in Great Britain or America today, where compositors, typists, and writers, in different parts of the country use the same spelling, no matter how different their pronunciations may be.

§3 Most OE primers therefore attempt to make things easier for the beginner by 'normalizing', i.e. regularizing, the spelling by eliminating all forms not belonging to the West-Saxon dialect. But difficulty arises because two stages can be distinguished—early West-Saxon (eWS), which is the language of the time of King Alfred (c. 900), and late West-Saxon (lWS), which is seen in the works of Ælfric (c. 1000). Professor Davis, in revising Sweet's *Anglo-Saxon Primer*, followed Sweet and used eWS as his basis. Quirk and Wrenn's *Old English Grammar*, however, normalizes on the basis of Ælfric's lWS. For the beginner, the most important difference is that eWS *ie* and *īe* appear in lWS texts as *y* and *ȳ*; this accounts for such differences as Sweet *ieldra*, *hīeran*, but Q. & W. *yldra*, *hȳran*. Another is that *ea* and *ēa* may be spelt *e* and *ē* in lWS (and sometimes in eWS) texts, e.g. *seah* and *scēap*, but *seh* and *scēp*. Since the other differences will scarcely trouble you and since there are some disadvantages in the use of lWS, the paradigms are given here in their eWS forms and the sound laws are discussed with eWS as the basis. Any important variations likely to cause difficulty—apart from those mentioned here—will be noted. Full lists of all dialectal variants will be found in the appropriate section of Campbell's *Old English Grammar*.

In the sections on syntax, the spelling of a standard edition has

9

generally been followed, though occasionally an unusual form has been silently regularized. This should ease the transition to non-normalized texts. For the real difficulty arises when the student leaves his primer and begins to read texts presented in the spelling of the MS(S), a practice which many editors adopt. The remarks made by Henry Sweet in the Preface to the Seventh Edition of his *Anglo-Saxon Reader* are still partly true: 'Of course, if a beginner attempts to cram up Old-English from this Reader without having mastered the Primer, the dialectal forms will cause him great irritation and waste of time; but that is no reason why I should double the bulk of the glossary by giving such regular variations as *heran*, *hieran*, *hyran*, *anda*, *onda* separate headings and cross-references'. He did, however, try to help by putting at the beginning of the glossary a list of the main variants. Thus he records that *y* must often be sought under *ie*, *i*, or *e*. It will certainly save you much annoyance and much time if you read the remarks at the head of the glossary in your own text-book to learn what practices your editor has adopted. You should do this before looking up a single word.

You should also note the editor's abbreviations. He will generally tell you the gender of a noun or the class of a verb, and this information is important. After all, you learn the paradigm *nama* (§22) or the principal parts of *scinan* (§93) so that you can recognize the number and case of similar nouns or the mood and tense of similar verbs. This is why the editor marks *guma* as a weak masculine noun and *drīfan* as a strong verb of Class I. You should take advantage of the help he gives you.

§4   As has been explained in the Foreword, this book, after a brief discussion of orthography and pronunciation, deals with accidence, word formation, and syntax (including word-order), and attempts simple explanations of those sound-changes which will help you to learn the inflexions. Other sound-changes, the metre of poetry, and semantics, are not discussed. It is important, however, to remember that many common words have changed their meaning. *Sellan* means 'to give', not just 'to give in exchange for money, to sell'. *Eorl* cannot always be translated 'earl' and *dēor* and *fugol* mean, not 'deer' and 'fowl', but 'any (wild) animal' and 'any bird' respectively. The Bibliography contains references to useful introductory discussions on all the topics not discussed in this book.

II ORTHOGRAPHY AND PRONUNCIATION

i ORTHOGRAPHY

§5 As a glance at the facsimile of any OE manuscript will show, the letters used by Anglo-Saxon scribes were sometimes very like and sometimes very unlike those used today, both in shape and function. Printers of Anglo-Saxon texts generally use the equivalent modern letter form. Hence the sounds [f] and [v] are both represented by *f*, and the sounds [s] and [z] by *s* because this is the usage of the scribes; on these and other differences in representing the consonants, see §9. On the value of *y*, which represents a vowel now lost, see §7.

The following symbols are not in use today: *æ* (ash), which represents the vowel in MnE 'hat', *þ* (thorn) and *ð* (eth), both of which represent MnE *th* as in 'cloth' and in 'clothe'. Capital *ð* is written *Ð*. To make the learning of paradigms as simple as possible, *þ* has been used throughout chapter III.

The early texts of the Methuen Old English Library used the runic 'wynn' *ƿ* instead of *w* and the OE letter *ȝ* for *g*. In the latest volumes, these have been discarded.

As is customary, the punctuation in quotations from OE is modern.

ii STRESS

§6 The stress usually falls on the first syllable, as in MnE, e.g. *mórgen* 'morning'. The prefix *ġe-* is always unaccented; hence *ġebídan* 'await'. Two main difficulties occur:

1. Prepositional prefixes, e.g. *for-*, *ofer-*, can be either accented (usually in nouns or adjectives, e.g. *fórwyrd* 'ruin') or unaccented (usually in verbs, e.g. *forwiernan* 'refúse').

2. Compound words in which both elements retain their full meaning, e.g. *sǽ-weall* 'sea-wall', have a secondary stress on the root syllable of the second element. There is some dispute about three-syllabled words with a long first syllable (see §26). Some say that *bindende* 'binding' and *timbrode* 'built' have a pattern like MnE 'árchàngĕls', not like 'hástĭlÿ'. But not everyone agrees.

iii VOWELS

§7 Short vowels must be distinguished from long vowels, which are marked (‾) in this book (except as noted above). Approximate

11

pronunciations of OE vowels for those working without a teacher are given as far as possible in terms of MnE words.

a as the first vowel in 'aha'
$\bar{a}$ as the second vowel in 'aha'
$æ$ as in 'mat'
$\bar{æ}$ as in 'has'[1]
e as in 'bet'
$\bar{e}$ approx. as in 'hate' [German *See*]
i as in 'tin'
$\bar{i}$ as in 'seen'
o as in 'hot'
$\bar{o}$ approx. as in 'goad' [German *so*]
u as in 'pull' [NOT 'hut']
$\bar{u}$ as in 'cool'
y as i, with lips in a whistling position [French *tu*]
$\bar{y}$ as $\bar{i}$, with lips in a whistling position [French *ruse*]

Vowels in unstressed syllables should be pronounced clearly. Failure to distinguish gen. sg. *eorles* from nom. acc. pl. *eorlas* is characteristic of ME, not of OE.

iv   DIPHTHONGS

§8   If you are not sure of the distinction between vowels and diphthongs, you should consult a simple manual of phonetics. It is important to realize that OE words such as *heall*, *hēold*, *hielt*, which contain diphthongs, are just as much monosyllables as MnE 'meat' and 'field' (in which two letters represent one vowel) or MnE 'fine' and 'base', which contain diphthongs. The diphthongs, with approximate pronunciations, are:

$$ea = æ + a$$
$$\bar{e}a = \bar{æ} + a$$
$$eo = e + o$$
$$\bar{e}o = \bar{e} + o$$
$$ie = i + e^{[2]}$$
$$\bar{i}e = \bar{i} + e$$

A short diphthong is equal in length to a short vowel, a long diphthong to a long vowel. But remember that, like the MnE word 'I',

---

[1] If you experiment, you will notice that the vowel in 'has' is longer than that in 'mat', though MnE [æ] is frequently described as a 'short vowel'.

[2] The original pronunciation of *ie* and *īe* is not known with any certainty. It is simplest and most convenient for our purposes to assume that they represented diphthongs as explained above. But by King Alfred's time *ie* was pronounced as a simple vowel (monophthong), probably a vowel somewhere between *i* and *e*; *ie* is often replaced by *i* or *y*, and unstressed *i* is often replaced by *ie*, as in *hiene* for *hine*. Probably *īe* had a similar sound.

they are diphthongs, not two distinct vowels such as we get in the *ea* of 'Leander'.

v CONSONANTS

§9 All consonants must be pronounced, e.g. *c* in *cnapa*, *g* in *gnæt*, *h* in *hlāf*, *r* in *þær*, and *w* in *writan* and *trēow*.

Double consonants must be pronounced. Thus *biden* and *biddan* differ as MnE 'bidden' and 'bad debt'.

Most of the consonants are pronounced in the same way as in MnE. The main exceptions are set out below.

The letters *s, f, þ* and *ð*, are pronounced voiced, i.e. like MnE *z, v*, and *th* in 'clothe', between vowels or other voiced sounds, e.g. *rīsan, hlāfas, papas*, and *hēafdes*. In other positions, including the beginning and end of words, they are voiceless, i.e. like MnE *s, f*, and *th* in 'cloth', e.g. *sittan, hlāf, pæþ*, and *oft*. This accounts for the different sounds in MnE 'path' but 'paths', 'loaf' but 'loaves', and the like.

At the beginning of a word ('initially') before a vowel, *h* is pronounced as in MnE 'hound'. Otherwise, it is like German *ch*.

Before *a, o, u*, and *y*, *c* is pronounced *k* and *g* is pronounced as in MnE 'good'. Before *e* and *i*, *c* is usually pronounced like *ch* in MnE 'child' and *g* like *y* in MnE 'yet'. In this book, the latter are printed *ċ* and *ġ* respectively, except in the examples quoted in chapters V and VI.

Between back vowels, *g* is pronounced like the *g* in German *sagen*. Those without a teacher can pronounce it as *w* in words like *dragan* and *boga*.

The combinations *sc* and *cg* are usually pronounced like MnE *sh* and *dge* respectively. Thus *scip* 'ship' and *ecg* 'edge' are pronounced the same in both OE and MnE.

Note

A more detailed account of the pronunciation of Old English will now be found in §§9-19 of *Old English Sound Changes for Beginners* by R. F. S. Hamer (Basil Blackwell, 1967).

III INFLEXIONS

Introduction

§10 Following (as most primers do) the conventional terminology, we distinguish in Old English the following parts of speech: nouns, adjectives, pronouns (including articles), verbs, adverbs, prepositions, conjunctions, and interjections.

§11 Like most inflected languages, OE distinguishes number, case, and gender, in nouns, pronouns, and adjectives. The numbers are singular and plural; a dual is found in the 1st and 2nd pers. pron. where, e.g. *wit* means 'we two', *ġit* 'you (ye) two'. The main cases are nominative, accusative, genitive, and dative, but in certain parts of the adjective and pronoun declensions an instrumental occurs; where it does not, the dative does its work.

§12 There are three genders—masculine, feminine, and neuter. Gender sometimes agrees with sex, e.g. *se mann* (masc.) 'the man', *sēo sweostor* (fem.) 'the sister', or with lack of it, e.g. *þæt scip* (neut.) 'the ship'. This is often called 'natural gender'. But grammatical gender is often opposed to sex, e.g. (with persons) *se wifmann* (masc.) 'the woman', *þæt wīf* (neut.) 'the woman', and (with inanimate objects) *se stān* (masc.) 'the stone', *sēo ġiefu* (fem.) 'the gift'. These opposing tendencies, which contribute to the later disappearance of grammatical gender in English, sometimes produce 'lack of concord'; see §187.2. Compounds follow the gender of the second element; hence *þæt wīf* (neut.) +*se mann* (masc.) = *se wifmann* (masc.).

§13 Generally, the gender of nouns must be learnt. The form of the demonstrative is the main clue (see §§16-17). The following nom. sg. endings, however, are significant:

Weak Masc. : *-a.*
Strong Masc. : *-dōm, -els*, agent nouns in *-end* and *-ere*, *-hād*, concrete nouns in *-ing* and *-ling*, *-scipe*.
Strong Fem. : *-nes(s)*, abstract nouns in *-ing/ung*, *-rǣden*, *-þo/þu.*
Strong Neut. : *-lāc.*

Notoriously ambiguous is the ending *-e*; see §77. On these endings, see further §§136-138.

§14 Verbs. The differences between strong and weak verbs and the system of conjugating the OE verb are described in §§87-89. New developments, many of them important for MnE, are outlined in §§199-203.

14

i PRONOUNS

§15 You are now ready to learn your first paradigms. The demonstrative *se* serves as a definite article. Both *se* 'that' and *þes* 'this' can be used with nouns, e.g. *se mann* 'the man', or as pronouns, e.g. *hē sorgaþ ymb þā* 'he is concerned about those (them)'.

§16 *se* 'the, that'

		Singular		Plural
	Masc.	Neut.	Fem.	All genders
Nom.	se	þæt	sēo, sīo	þā
Acc.	þone	þæt	þā	þā
Gen.	þæs	þæs	þǣre	þāra, þǣra
Dat.	þǣm, þām	þǣm, þām	þǣre	þǣm, þām
Inst.	þȳ, þon	þȳ, þon		

§17 *þes* 'this'

		Singular		Plural
	Masc.	Neut.	Fem.	All genders
Nom.	þes	þis	þēos	þās
Acc.	þisne	þis	þās	þās
Gen.	þisses	þisses	þisse	þissa
Dat.	þissum	þissum	þisse	þissum
Inst.	þȳs	þȳs		

§18 3rd Pers. Pron.

		Singular		Plural
	Masc.	Neut.	Fem.	All genders
Nom.	hē 'he'	hit 'it'	hēo, hīo 'she'	hīe, hī 'they'
Acc.	hine	hit	hīe, hī	hīe, hī
Gen.	his	his	hire	hira, hiera, hiora
Dat.	him	him	hire	him

§19 The following similarities in these declensions may be noted:

1. neut. gen. dat. inst. are the same as the corresponding masc. forms;
2. nom. and acc. neut. sg. are the same;
3. gen. and dat. fem. sg. are the same;
4. pl. is the same for all genders;
5. acc. fem. sg. is the same as nom. and acc. pl.

Note too the way in which the masc. and neut. sg., while agreeing with one another except in the nom. and acc., differ markedly in inflexion from the fem.

§20 *Hwā* is interrogative 'who?' or indefinite 'anyone, someone'. It is not a relative pronoun in OE; see §164.

	Masc. and Fem.	Neut.
Nom.	hwā	hwæt
Acc.	hwone	hwæt
Gen.	hwæs	hwæs
Dat.	hwǣm, hwām	hwǣm, hwām
Inst.	hwȳ	hwȳ, hwon

Note the similarities between *hwā* and *se*. The main difference, of course, is that the masc. and fem. of *hwā* are the same. This is easily understandable if we think of what *hwā* means.

§21   1st and 2nd Pers. Prons.

	Singular	Dual	Plural
Nom.	iċ 'I'	wit 'we two'	wē 'we'
Acc.	mē	unc	ūs
Gen.	mīn	uncer	ūre
Dat.	mē	unc	ūs

	Singular	Dual	Plural
Nom.	þū 'thou'	ġit 'you two'	ġē 'you'
Acc.	þē	inc	ēow
Gen.	þīn	incer	ēower
Dat.	þē	inc	ēow

The easiest way to learn these is to compare them with their MnE equivalents (the main differences are in pronunciation) and with one another.

ii   Nouns and Sound-Changes relevant to them

Weak Nouns

§22   The basic paradigm of the weak or *-an* nouns is *nama* 'name', the weak masc. noun:

	Singular	Plural
Nom.	nama	naman
Acc.	naman	naman
Gen.	naman	namena
Dat.	naman	namum

Notes
1. Any noun with the nom. sg. ending *-a* is weak masc.
2. All other cases have the ending *-an* except gen. pl. *-ena* and dat. pl. *-um*.

Once *nama* is known, the rest follows quite simply without learning further paradigms.

§23   The weak fem. noun *sunne* 'sun' is declined exactly as *nama* apart from the nom. sg.

§24 The weak neut. noun *ēage* 'eye' is declined exactly as *nama* except that, as in all neut. nouns, the nom. and acc. sg. are the same.

§25 Nouns with a nom. sg. ending in a long vowel or diphthong form their oblique cases by adding the consonant of the inflexional ending. So *ġefēa* (masc.) 'joy' has oblique cases *ġefēa/n* except for gen. pl. *ġefēa/na* and dat. pl. *ġefēa/m*.

Some Technical Terms

§26 You now need to know some phonological terms. 'Short vowel' as in MnE 'hit' and 'long vowel' as in the second syllable in MnE 'machine' will present no difficulty. The word *wer* 'man' has a short vowel and is a short syllable. The word *stān* 'stone' has a long vowel and is a long syllable. Such words as *cniht* 'young man' and *cræft* 'strength' have a short vowel. But, since the short vowel is followed by *two* consonants, the syllable is long; cf. the rules of Latin prosody. To summarize, we have:

short-stemmed monosyllables[1]	*wer, bæc*
long-stemmed monosyllables	*stān, cniht*
short-stemmed dissyllables	*miċel, yfel*
long-stemmed dissyllables	*ēþel, engel*

Forms like *metodes* and *bysiġe* are called 'trisyllabic' and the *o* or *i* is sometimes called the 'medial vowel'.

§27 It is also important to distinguish open and closed syllables. An open syllable ends in a vowel, e.g. *hē* 'he'; a closed syllable ends in a consonant, e.g. *stān* 'stone'. This is clear enough. But difficulty arises with dissyllables. You must take on trust that the gen. sg. *stānes* is divided *stā/nes* (cf. MnE 'stone' but 'sto/ning'), while the infinitive *limpan* divides *lim/pan* (cf. MnE 'limb pad'). So we have:

open syllables	*hē*	*stā/nes*
closed syllables	*stān*	*lim/pan*

§28 'Sometimes', it has been observed, 'things may be made darker by definition.' This must not deter us from attempting to define high and low vowels and back and front vowels. The adjectives 'high, low, back, front' all refer to the position in the mouth occupied by some part of the tongue. The tip of the tongue is not usually important; here it is assumed to be near or touching the lower front teeth. We are concerned with the movement of that part of the tongue which is highest when we pronounce a particular vowel.

---

[1] The 'stem' of a word may be defined as that portion to which the inflexional ending is added, e.g. *scip* + *-es* = gen. sg. *scipes*. The stem of words ending in a vowel can usually be found by dropping the final vowel. So *ende* has stem *end-* + *-es* = gen. sg. *endes*.

GOE C

§29 What follows is a conventionalized diagram showing the parts of the mouth in which the vowels are pronounced.

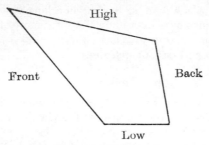

In the front vowels, the 'front' of the tongue is raised towards the hard palate. In the back vowels, the 'back' of the tongue is raised towards the soft palate. To understand this, you may well need the help of a tutor and of a book on the phonetics of your own 'accent' of English. But you can try the following experiment, observing with the aid of a mirror the movements of jaw, lips, and tongue:

1. Practise individually the sounds you have learnt for the OE vowels *i, e, æ, a, o, u.*

2. Sing them in a rough scale in the order given in 1, with the tip of the tongue near or touching the lower front teeth.

§30 Observe:

1. with *i, e, æ,*
   (a) a gradual lowering of the jaw;
   (b) a gradual lowering of the (front of the) tongue;
   (c) the roughly natural position of the lips, i.e. neither unduly spread out nor rounded;
   (d) a general feeling that the sounds are being made in the front of the mouth.

2. with the transition from *æ* to *a* a backward and slightly downward movement of the tongue.

3. with *a, o, u,*
   (a) progressive raising of the jaw and of the (back of the) tongue;
   (b) the way in which the lips become more rounded, i.e. form a progressively smaller circle;
   (c) the general feeling of 'backness'.

§31 From this, it should be clear why *i, e, æ,* are called front vowels and *a, o, u,* back vowels. Another way of feeling the difference is to pronounce the diphthongs made up of *i + u, e + o,* and *æ + a,* for if you do this you will feel the backward movement of the tongue. (The two latter sounds will be close to the OE diphthongs *eo* and *ea* respectively.) But you will not feel a great downward movement; roughly speaking, *i* and *u* are pronounced with the highest part of the tongue about the same height in the mouth. Similarly with *e* and *o* and with *æ* and *a*. Now, if you draw the vowel diagram again and try to plot these vowels as you pronounce them, you will get something like this:

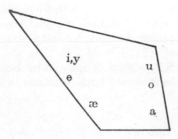

Since we can distinguish *i*, *u*, as high vowels and *æ*, *a*, as low vowels, we can now describe *i* as a high front vowel, *a* as a low back vowel, and so on.

§32   Of course, this is far from being a scientific description of the vowel sounds and you will need to consult a book on phonetics if you wish to learn more. Its incompleteness is illustrated by the fact that OE possesses another high front vowel *y* which (unlike the high front vowel *i*) has lip rounding. (If you try to pronounce the second vowel in 'machine' and to whistle at the same time, you will get a rather strained and tense *ȳ*.) But this outline will suffice for our present purposes.

Strong Nouns like *stān* (masc.) and *scip* (neut.)

§33   Here we can take the masc. and neut. nouns together and deal with the fem. separately; cf. §19. The basic paradigm is the masc. *stān*:

	Singular	*Plural*
Nom.	stān	stānas
Acc.	stān	stānas
Gen.	stānes	stāna
Dat.	stāne	stānum

Notes
1. nom. and acc. sg. the same;
2. nom. and acc. pl. the same—the characteristic strong masc. *-as* which gives the MnE 's' plural;
3. gen. pl. in *-a*;
4. dat. pl. in *-um*.

§34 In the neut. we find

	Singular	Plural	Singular	Plural
Nom.	scip	scipu	word	word
Acc.	scip	scipu	word	word
Gen.	scipes	scipa	wordes	worda
Dat.	scipe	scipum	worde	wordum

These differ from *stān* and from one another only in the nom. and acc. pl. where the short-stemmed *scip* has *scipu* while the long-stemmed *word* remains unchanged; for this absence of *-u*, cf. *ġiefu/lār* (§48) and *sunu/hand* (§61).

Ċild 'child' may follow *word* or may add *r* before the pl. endings —*ċildru, ċildra, ċildrum*; hence MnE 'children', with final *n* from the weak declension. *Ǣġ* 'egg' has nom. acc. pl. *ǣġru*.

§35 Many nouns are exactly like *stān* (e.g. *āþ* 'oath', *dōm* 'judgement', *wer* 'man'), like *scip* (e.g. *god* 'god', *hof* 'dwelling'), or like *word* (e.g. *hūs* 'house', *wif* 'woman'). But some differ in that, while THEY HAVE PERFECTLY NORMAL ENDINGS like those of *stān, scip*, or *word*, THEY SHOW SOME ABNORMALITY IN THE STEM (see §26, note) as the result of certain 'sound-changes' or 'sound-laws'. These 'sound-laws' are not laws in the same sense as the law of gravity is one. People who jump off cliffs always have fallen and (as far as we know) will continue to fall, irrespective of what language they spoke or speak. But each language undergoes different changes at different periods. And the 'sound-laws' in which these changes are summed up are the result of observation by later scholars. Sometimes one of these 'laws' appears not to operate. This, however, is usually because something in a particular word or form prevented it. In such cases, another 'sound-law' was deduced to explain the exception. Thus the sound which was Gmc. *a* usually turns up in OE as *æ*. But in the nouns discussed in §36 we sometimes find *æ*, sometimes *a*. It was as a result of observing such differences that famous scholars first deduced the sound-changes. We can follow in their steps by examining the full paradigms of two nouns, noting the similarities and dissimilarities between them and regular nouns of the same declension, and so deducing the sound-changes necessary to explain the forms we have.

§36 These nouns are *dæġ* (masc.) 'day' and *fæt* (neut.) 'vessel':

	Singular	Plural	Singular	Plural
Nom.	dæġ	dagas	fæt	fatu
Acc.	dæġ	dagas	fæt	fatu
Gen.	dæġes	daga	fætes	fata
Dat.	dæġe	dagum	fæte	fatum

Observe:

1. that their endings are the same as in *stān* and *scip* respectively;
2. that they are short-stemmed monosyllables;
3. that the stem vowel of the nom. sg. is *æ*;
4. that both have *æ* throughout sg., *a* throughout pl.;
5. that where they have *a*, the ending is, or begins with, a back vowel.
6. that where they have *æ*, there is either no ending or an ending which is, or begins with, a front vowel.

Hence we can deduce that *æ* is found in a closed syllable (*dæġ*) or in an open syllable + a front vowel (*dæġes*), but appears as *a* in an open syllable + a back vowel (*dagas*). A simple rule is that these monosyllabic nouns have *æ* in the sg. stem, *a* in the pl. stem.

§37 Long-stemmed monosyllables ending in a vowel or diphthong + *h* take the endings of *stān* or *scip* but show absorption of *h* when it occurs between two vowels. Subsequently the unaccented vowel is also absorbed. Thus the gen. sg. of *scōh* (masc.) 'shoe' is **scōhes > *scōes > scōs*. The paradigm is:

Singular: *nom.* scōh, *acc.* scōh, *gen.* scōs, *dat.* scō
Plural: *nom.* scŏs, *acc.* scŏs, *gen.* scōna (§38), *dat.* scōm.

§38 The same thing happens in short-stemmed monosyllables ending in a vowel or diphthong + *h*. But even without the *h* and the vowel, these words appear to have taken roughly the same time to pronounce. (A little experimenting will convince you that this is reasonable.) Hence the stressed vowel or diphthong is lengthened. So we get (I give the recorded forms)

> *eoh* (masc.) 'horse', but gen. sg. *ēos*
> *feoh* (neut.) 'money', but gen. sg. *fēos*, dat. sg. *fēo*.

Theoretically, the gen. pl. of *feoh* should be **fēo < *feoha*, but *fēona*, with the weak ending *-ena*, occurs—doubtless because *fēo* was ambiguous. So also *scōna* (§37).

§39 Loss of *h* with lengthening of the stem vowel or diphthong occurs between *r* or *l* and a vowel in monosyllabic nouns like *mearh* (masc.) 'horse' and *wealh* (masc.) 'foreigner'. The endings are those of *stān*.

	Singular	Plural	Singular	Plural
Nom.	mearh	mēaras	wealh	wēalas
Acc.	mearh	mēaras	wealh	wēalas
Gen.	mēares	mēara	wēales	wēala
Dat.	mēare	mēarum	wēale	wēalum

Note

Here the diphthong of the first syllable has been shown lengthened (as in *fēos*), so that the first syllable of *mēares* is the same length as *mearh*. But metrical and place-name evidence shows that forms with a short diphthong, e.g. *meares*, also occurred under the influence of the short sound in *mearh*; in these, the whole word is the metrical equivalent of *mearh*.

§40   The forms of *bearo, -u* (masc.) 'grove' and *searo, -u* (neut.) 'device' are

	Singular	Plural	Singular	Plural
Nom.	bearo	bearwas	searo	searo
Acc.	bearo	bearwas	searo	searo
Gen.	bearwes	bearwa	searwes	searwa
Dat.	bearwe	bearwum	searwe	searwum

Thus they add the endings of *stān* and *word* respectively to the stems which before vowels become *bearw-* and *searw-* respectively; cf. §71

§41   We turn now to dissyllabic nouns which take the endings of *stān, scip,* or *word.*

Compounds like *ġewrit* 'writing' and *ġebed* 'prayer' (both neut.), where the stress falls on the second syllable, follow *scip.*

Dissyllabic nouns which are compounds of two nouns, or of an adjective or adverb and a noun, have the second element declined, but not the first, e.g. *hron-fisc* (masc.) 'whale', *hēah-clif* (neut.) 'high cliff', and *in-gang* (masc.) 'entrance'.

Other dissyllables with their stress on the first syllable may follow one of four patterns:

		Masc.		Neut.
(a)	´ ◡ —	*cyning* 'king'		*færeld* (also masc.) 'journey'
(b)	´ —	*Hengest* 'Hengest'		*īsern* 'iron'
(c)	´ ◡	*engel* 'angel'		*hēafod* 'head'
(d)	◡ ◡	*metod* 'creator'		*werod* 'troop'

Types (a) and (b) are quite regular and follow *stān* or *word* without any variations of stem or ending.

§42   Type (c)—long-stemmed dissyllables—add the endings of *stān* or *scip.* But they lose the medial vowel when an ending is added:

	Singular	Plural	Singular	Plural
Nom.	engel	englas	hēafod	hēafdu
Acc.	engel	englas	hēafod	hēafdu
Gen.	engles	engla	hēafdes	hēafda
Dat.	engle	englum	hēafde	hēafdum

Note

This loss of the medial vowel occurs only when an inflexional ending beginning with a vowel is added or (to put it another way) when this medial vowel is in an open syllable. Thus *engel* and *hēafod* have dat. pl. *englum* (NOT **enge/lum*—medial *e* is in an open syllable) and *hēafdum* (NOT **hēafo/dum*—*o* is in an open syllable). Since all the endings of *stān* and *scip* begin with a vowel, the simple statement made above suffices here. But the qualification is important for adjectives; see §68.

§43   Nouns of type (*d*)—short-stemmed dissyllables—are

	Singular	Plural	Singular	Plural
Nom.	metod	metodas	werod	werod
Acc.	metod	metodas	werod	werod
Gen.	metodes	metoda	werodes	weroda
Dat.	metode	metodum	werode	werodum

The masc. nouns therefore follow *stān* exactly. The neut. nouns remain unchanged in the nom. and acc. pl.; in other words, they are like *word*, not *scip*.

§44   But, as Dr. Johnson wisely observed, 'it may be reasonably imagined that what is so much in the power of men as language will very often be capriciously conducted'. For analogy often interferes with the historically-correct forms given in §§42-43. A child learning to speak English today hears those around him forming past tenses of verbs by adding the sound *t*, e.g. 'baked', or *d*, e.g. 'sighed'. So quite naturally he says 'I maked a mud-pie today' or 'I buyed a hat in the shop today'. Thus the process of analogy can produce forms not accepted by most speakers of English today. But since we now have pretty strict notions of 'correctness', we tend to say to children 'No dear, I made a mud-pie' or 'I bought a hat', thereby helping to preserve the now-accepted form.

But many such variant forms are recorded in Old English texts. Alongside the regular nom. and acc. pls. *hēafdu* and *werod*, we find *hēafod*, *hēafodu*, and *weredu*.

Similarly, the process of analogy and earlier differences in some of the words themselves cause type (*d*) nouns ending in *l*, *r*, *m*, or *n*, to appear sometimes with no medial vowel in oblique cases. Thus *fugol* (masc.) 'bird' appears, like *engel*, without the medial vowel, and *wæter* may have gen. sg. *wæteres* or *wætres*, and nom. and acc. pl. *wæter*, *wætru*, or *wæteru*.

Hæleþ (masc.) 'man' and *mōnaþ* (masc.) 'month' may have nom. and acc. pl. the same or may add *-as*.

Masculine and Neuter Nouns in -e

§45   Masc. nouns in *-e* are always strong, for weak masc. nouns have nom. sg. in *-a*. Neut. nouns in *-e* can be strong or weak (see

§24). Historically speaking, strong nouns in -e belong either to a sub-class of the *stān/scip* declension or to another declension. As a general rule, it is safe to say that they drop the -e of the nom. sg. and add the endings of *stān* or *scip* as appropriate. Examples are:

masc.: *ende* 'end', *here* 'army', *wine* 'friend', *stede* 'place'; neut. : *wīte* 'punishment', *riċe* 'kingdom', *spere* 'spear'.

The long-stemmed neuters, being dissyllabic in nom. sg., remain dissyllabic in the nom. acc. pl. *witu, riċu*.

§46 Words like *wine* and *stede* may have nom. and acc. pl. *wine* and *stede*.

A few masc. nouns have only the -e form in the nom. and acc. pl.; they include names of people, e.g. *Seaxe* 'Saxons' and *Dene* 'Danes', and the common nouns *ielde* 'men' and *lēode* 'people'.

Other forms you need to be able to recognize in your reading are:

1. nom. acc. pl. *riċiu* alongside *riċu* 'kingdoms';
2. forms with -(i)ġ(e)-, e.g. nom. acc. pl. *her(i)ġ(e)as* alongside *heras* 'armies'.

Strong Feminine Nouns

§47 The basic paradigm is *ġiefu* 'gift':

	Singular	Plural
Nom.	ġiefu	ġiefa, -e
Acc.	ġiefe	ġiefa, -e
Gen.	ġiefe	ġiefa, -ena
Dat.	ġiefe	ġiefum

Note the following endings:

1. -e in acc. gen. and dat. sg.;
2. alternative nom. acc. pls. -a, -e;
3. weak -ena in gen. pl. alongside -a;
4. dat. pl. in -um.

§48 The long-stemmed monosyllable *lār* 'teaching' is identical except for nom. sg.; for absence of -u cf. *scipu/word* (§34) and *sunu/hand* (§61).

	Singular	Plural
Nom.	lār	lāra, -e
Acc.	lāre	lāra, -e
Gen.	lāre	lāra, -ena
Dat.	lāre	lārum

§49 Some fem. monosyllables with long front vowels, e.g. *cwēn* 'queen', originally had nom. and acc. sg. the same and -e in nom. acc. pl. Later most of them (by a perfectly natural confusion) sometimes followed *lār*. But it is important to note that *brȳd* 'bride', *cwēn* 'queen', *dǣd* 'deed', etc. may be acc. as well as nom. sg. in your texts, and that all the long-stemmed fem. monosyllables may have *-a* or *-e* in nom. acc. pl.

§50   Long-stemmed dissyllables, e.g. *sāwol* 'soul' and *ċeaster* 'city', take the endings of *lār*, but (like *engel* and *hēafod*) lose the medial vowel in trisyllabic forms.

§51   Some abstract nouns ending in *-þu* and *-u(-o)* can remain unchanged in the oblique cases, e.g. *iermþu* 'poverty' and *ieldu* 'age'.

i-Mutation

§52   A sound-change which affects certain nouns and verbs must now be explained. The vowel *i* and the related consonant written in phonetic script [j] and pronounced as the first consonant in MnE 'yes' are high front sounds. When in OE one of these followed a stressed syllable, the vowel of that stressed syllable was subject to what is called '*i*-Mutation'.[1] In simple terms, the organs of speech and the mind of the speaker got ready for the high front sound too soon and in the process

the low front vowels were dragged up or 'raised'

and the back vowels were pulled forward or 'fronted'.

The *i* or [j] is usually lost but may appear in OE as *e* or *i*.

§53   This change can be explained (unscientifically) in terms of the diagram in §31 as follows:

1. The low front vowels *æ* and *e* move up one place.
2. The back vowels *a* and *o* are pushed straight forward to the corresponding front position.
3. *u* keeps its lip-rounding and goes forward to the rounded *y* described in §32.

The sections which follow give a Table of Correspondences in which the unmutated vowel (as it appears in OE) is shown on the left, and the OE mutated equivalent on the right.

Table of Correspondences

§54   The low front vowels are raised; only the short ones are affected.

$$ \breve{æ} \quad : \quad \breve{e} $$
$$ \breve{e} \quad : \quad \breve{i} $$

Note

   i is not affected because it cannot go any higher.

[1] Unstressed vowels are sometimes affected. But this need not concern us here.

§55 The back vowels are fronted; both short and long are affected here.

$$\begin{array}{ccc}
\breve{a} & : & \widebreve{æ} \\
\breve{o} & : & \breve{e} \\
\breve{u} & : & \breve{y} \\
\end{array}$$

But   ă + m, n   :   ĕ + m, n.

§56 The diphthongs *ea* and *eo* (short and long) are affected.

$$\begin{array}{ccc}
\breve{e}a & : & \breve{i}e \\
\breve{e}o & : & \breve{i}e \\
\end{array}$$

§57 Thirteen sounds are therefore affected—2 front vowels, 7 back vowels (including *ă* in two ways), and 4 diphthongs. You should cull your own examples. A very good way to find some is to look at the strong verbs and to compare the stem vowel of the infinitive with the stem vowel of the 2nd and 3rd pers. sg. pres. ind.; see §112.1 and Appendix A. In most of them you will find the non-mutated vowel in the infinitive and its mutated equivalent in the 2nd and 3rd pers. sg. pres. ind. The *i* which caused *i*-mutation in these two forms has either disappeared or become *e*.

Nouns affected by *i*-Mutation

§58 Typical paradigms for those masc. and fem. nouns affected by *i*-mutation are *mann* (masc.) 'man' and *bōc* (fem.) 'book':

	Singular	Plural	Singular	Plural
Nom.	mann	menn	bōc	bēċ
Acc.	mann	menn	bōc	bēċ
Gen.	mannes	manna	bēċ, bōce	bōca
Dat.	menn	mannum	bēċ	bōcum

Note the following points:

1. nom. and acc. sg. the same;
2. gen. sg. like *stān* and *lār* respectively;
3. gen. and dat. pl. regular;
4. the mutated equivalent of the vowel of the nom. sg. appears in the dat. sg. and nom. and acc. pl. (with no inflexional ending);
5. the gen. sg. with the mutated vowel in the fem. nouns. This should not cause difficulty because the gen. and dat. sg. fem. are usually the same. *Bōce* arises by analogy with *lāre*.

Most of the masc. examples can be recognized by thinking of the MnE plural of the corresponding word, e.g. 'foot' (*fōt*), 'man' (*mann*), 'tooth' (*tōþ*). Most of the fem. nouns have become regular in MnE, e.g. 'book' (*bōc*), 'oak' (*āc*), 'goat' (*gāt*), but a few survive, e.g. 'goose' (*gōs*), 'louse' (*lūs*), 'mouse' (*mūs*).

§59   The nouns *frēond* 'friend' and *fēond* 'enemy', which are formed from pres. ptcs. of verbs, can follow *stān* or can have *īe* in dat. sg. and nom. and acc. pl.; cf. *mann*.

§60   Nouns ending in -*r* which denote relationship are: *fæder* 'father' and *brōþor* 'brother' (both masc.), *mōdor* 'mother', *dohtor* 'daughter', and *sweostor* 'sister' (all fem.). It is difficult to systematize these nouns, for many analogical variations exist, but the following observations may help:

1. All are regular in the gen. and dat. pl., ending in -*a* and -*um* respectively and losing the medial vowel if long-stemmed (§42).

2. All can have the nominative singular form in all remaining cases except for

(*a*) *fæder* which takes -*as* in nom. acc. pl.;

(*b*) *brōþor, mōdor, dohtor*, which show *i*-mutation in the dat. sg. and sometimes by analogy in the gen. sg.

u-Nouns

§61   A few masc. and fem. nouns belong to the *u*-declension. They may be short-stemmed dissyllables with final -*u*, e.g. *sunu* (masc.) 'son' and *duru* (fem.) 'door', or long-stemmed monosyllables, e.g. *feld* (masc.) 'field' and *hand* (fem.) 'hand'; for the absence of -*u* in the latter cf. *scipu/word* and *ġiefu/lār*. Typical paradigms are *sunu* (masc.) and *hand* (fem.):

	Singular	Plural	Singular	Plural
Nom.	sunu	suna	hand	handa
Acc.	sunu	suna	hand	handa
Gen.	suna	suna	handa	handa
Dat.	suna	sunum	handa	handum

Notes
1. Nom. and acc. sg. are the same.
2. All other cases end in -*a* except of course the dat. pl. -*um*.

Other nouns which belong here are *wudu* 'wood', *ford* 'ford', and *weald* 'forest'—all masc.

§62   Masc. nouns like *feld* and fem. nouns like *duru/hand* are all to some extent influenced by *stān* and *ġiefu/lār* respectively and so hover uneasily between two declensions; hence gen. sg. *feldes* and the like. But the most important point to note here is that the ending -*a* is sometimes a dat. sg. in the texts, e.g. *felda, forda, wealda*.

iii ADJECTIVES
Introduction

§63 Most adjectives can be declined strong or weak. Important
exceptions are *ōþer* and the poss. adjs. *mīn, þīn,* etc., which are
declined strong, and comparatives, which end in -*a* in nom. sg. masc.,
e.g. *blindra* 'blinder', and are declined weak.
On participles, see §111.

§64 Which form of the adjective is used depends, not on the
type of noun with which it is used, but on how it is used. The strong
form is used when the adj. stands alone, e.g. 'The man is old' *se mann
is eald,* or with a noun, e.g. 'old men' *ealde menn.* The weak form
appears when the adj. follows a dem., e.g. 'that old man' *se ealda
mann,* or a poss. adj., e.g. 'my old friend' *mīn ealda frēond.* You can
remember that the strong forms stand alone, while the weak forms
need the support of a dem. or poss. pron.

Weak Declension

§65 The paradigm is *tila* 'good':

	Masc.	Singular Neut.	Fem.	Plural All genders
Nom.	tila	tile	tile	tilan
Acc.	tilan	tile	tilan	tilan
Gen.	tilan	tilan	tilan	tilra, -ena
Dat.	tilan	tilan	tilan	tilum

The long-stemmed *gōda* 'good' is declined exactly the same. Here
the endings are identical with those of the weak noun of the same
gender with one addition—the strong form of gen. pl. *tilra* is generally preferred to -*ena*, except in eWS. The dat. pl. -*um* is frequently
replaced by -*an* in WS texts and in lWS -*an* is found in the gen. pl.
too. Stem changes in the weak declension of the adjectives follow
the rules set out in §§68-73.

Strong Declension

§66 The paradigm is *til* 'good', which has a separate inst. form
in the masc. and neut. sg.:

	Masc.	Singular Neut.	Fem.
Nom.	til	til	tilu
Acc.	tilne	til	tile
Gen.	tiles	tiles	tilre
Dat.	tilum	tilum	tilre
Inst.	tile	tile	

Adjectives 29

	Plural		
	Masc.	*Neut.*	*Fem.*
Nom.	tile	tilu	tile, -a
Acc.	tile	tilu	tile, -a
Gen.	til*ra*	til*ra*	til*ra*
Dat.	tilum	tilum	tilum

Notes

1. Nom. and acc. pl. masc. end in *-e*, e.g. *cwice eorlas* 'living noble-men'; the ending *-as* belongs to the nouns only.
2. All the other endings are familiar. Those italicized have already been met in the pronouns (§§16-18). The remainder are endings found in *stān, scip,* and *ġiefu,* respectively.

§67 The long-stemmed monosyllable *gōd* 'good' varies only in the nom. sg. fem. *gōd* as against *tilu* (cf. *lār/ġiefu*) and in the nom. and acc. neut. pl. *gōd* as against *tilu* (cf. *word/scipu*).

Stem Changes in Adjectives

§68 Long-stemmed dissyllables such as *hāliġ* add the weak or strong endings given above as appropriate. The medial vowel is not lost before endings beginning with a consonant, i.e. in closed syl-lables—hence *hāliġ/ne, hāliġ/re, hāliġ/ra*.

When the ending begins with a vowel, the medial vowel sometimes disappears; cf. the nouns *engel* and *hēafod* (§42) and *sāwol* (§50). Thus *hāliġ* has gen. sg. masc. strong *hālġes*. But analogical varia-tions are common, and we find *hāligan* alongside *hālgan, hāliġes* alongside *hālġes* and so on.

In the nom. sg. fem. and the nom. and acc. pl. *hāliġ* (cf. *lār/word*), *hāligu* (cf. *ġiefu/scipu*), and *hālgu* (with loss of vowel) are all found.

§69 Short-stemmed dissyllabic adjectives show forms with no medial vowel more frequently than the corresponding nouns (§§43-44). Thus *miċel* 'great' may have acc. sg. fem. *miċele* or *miċle*, while *moniġ* 'many' and *yfel* 'evil' have dat. pl. *monigum* or *mongum* and gen. sg. masc. *yfeles* or *yfles*, respectively.

§70 Short-stemmed monosyllabic adjectives with the stem-vowel *æ* follow *glæd* 'glad', here declined strong:

	Singular		
	Masc.	*Neut.*	*Fem.*
Nom.	glæd	glæd	gladu
Acc.	glædne	glæd	glade
Gen.	glades	glades	glædre
Dat.	gladum	gladum	glædre
Inst.	glade	glade	

	Masc.	*Plural* *Neut.*	*Fem.*
Nom.	glade	gladu	glade
Acc.	glade	gladu	glade
Gen.	glædra	glædra	glædra
Dat.	gladum	gladum	gladum

Here *æ/a* fluctuation occurs. As in the nouns (§36), we find *æ* in a closed syllable, i.e. in the simple form *glæd* and when an ending beginning with a consonant is added, e.g. *glæd/ne*. In open syllables, however, the adjectives have *a* irrespective of whether a front or back vowel follows, e.g. *gla/des, gla/dum*. This is the result of analogy.

§71 Adjectives like *ġearo, -u* 'ready' take the endings of *gōd*. Hence in the strong declension, they remain unchanged in the nom. sg. all genders, acc. sg. neut., and nom. and acc. pl. Before consonants, the stem is *ġearo-* —hence *ġearone, ġearore, ġearora*, but before vowels it is *ġearw-* —hence *ġearwes, ġearwum*; cf. §40. Write out the paradigm. Then see A. Campbell, *O. E. Grammar*, §649.

§72 Adjectives such as *hēah* 'high' and *fāh* 'hostile' usually lose their final *h* and contract where possible; cf. §§37 and 38. *Hēah* may have acc. sg. masc. strong *hēanne* or *hēane*.

§73 Adjectives in *-e*, e.g. *bliþe*, behave like the corresponding nouns. Hence they drop the *-e* and add the endings of *til*.

Comparison of Adjectives

§74 Most adjectives add the endings *-ra, -ost* to the stem. Thus we find *lēof* 'dear', *lēofra* 'dearer', *lēofost* 'dearest'. Similarly *glæd* 'glad', *glædra* 'gladder', but *gladost* 'gladdest' (see §70). The comparative is declined weak, the superlative strong or weak (see §64).

§75 Some adjectives, however, add the endings *-ra, -est*, and show an *i*-mutated vowel in the stem, e.g.

eald 'old'	ieldra	ieldest
ġeong 'young'	ġingra	ġingest
lang 'long'	lengra	lengest
strang 'strong'	strengra	strengest
hēah 'high'	hīerra	hīehst

§76 Irregular are:

lȳtel 'little'	lǣssa	lǣst
miċel 'great'	māra	mǣst
yfel 'bad'	wiersa	wierst
gōd 'good'	betera, sēlra	betst, sēlest

These, of course, can be compared with their MnE equivalents.

iv OBSERVATIONS ON NOUN, ADJECTIVE, AND PRONOUN DECLENSIONS

§77 The weak declension of nouns and adjectives, with *-an* throughout except in a few easily remembered places (see §§22-25), presents little difficulty. The weak masc. noun can always be recognized by *-a* in nom. sg. Unfortunately *-e* of the weak fem. and neut. is also found in strong masc. and neut. nouns. But a noun with final *-e* in nom. sg. cannot be strong fem.

§78 Nouns with their nom. sg. ending in a consonant are strong, but can be any gender. See again §13.

§79 In the strong nouns and the strong declension of the adj., the characteristic endings should be noted. The gen. pl. of the noun is *-a*, of the adj. *-ra*. But the weak ending *-ena* is found in nouns like *feoh/fēona* and *ġiefu/ġiefa* or *ġiefena*, and in the adj. The endings *-ne* (acc. sg. masc.) and *-re* (gen. and dat. sg. fem.) are found in adjs. (strong forms) and prons.

§80 Certain similarities may be noted in the declension of strong nouns, the strong form of the adj., and the dem. and pers. prons. (less 1st and 2nd pers.; on these, see §21). These are:

1. neut. sg. nom. and acc. are always the same;
2. nom. and acc. sg. of masc. NOUNS are always the same;
3. nom. and acc. pl. are always the same;
4. gen. and dat. fem. sg. are always the same (with the reservations made in §§58 and 60);
5. within the same declension
   (*a*) masc. and neut. gen. sg. are the same;
   (*b*) masc. and neut. dat. sg. are the same;
   (*c*) masc. and neut. inst. sg. are the same.

§81 A possible source of confusion is the fact than in prons. and adjs., the acc. fem. sg. is the same as nom. and acc. pl., e.g. *þā/þā*, *þās/þās*, *hīe/hīe*, *cwice/cwice*. This last form *cwice* is properly the masc. pl. But in later texts, it is often used for all genders.

v NUMERALS

§82 The numerals from 1-10 are:

	Cardinal	*Ordinal*
1	ān	forma
2	twēgen	ōþer
3	þrīe	þridda
4	fēower	fēorþa
5	fīf	fīfta
6	siex	siexta

	Cardinal	Ordinal
7	seofon	seofoþa
8	eahta	eahtoþa
9	nigon	nigoþa
10	tīen	tēoþa

§83   When declined strong, ān means 'one'; when declined weak āna, it usually means 'alone'.

Ordinals are declined weak, except ōþer which is always strong.

§84   Twēġen 'two' and bēġen 'both' are declined alike. In the nom. and acc. they have:

Masc.	twēġen	Neut.	twā	tū	Fem.	twā
	bēġen		bā	bū		bā

The gen. and dat. are the same for all genders:

twēġra, twēġ(e)a;   bēġra, bēġ(e)a
twǣm;   bǣm

§85   In the nom. and acc. of þrīe 'three' we find:

Masc.	þrīe	Neut.	þrēo	Fem.	þrēo

The gen. and dat. are þrēora, þrim.

§86   A knowledge of the remaining numerals is not essential at first. The meaning of many is obvious, e.g. twēntiġ, þritiġ, fēowertiġ, fīftiġ, and those which occur in your texts will almost certainly be glossed. Full lists will be found in any of the standard grammars. Roman numerals are often used.

vi   STRONG VERBS AND SOUND-CHANGES
RELEVANT TO THEM
Introduction

§87   Like MnE, OE has two types of verbs—weak and strong. The weak verb forms its preterite and past participle by adding a dental suffix, the strong verb by changing its stem vowel; cf. MnE 'laugh, laughed' and 'judge, judged' with MnE 'sing, sang, sung'. The strong verbs are nearly all survivals from OE; new verbs when made up or borrowed today join the weak conjugation. Thus the strong verb 'drive, drove, driven' survives from OE. When in the thirteenth century 'strive' was borrowed from the French, it followed the pattern of 'drive' because the two infinitives rhymed; hence we get MnE 'strive, strove, striven'. But we conjugate the comparatively new verb 'jive', not 'jive, jove, jiven', but 'jive, jived', i.e. as a weak verb.

§88   Such patterns as 'drive, drove, driven' and 'jive, jived' are called the 'principal parts' of the verbs. It is essential for you to know the principal parts of the Old English verbs. This is important because, if you do not know the patterns which the various verbs display in their principal parts, you will be unable to find out their meaning. You will be in the same position as a foreign student of English looking up 'drove (verb)' in his dictionary. For he can only find out what it means by knowing that it is the preterite of 'drive'.

§89   Both weak and strong verbs in OE distinguish:

1. two tenses—present and preterite;

2. indicative, subjunctive, and imperative, moods, in addition to infinitives and participles;

3. two numbers—singular and plural. The dual is found only in the 1st and 2nd person pronouns and is used with plural verb forms;

4. three persons, but only in the singular of the present and preterite indicative. All plurals and the singular of the subjunctives are the same throughout;

5. one voice only—the active. One true passive form survives from an earlier stage of the language, viz. *hātte* 'is called, was called'.

On the syntax of these forms and on the beginnings of new methods of expressing verbal relationships, see §§195 ff.

Principal Parts of the Strong Verbs

§90   These verbs show a change of vowel in the stressed syllable in the principal parts. This is known as 'gradation' and the vowels which change—e.g. *ī, ō, i* in 'drive, drove, driven'—are known as the 'gradation' series. The origin of these is to be found in the shifting stress of the original IE language (which later became fixed, usually on the first syllable, in OE). We can see how the pronunciation of a vowel can change according to the amount of stress the syllable carries if we compare the pronunciation of the following three versions of the same MnE sentence:

Cán he do it?
Can hé do it?
Can he dó it?

In the first, the vowel of 'can' has its full value; in the second, a reduced value; and in the third, it has almost disappeared and has what is sometimes called 'zero' value. Such variations in IE may well have been perpetuated when the stress became fixed.

§91   No MnE strong verb has more than three vowels in its gradation series; some, e.g. 'bind, bound, bound', have only two. But in OE, four parts of the verb may be distinguished by different vowels—the infinitive, two preterites, and the past participle, e.g. *crēopan* 'creep', *crēap, crupon, cropen.* But (for various reasons) the same vowel may occur more than once in the same verb. So we find,

GOE D

with three different vowels, *bindan* 'bind', *band, bundon, bunden*, and, with two only, *faran* 'go', *fōr, fōron, faren*.

§92 Many primers show five vowels for the strong verbs, viz. inf. (*crēopan*), 3rd sg. pres. ind. (*crīepþ*), pret. sg. or 1st pret. (*crēap*), pret. pl. or 2nd pret. (*crupon*), past ptc. (*cropen*). The 3rd sg. pres. ind. is not part of the gradation series; its stem vowel is the *i*-mutated equivalent of the vowel of the inf. and can be deduced from that vowel; see §57. So, when we learn a strong verb, we need to remember four vowels—those of the inf., two preterites, and the past ptc. There are in OE seven different 'classes' of verbs, each with a different gradation series. Each type can be recognized by its 'uniform' in the same way as football teams can be distinguished one from the other. So, in addition to the vowels, we need to know the 'uniform' or recognition symbol which will enable us to tell the class to which a verb belongs.

§93 Verbs characteristic of these classes are:

Class	Inf.	1st Pret.	2nd Pret.	Past Ptc.
I	scīnan 'shine'	scān	scinon	scinen
II	crēopan 'creep'	crēap	crupon	cropen
	brūcan 'enjoy'	brēac	brucon	brocen
III	breġdan 'pull'	bræġd	brugdon	brogden
IV	beran 'bear'	bær	bǣron	boren
V	tredan 'tread'	træd	trǣdon	treden
VI	faran 'go'	fōr	fōron	faren
VII	(a) healdan 'hold'	hēold	hēoldon	healden
	(b) hātan 'command'	hēt	hēton	hāten

Roman numerals are here used for the classes of strong verbs, arabic numerals for those of the weak verbs. Thus *scīnan* I 'shine' and *lufian* 2 'love' tell us both the type and class of verb. Some books call class VII 'reduplicating' (abbreviation 'rd.').

§94 From a study of these and of the lists of strong verbs set out in Appendix A, the following gradation series will emerge:

Class	Recognition Symbol	Inf.	1st Pret.	2nd Pret.	Past Ptc.
I	*ī* + one cons.	ī	a	i	i
II	*ēo* + one cons. ⎫ *ū* + one cons. ⎬	ēo ⎫ ū ⎬	ēa	u	o
III	See §102				
IV	*e* + one cons.[1]	e	æ	ǣ	o
V	*e* + one cons.[2]	e	æ	ǣ	e
VI	*a* + one cons.[3]	a	ō	ō	a
VII	See §104				

[1] Usually a liquid (*l, r*). But note *brecan* 'break'. On the verbs with nasals, 103.2.

[2] Usually a stop (*p, t, c, d, g*) or spirant (*f, þ, s*).

[3] *Standan* 'stand', with *-n-* in inf. and past ptc., belongs here.

§95   The gradation series of verbs in classes I and II are quite regular. Class III presents special difficulties because the stem vowels of most verbs are affected by one of several sound laws. For purposes of explanation, we can take the verb *breġdan* 'pull' as the basic paradigm in terms of which all the other verbs can be explained. *Breġdan* shows the following pattern

III   *e* + TWO cons.   e   æ   u   o

A few other verbs, e.g. *streġdan* 'strew', *berstan* 'burst', *perscan* 'thresh',[1] show the same vowel pattern. But the remainder fall into four groups which are represented by the verbs *weorpan* 'throw'/ *feohtan* 'fight', *helpan* 'help', *ġieldan* 'pay', and *drincan* 'drink'. To understand the variations in these verbs, we have to know something about certain sound-changes.

Breaking

§96   The first of these is the diphthongization of a front vowel when it is followed by a consonant or group of consonants produced in the back of the mouth. When moving from a front vowel to a back consonant, the organs of speech do NOT perform the equivalent of the quick march, in which one foot is lifted cleanly from the ground and put down again 30 inches or so further on. They glide more or less smoothly from one position to another, as your feet do when you are dancing a waltz. You can see the result of this process in an exaggerated form if you imagine that you have fallen overboard from a ship and are calling out 'Help'. If you call out loudly and long (you had better do this in a desert place!), you will find that the vowel of the word 'Help' is 'broken' as you glide from the front position of *e* to the back position of *lp*. If you spell it as you are pronouncing it, you will write something like 'Heulp'. Try the same experiment with words like 'bell', 'fell', 'tell'. You will probably find that a 'glide' develops between the short front vowel *e* and the following *l*. A similar process took place in OE. It is called 'breaking'.

§97   For our purposes, its most important effects are:
1. before *h*, *h* + cons., *r* + cons.[2]

    ă̆e   >   ĕa
    ĕ   >   ĕo

In terms of the diagram in §31, the organs of speech glide back to the back vowel nearest in height to the front vowel from which they

---

[1] *Berstan* and *perscan* were originally **brestan* and **prescan*, with two medial consonants. But the *r* 'changed places'. This change, known as 'metathesis', is not uncommon; cf. OE *brid* with MnE 'bird'.

[2] Here *r* was probably made with the tip of the tongue curved back.

started. (See §8, where I assume that the symbol *ea* is pronounced *æa*.)

2. before *l* (here made in the back of the throat) + cons.

$$\breve{æ} \quad > \quad \breve{e}a$$

But *ĕ* is not usually affected before *l*. We can call this 'limited breaking'; it occurs before *l*, with which the word 'limited' begins!

Note

    ĕ does break before *lh*. See §133.2 for an example.

3. before *h* and *h* + cons.

$$\bar{\imath} \quad > \quad \bar{\imath}o \quad > \quad \text{very often } \bar{e}o$$

§98   We can now return to the verbs of class III where the basic gradation series is *e*, *æ*, *u*, *o* (§95). If we examine *weorpan* and *feohtan*, we find

weorpan	wearp	wurpon	worpen
feohtan	feaht	fuhton	fohten

Here the medial cons. groups -*rp*- and -*ht*- cause *e* and *æ* to break but do not affect the back vowels *u* and *o*. Hence we get as the gradation series, NOT *e*, *æ*, *u*, *o*, but *eo*, *ea*, *u*, *o*.

§99   In *helpan*, however, the medial group -*lp*- produces only limited breaking and so we get

helpan	healp	hulpon	holpen

where only the 1st pret. *ea* differs from the basic series of *bregdan*, the *e* of the infinitive remaining unchanged.

Influence of initial *ġ*, *sc*, *ċ*

§100   The results of the next sound-change to affect the verbs of class III are seen most commonly in the WS dialect, with which we are mainly concerned. Here the initial palatal consonants *ġ*, *sc*, and *ċ*, caused the following front vowels *ĕ* and *ǣ* to become *ĭe* and *ĕa* respectively. The effect may be produced by an emphatic pronunciation of these consonants, which will produce a glide between the consonant and vowel. A modern parallel may be found in the prolonged 'Yes' in the sentence 'Well, yes, I suppose so' used when one gives hesitating assent or grudging permission; we might spell our pronunciation something like 'Yies'. This change is sometimes called 'palatal diphthongization' (p.d. for short). It is because of it that we find the inf. *ġieldan*. For further examples, see §103.1.

Note

    The pret. *ġeald* could be the result of breaking or of p.d. But such forms as *ćeorfan*, which show *eo<e* as the result of breaking, suggest that breaking took place before p.d.; if it had not, we should have had **ćierfan* by p.d. P.d. can take place in such forms as *ġieldan* because *e* did not break before *-ld-* and hence remained until p.d. took place.

Influence of Nasals

§ **101**   The last sound-change which affects verbs of class III is found in verbs in which the first of the two medial consonants is a nasal *m* or *n*. In these circumstances, *i* appears instead of *e*, *a* instead of *æ*, and *u* instead of *o*. So we get

drincan   dranc   druncon   druncen

with *i*, *a* (sometimes *o*; see § 103.2), *u*, *u* instead of *e*, *æ*, *u*, *o*.

Summary of the Strong Verbs of Class III

§ **102**   The following table summarizes class III verbs. Each of series (*b*)-(*e*) is to be explained by the appropriate sound-change operating on series (*a*). See also §§ 116 and 133.5.

Sound-Change	Symbol	Example	Gradation Series			
(*a*) Basic Series	*e* + 2 cons.	*breġdan*	e	æ	u	o
(*b*) Breaking before *r* + cons. *h* + cons.	*eo* + *r* + cons. *eo* + *h* + cons.	*weorpan* ⎫ *feohtan* ⎭	eo	ea	u	o
(*c*) Limited break- ing before *l* + cons.	*e* + *l* + cons.	*helpan*	e	ea	u	o
(*d*) Palatal diph- thongization	palatal + *ie* + 2 cons.	*ġieldan*	ie	ea	u	o
(*e*) Nasal	*i* + nasal + cons.	*drincan*	i	a	u	u

The Effects of Sound-Changes on other Strong Verbs

§ **103**   Some of these sound-changes affect verbs of other classes.
1. P.d. is seen in:
Class IV *scieran* 'cut', which has *ie*, *ea*, *ēa*, *o* instead of *e*, *æ*, *ǣ*, *o*,
Class V *ġiefan* 'give' with *ie*, *ea*, *ēa*, *ie*, instead of *e*, *æ*, *ǣ*, *e*,
and in the class VI infinitive *scieppan* 'create'.
2. Nasals influence class IV *niman* 'take' with *i*, *a/o*, *ā/ō* (fluctua-

tion between *a* and *o* is not uncommon before nasals) and *u* instead
of *e*, *æ*, *ǣ*, *o*. On *niman* and *cuman* 'come' see also § 109.

3. Breaking before *h* with subsequent loss of *h* between a diphthong and a vowel (see §§ 37-38) affects the infinitives of the contracted verbs of classes I, V, and VI. The stages can be set out thus:

I   *wrīhan > *wrēohan > wrēon 'cover'
V   *sehan > *seohan > sēon 'see'
VI   *slahan > *slæhan[1] > *sleahan > slēan 'strike'.

4. The infinitives of contracted verbs of class II are affected by
loss of *h* only, e.g.

     *tēohan > tēon 'draw'.

5. The contracted verbs of class VII—*fōn* 'take' and *hōn* 'hang'—
have a complicated phonology; detailed explanation would be out
of place here. But see § 108.

6. On the principal parts of contracted verbs, see §§ 107-108. On
3rd sg. pres. ind. of contracted verbs, see § 114. On the 'weak presents' of classes V-VII, see § 116.

Strong Verbs of Class VII

§ 104   Strong verbs of class VII show the following characteristics:
1. the same stem vowel in inf. and past ptc. (except *wēpan*);
2. the same stem vowel in 1st and 2nd pret.—either *ēo* or *ē*. On
this basis the two sub-classes (*a*) and (*b*) are distinguished.

Important verbs here are: *cnāwan* 'know', *feallan* 'fall', *weaxan*
'grow' (all VII(*a*)), and *drǣdan* 'fear' and *lǣtan* 'let' (both VII(*b*)).
It is worth noting that none of them can be mistaken for strong
verbs of any other class, for the stem vowels of the inf. are different.
But see further §§ 131-134.

Grimm's Law and Verner's Law

§ 105   Certain consonant changes which distinguish the Gmc.
languages from the other IE languages were first formulated by the
German philologist Grimm (of the Fairy Tales) and hence are known
as Grimm's Law. But the fact that the expected consonant did not
always appear in the Gmc. languages puzzled philologists until the
Danish grammarian Karl Verner explained that the differences de-
pended on the position of the stress in the original IE form of the
word.

§ 106   Grimm's Law accounts (*inter alia*) for the variations be-

---

[1] This variation must be taken on trust. (Those interested can compare
§§ 35-36.)

tween Latin (which in the examples cited keeps the IE consonant) and OE seen in such pairs as

Lat.	piscis	OE	fisc	(p/f)
Lat.	frater	OE	brōþor	(t/þ)
Lat.	genus	OE	cynn	(g/c)
Lat.	dentem	OE	tōþ	(d/t)

But, if *fisc* corresponds to *piscis* and *brōþor* to *frāter*, we should expect **fæþer* alongside *pǽter*. But we have *fæder*. Verner explained exceptions like this.

We can see the sort of thing which happened if we compare MnE 'éxcellent' and 'ábsolution' on the one hand with MnE 'exám.' and 'absólve' on the other. In the first pair, the stress falls on the first syllable and the consonants which follow are voiceless; we could spell the words 'eks-' and 'aps-'. In the second pair, the stress is on the second syllable, the consonants are voiced, and the words could be spelt 'egz-' and 'abz-'. Similar variations, said Verner, arose in Pr. Gmc. because of similar differences. Greek φράτηρ – Latin *frāter* was stressed on the first syllable. Hence in its Pr. Gmc. equivalent the medial *t* developed regularly by Grimm's Law to voiceless *þ* (cf. MnE 'cloth') in Pr. OE.[1] But Greek πατήρ = Latin *páter* was stressed on the second syllable. So in Pr. Gmc. the voiceless *þ* which arose from the *t* by Grimm's Law was voiced to the sound in MnE 'clothe'. This voiced sound subsequently became *d*.

§ 107   Many standard histories of the English language explain these two Laws in detail; for us their most important effect is seen in the OE strong verbs, where Verner's Law accounts for certain variations in the medial consonant. Thus in class I we find

> snīþan   snāþ   snidon   sniden

Here the *þ* of the inf. and 1st pret. is the consonant we should expect by Grimm's Law. The *d* of the 2nd pret. and past ptc. is the Verner's Law form. Similarly we find

> II   cēosan   cēas   curon   coren

and in contracted verbs (which originally had *h* in the inf.; see §§103.3 and 103.4)

> I   wrēon   wrāh   wrigon   wrigen
> V   sēon   seah   sāwon   sewen

In these strong verbs, the Verner's Law forms occur in the 2nd pret. and the past ptc., while the inf. and 1st pret. are regular. This is historically 'correct'; we see from the verbs marked † in Appendix A that by Verner's Law TH in the inf. and 1st pret. is LIKELY to

---

[1] Its voicing (§9) comes later; see A. Campbell, *Old English Grammar*, §444.

be replaced by D in the 2nd pret. and past ptc., s by R, and (mostly in contracted verbs) H by G, w, or (in *hōn* and *fōn*: see below) by NG.[1]

§108 The word 'LIKELY' is emphasized because the Verner's Law forms sometimes occur where historically they should not. Thus the principal parts of the contracted verbs of class VII are

hōn	hēng	hēngon	hangen
fōn	fēng	fēngon	fangen

Here the Verner's Law *ng* is extended into the 1st pret.; the same may be true of the *g* in

VI	slēan	slōg	slōgon	slǣgen[2]

Sometimes, on the other hand, the Verner's Law forms are completely eliminated, as in *mīþan* I 'conceal' and *rīsan* I 'rise'; this has happened to all Verner's Law forms in MnE except 'was/were'. This process of systematizing or regularizing by the elimination of odd forms is sometimes called 'levelling'. But, as we see from verbs like *scrīþan*, with past ptc. *scriden* or *scripen*, its results are often capricious because it is not conducted consciously and logically.

§109 These and other levellings which occur in OE can be seen as the first signs of two great changes which overtook the strong verbs as English developed through the centuries. First, we today distinguish fewer classes of strong verbs. For example, the verbs of class V have gone over to class IV. Thus, while OE *specan*, *tredan*, *wefan*, have *e* in their past ptcs., MnE 'speak', 'tread', 'weave', have *o*; cf. *beran* IV. Second, while in OE the stem vowels of the 1st and 2nd prets. are different except in classes VI and VII, they are today the same (again except in 'was/were'). The beginnings of this process are seen in *cuman* IV 'come' and *etan* V 'eat', where the vowel of the 2nd pret. is found in the 1st pret. too. The marked confusion of forms in *niman* IV 'take' also results from this levelling. Perhaps you can work out for yourself why *findan* has a 1st pret. *funde*.

Conjugation of the Strong Verb

§110 Our wanderings through what have been called 'the dusty deserts of barren philology' lead us now to the conjugation of the strong verb, here exemplified by *bēodan* II. Points which must be carefully noted when conjugating these and all strong verbs are set out below; on the uses of the tenses and moods, see §§195-198 and 173-179.

[1] Verner's Law forms are also seen in such related pairs as *cēosan* 'choose'/ *cyre* 'choice' and *rīsan* 'rise'/*rǣran* 'raise'. See §136.

[2] But *slōh* does occur, and ME forms suggest that the *g* in *slōg* may be merely a spelling variant of *h*.

§111 *Bēodan* 'command' is conjugated:

	Present Indicative	Preterite Indicative
Sg. 1	bēode	bēad
2	bīetst	bude
3	bīett	bēad
Pl.	bēodaþ	budon

	Present Subjunctive	Preterite Subjunctive
Sg.	bēode	bude
Pl.	bēoden	buden

Before a 1st or 2nd pers. pron., the plural endings can be reduced to -*e*, e.g. *wē bēodaþ* but *bēode wē*.

Imp. Sg.	bēod	*Pl.*	bēodaþ
Inf.	bēodan	*Infl. Inf.*	tō bēodenne
Pres. Ptc.	bēodende	*Past Ptc.*	(ġe-)boden

Participles may be declined like adjectives. Strong and weak forms occur, as appropriate.

§112 In the present tense, note:

1. The stem vowel of the inf. appears throughout except in 2nd and 3rd pers. sg. pres. ind., where its *i*-mutated equivalent is found if there is one. Hence *scīnan/scīnþ* but *bēodan/bīett*.

2. The reduction of the endings of 2nd and 3rd pers. sg. pres. ind. (which is common in WS) whereby the *e* of the endings -*est* and -*eþ* disappears. If this leaves a combination which is difficult to pronounce, it is simplified. So from *bīdan* 'wait for', we get *bīdeþ* > **bīdþ* > **bītþ* > *bītt*. (Try this simple phonetic process for yourself.) Similarly, *bīteþ* from *bītan* 'bite' is also reduced to *bītt*. Hence theoretically *se mann bītt þæt wīf* could mean 'the man is waiting for the woman' or 'the man is biting the woman'.[1] But, in the absence of newspaper reporters in Anglo-Saxon times, this ambiguity does not cause practical difficulty. The most important consequences for you are that 2nd pers. sg. pres. ind. ending in -*tst* and 3rd pers. sg. pres. ind. ending in -*tt* may be from verbs with -*tan* (e.g. *bītan*), -*dan* (e.g. *bīdan*), or -*ddan* (e.g. *biddan*). Since -*sest* and -*seþ* both become -*st*, *cīest* may be either 2nd or 3rd pers.[2]

3. The endings of the imp.—sg. NIL, pl. -*aþ*.
4. The imp. pl. is the same as the pres. ind. pl.
5. The subj. endings sg. -*e* and pl. -*en*, which also occur in the pret.
6. The pres. subj. sg. is the same as the 1st pers. sg. pres. ind.

§113 In the preterite tense, note:

[1] *Bīdan* 'wait for' can take gen. or acc.   [2] See further, Appendix A.

1. The so-called pret. sg. occurs in TWO PLACES ONLY—1st and 3rd sg. pret. ind. Hence it is better called the 1st pret.

2. The vowel of pret. pl. (better called the 2nd pret.) is found in all other places in the pret. Hence *þu drife* and *þu bude* may be either pret. ind. or pret. subj.

3. In actual practice, a similar ambiguity exists throughout the pret. pl. Many primers and grammars show *-on* as the ind. ending and *-en* as the subj. ending. But (generally speaking) this distinction does not hold in the MSS. This is because the process which led to the reduction of all the inflexional endings to *-e*, *-es*, *-en*, and so on, in ME had already begun in OE. MnE, with its fixed spelling system, still spells differently the second syllables of 'pukka', 'beggar', 'baker', 'actor', and (in some places) 'honour', all of which are pronounced the same by many speakers in Great Britain, and by some in other countries. But in OE the spelling system tended to be more phonetic and we often find scribes writing down in the MSS forms which represent the pronunciation they actually used and not the forms which are shown in the grammars. As a result, you may find in your reading pret. pl. forms ending, not only in *-on* and *-en*, but also in *-æn*, *-an*, and *-un*. Any of these may be ind. or subj. Hence the only places in the pret. of the strong verbs where ind. and subj. are clearly distinguished are the two places where the ind. has the 1st pret. form; see 1 above.

4. The variations in the medial cons. caused by Verner's Law; see §§107-108.

§114 Two groups of strong verbs present special difficulties in the present tense. The first—those in classes V and VI with weak presents—are discussed in §116. The others are the contracted verbs, exemplified here by *sēon* V 'see'. Only the present tense is given, for in the pret. it follows the rules given above.

		Present Indicative			*Present Subjunctive*
Sg.	1	sēo			sēo
	2	si(e)hst			sēo
	3	si(e)hþ			sēo
Pl.		sēoþ			sēon
Imp. Sg.		seoh	*Pl.*		sēoþ
Inf.		sēon	*Infl. Inf.*		tō sēonne
Pres. Ptc.		sēonde			

Note

We have already seen in §103.3 that *sēon* is a form produced by breaking and loss of *h*. The whole of the pres. tense except 2nd and 3rd sg. pres. ind. (forms which must always be viewed with suspicion in both strong and weak verbs) is affected by these two sound-changes, e.g.

1st sg. pres. ind. *ić sehe > *ić seohe > *ić sēoe > ić sēo

and so on for the other forms. But the 2nd and 3rd sg. pres. ind. are different. The vowels will have to be taken on trust for the moment. But *h* occurs in these forms because the *e* of the ending disappeared (see §112.2) before the *h* could be lost between vowels. Because the *h* did not disappear, the vowels remained short; cf. the imp. sg. *seoh*.

You may care to note that the pres. subj. sg. is the same as the 1st pers. sg. pres. ind. (*sēo*) and that the subj. pl. and the inf. are the same (*sēon*). This is true of all contracted verbs.

vii Weak Verbs and Sound-Changes
relevant to them
Introduction

§115 There are three classes of weak verbs in OE. As in MnE, these verbs form their pret. and their past ptc. by the addition of a dental suffix. Normally the stem vowel is the same throughout; for exceptions, see §§122-123 and 126. As will become apparent, the inflexional endings of the strong and weak verbs have much in common.

Class 1

§116 Class 1 of the weak verbs is divided into two sub-classes:
(a) exemplified by *fremman* 'do' and *nerian* 'save';
(b) exemplified by *hieran* 'hear'.

Present Indicative

	(a)	(a)	(b)
Sg. 1	fremme	nerie	hiere
2	fremest	nerest	hierst
3	fremeþ	nereþ	hierþ
Pl.	fremmaþ	neriaþ	hieraþ

Imperative

	(a)	(a)	(b)
Sg.	freme	nere	hier
Pl.	fremmaþ	neriaþ	hieraþ

Present Subjunctive

	(a)	(a)	(b)
Sg.	fremme	nerie	hiere
Pl.	fremmen	nerien	hieren

Preterite Indicative

	(a)	(a)	(b)
Sg. 1	fremede	nerede	hierde
2	fremedest	neredest	hierdest
3	fremede	nerede	hierde
Pl.	fremedon	neredon	hierdon

Preterite Subjunctive

	(a)	(a)	(b)
Sg.	fremede	nerede	hīerde
Pl.	fremeden	nereden	hīerden

Inf.	fremman	nerian	hīeran
Infl. Inf.	tō fremmenne	tō nerienne	tō hīerenne
Pres. Ptc.	fremmende	neriende	hīerende
Past Ptc.	(ġe-)fremed	(ġe-)nered	(ġe-)hīered

Participles may be declined like adjectives.

Like *fremman* are most verbs with short vowel + a double consonant, e.g. *cnyssan* 'knock'. The strong verbs of classes V and VI such as *biddan* 'pray' and *hebban* 'lift' are like *fremman* THROUGHOUT THE PRESENT.[1]

Like *nerian* are nearly all verbs ending in -*rian* (for exceptions, see §132.1). The class VI strong verb *swerian* is like *nerian* THROUGHOUT THE PRESENT.

Like *hīeran* are verbs with a long vowel + a single consonant, e.g. *dēman* 'judge', and verbs with a short vowel + two consonants not the same, e.g. *sendan* 'send'. A few verbs of the same pattern as *fremman*, but with a different history, also belong here; they include *fyllan* 'fill'. The strong verb *wēpan* (class VII(a)) is like *hīeran* THROUGHOUT THE PRESENT. Its past ptc. is *wōpen*.

As is shown in §117, all the verbs of this class have an *i*-mutated vowel throughout the stem except those discussed in §§122-123.

§117 A glance at the conjugation of these three verbs will show that *fremman* sometimes loses an *m*, *nerian* its *i*, and that (compared with *fremman* and *nerian*) *hīeran* sometimes loses an *e* in the inflexional endings. These 'losses' (an unhistorical name, as we shall see below) occur in the following places:

1. 2nd and 3rd sg. pres. ind.;
2. imp. sg.;
3. throughout the pret. The pret. stems of these three verbs are respectively *fremed-* (with one *m*), *nered-* (with no *i*), and *hierd-* (with no *e*);
4. in the past ptc., except that *hīeran* usually has *hīered*.

Note

These variations can be explained briefly as follows. The infinitive

---

[1] The only verbs with double medial cons. which are strong throughout belong to class III (e.g. *swimman*, *winnan*) and to class VII (e.g. *bannan*, *feallan*). Verbs whose infinitives rhyme with any of these four are always strong. See further §133.5.

of *fremman* was once **framjan*.[1] The *j*—a high front sound—operated like *i* and caused *i*-mutation of *a*, which before *m* became *e*. But *j* had another property denied to *i*; in short-stemmed words it caused lengthening or doubling of any cons. (except *r*) which preceded it, and then disappeared. So **framjan* > *fremman*. In **nærjan* the *j* merely caused *i*-mutation and remained as *i*; hence *nerian*.

But in the places where *fremman* 'loses' an *m*, the inflexional ending originally began with *i*. So e.g., the 3rd sg. pres. ind. of **framjan* was **framjiþ*. Here the *j* was absorbed into the *i* before it could cause doubling; so we get **framiþ*. The *i* caused *i*-mutation and then became *e*, giving *fremeþ*. Similarly **nærjiþ* > **næriþ* > *nereþ*. Similarly, absence of *j* in the pret. gave *fremede* and *nerede*. In *hīeran* and the other verbs of sub-class (b), the details and the results are different, and can be taken on trust for the time being.

§118 Once these variations are understood, we can observe certain similarities in the inflexional endings of the weak verbs of class 1 and those of the strong verbs. These are:

1. The pres. ind. endings of the weak verbs are the same as the endings of the strong verbs. The *-est* and *-eþ* of the 2nd and 3rd sg. pres. ind. are subject to the same reductions as occurred in these forms in the strong verbs (§112.2). However, the weak verbs generally show more unreduced forms than the strong verbs.

2. The pres. and pret. subj. endings are the same in both weak and strong verbs.

3. The pres. subj. sg. is the same as the 1st pers. sg. pres. ind.

4. The endings of the pret. pl. ind. are the same.

5. The endings of the imp. pl., the pres. ptc., and the infs. respectively are the same.

6. The imp. pl. is the same as the pres. ind. pl.

§119 Important differences are seen in

1. the imp. sgs. *freme* and *nere*, where the strong verbs have no final *-e*; cf. *hier* (see §117.2);

2. the pret. ind. sg., where the endings are *-e, -est, -e*.

§120 As in the strong verbs, the pret. pl. endings *-on* and *-en* are ambiguous; see §113.3. In lWS the 2nd sg. ending *-est* is often extended to the subj. Hence the pret. ind. and subj. can no longer be distinguished in the weak verbs.

§121 Certain simplifications occur in the pret. and the past ptc.:

1. If in forming the pret. a double consonant followed another

---

[1] *j* here and elsewhere is the sound written [j] in phonetic script and pronounced something like MnE *y* in 'year'. It is a high front sound which can be made by saying *i* and then closing the gap between the tongue and the hard palate.

consonant, it was simplified. Hence *sendan* has pret. *sende*, not
*sendde.

2. A ptc. such as *sended* may be simplified to *send*.

3. After voiceless sounds (e.g. *p*, *s*, *t*) the dental suffix becomes *t*,
e.g. *mētan* 'meet' has *mētte*; cf. MnE 'judged' with 'crept'.

4. *-cd-* appears as *-ht-*. Hence *tǣċan* 'teach' has pret. *tǣhte*, past
ptc. *(ġe-)tǣht*.

§122 In MnE we have some weak verbs which change their stem
vowel in the pret. and the past ptc. as well as adding the dental
suffix. They include 'sell/sold', 'tell/told', 'seek/sought', 'buy/bought',
'bring/brought', and 'think/thought', which were weak verbs of
class 1 in OE and had the same irregularity even then. There were
more of them in OE, for some have disappeared, e.g. *reċċan* 'tell',
and some have become regular weak verbs, e.g. *streċċan* 'stretch'.[1]
It is simplest just to learn these in the first instance. The most
important ones are:

Inf.	Pret. Sg.	Past Ptc.
sēċan 'seek'	sōhte	sōht
sellan 'give'	sealde	seald
cwellan 'kill'	cwealde	cweald
þenċan 'think'	þōhte	þōht
brenġan 'bring'	brōhte	brōht
þynċan 'seem'	þūhte	þūht
byċgan 'buy'	bohte	boht
wyrċan 'work'	worhte	worht

§123 The irregularity of these verbs is due to the fact that there
was no *i* in the pret. or the past ptc. to cause *i*-mutation. Hence,
while their present tenses have an *i*-mutated vowel like all the other
verbs of this class, the vowel of the pret. and past ptc. is unmutated.
This can be seen clearly by comparing *sēċan* (< **sōkjan*) with
sōhte/sōht. Unfortunately the parallels in most verbs are obscured
by other sound-changes which affected the vowel of the pret. and
past ptc. They are:

1. Breaking, e.g. *cwellan/cwealde*. Here the *æ* which once occurred
throughout has been *i*-mutated to *e* in the pres. and broken to *ea*
by the *ld* in the pret.

2. Loss of *n* before *h* with lengthening of the preceding vowel so
that the word takes the same time to pronounce. This accounts for
þenċan/þōhte, *þynċan/þūhte*, and *brenġan/brōhte*. Note that the strong
inf. *bringan* usually replaces *brenġan*.

[1] As you will see from §121.4, the verb *tǣċan* 'teach' usually has the same
vowel throughout in WS, but *tāhte*, *tāht*, do occur.

3. A change by which Gmc. *u* under certain conditions became OE *o*. This accounts for the variations in *bycgan/bohte* and *wyrċan/worhte*, where an original *u* has been *i*-mutated to *y* in the pres. and has changed to *o* in the pret.

Class 2

§124   The weak verbs of class 2 present few problems. The traditional paradigm is *lufian* 'love' The long-stemmed *lōcian* 'look' has exactly the same endings.

	Pres. Ind.	*Pret. Ind.*
Sg. 1	lufie	lufode
2	lufast	lufodest
3	lufaþ	lufode
Pl.	lufiaþ	lufodon

	Pres. Subj.	*Pret. Subj.*
Sg.	lufie	lufode
Pl.	lufien	lufoden

Imp. Sg.	lufa	*Pl.*	lufiaþ
Inf.	lufian	*Infl. Inf.*	tō lufienne
Pres. Ptc.	lufiende	*Past Ptc.*	(ġe-)lufod

All weak verbs of class 2 end in *-ian*. However, most verbs ending in *-rian* belong, not to class 2, but to class 1(*a*) following *nerian*. But *andswarian* 'answer', *gadrian* 'gather', *timbrian* 'build', and one or two other verbs in *-rian*, usually follow *lufian*.

§125   Points to note in the conjugation of *lufian* are:

1. The *i* disappears in the 2nd and 3rd sg. pres. ind., the imp. sg., all forms of the pret., and the past ptc. These are exactly the same places where *fremman* 'loses' its *m*, *nerian* its *i*, and *hieran* its *e*.

2. The *-a* in 2nd and 3rd sg. pres. ind. *lufast, lufaþ*, and in imp. sg. *lufa*. So far the verb ending *-aþ* has always signified imp. or pres. ind. pl. In these verbs, *-aþ* is sg., *-iaþ* pl. Beware of this when reading your texts.

3. The *-od* in the pret. stem *lufod-* and in the past ptc. *lufod* where *fremman* has *-ed*.

Apart from these differences, the weak verbs of classes 1 and 2 are conjugated the same.

Class 3

§126   Class 3 contains four weak verbs—*habban* 'have', *libban* 'live', *secgan* 'say', and *hycgan* 'think'. These are conjugated:

Present Indicative

Sg. 1	hæbbe	libbe	secge	hycge
2	hæfst	leofast	sægst	hyġst
	hafast	lifast	seġ(e)st	hogast
3	hæfþ	leofaþ	sægþ	hyġþ
	hafaþ	lifaþ	seġ(e)þ	hogaþ
Pl.	habbaþ	libbaþ	secgaþ	hycgaþ
Imp. Sg.	hafa	leofa	sæġe	hyġe, hoga
Pret. Ind. Sg.	hæfde	lifde	sæġde	hogde

With these parts, you can construct the rest of these verbs for yourself, following the conjugation of *fremman* and the rules set out in §118.

To help you with the pres. ind. sg. and imp. sg., see §117.

viii OTHER VERBS
Bēon

§127   *Bēon* 'be' has forms from different stems.

Indicative	*Pres.*	*Pres.*	*Pret.*
Sg. 1	eom	bēo	wæs
2	eart	bist	wǣre
3	is	biþ	wæs
Pl.	sindon, sint	bēoþ	wǣron

Imp. Sg.	bēo, wes	*Pl.*	bēoþ, wesaþ
Pres. Subj. Sg.	bēo	*Pl.*	bēon
	sīe		sīen
Pret. Subj. Sg.	wǣre	*Pl.*	wǣren

On the distinction in meaning between *eom* and *bēo*, see §196.

Dōn and ġān

§128   *Dōn* 'do' and *ġān* 'go' have:

Present Indicative

Sg. 1	dō	gā
2	dēst	gǣst
3	dēþ	gǣþ
Pl.	dōþ	gāþ
Imp. Sg.	dō	gā
Pret. Ind. Sg.	dyde	ēode
Past Ptc.	ġedōn	ġegān

Note

     i-mutation in 2nd and 3rd pers. sg. pres. ind.

The remaining forms can be constructed with the help of §118.

Willan

§ 129   *Willan* 'wish, will' has:

		Pres. Ind.	Pres. Subj.
Sg.	1	wille	wille
	2	wilt	wille
	3	wil(l)e	wille
Pl.		willaþ	willen
Pret.		wolde	

Preterite-Present Verbs

§ 130   Some very common verbs have a strong past tense with a present meaning (cf. Lat. *novi* 'I know') and a new weak past tense. Thus *wāt* 'I know, he knows' *witon* 'they know' belongs to class I; cf. *scān, scinon.* Its new past tense is sg. *wiste* pl. *wiston.* Such verbs are called preterite-present verbs. The most important ones are:

Meaning	Pres. Ind. Sg. 1, 3	2	Pres. Ind. Pl.	Pret. Sg.
'possess'	āh	āhst, āht	āgon	āhte
'grant'	ann	—	unnon	ūþe
'can, know how to'	cann	canst	cunnon	cūþe
'avail, be of use'	dēah	—	dugon	dohte
'dare'	dearr	dearst	durron	dorste
'remember'	ġeman	ġemanst	ġemunon	ġemunde
'be able'	mæġ	meaht	magon	mihte, meahte
'be allowed to, may'	mōt	mōst	mōton	mōste
'be obliged to'	sceal	scealt	sculon	sceolde
'need'	þearf	þearft	þurfon	þorfte
'know'	wāt	wāst	witon	wiste

ix   Is A VERB STRONG OR WEAK? TO WHICH CLASS DOES IT
BELONG?

§ 131   If we assume that you can recognize on sight the strong contracted verbs, the four weak verbs of class 3 (§ 126), and the verbs discussed in §§ 127-130, the system set out below will enable you to answer the questions at the head of this section.

Verbs in -*ian*

§ 132   1. Verbs in -*rian* are class 1 weak.

Exceptions: (*a*) *swerian* 'swear' (class VI strong with a weak
present);

(*b*) *andswarian* 'answer' and a few other verbs
which can follow *lufian* 'love'; see § 124.

2. All other verbs in -*ian* are class 2 weak.

GOE E

Verbs in -*an*

§133   These are either strong or class 1 weak. You will find that
the recognition symbols for the strong verbs set out in §94 are almost
always reliable. Thus if a verb ending in -*an* has *ī* + one cons. in
the infinitive, it is probably class I strong. If it has *ū* + one cons.,
it is probably class II strong. And so on. Exceptions include:

1. The strong verbs of classes V, VI, and VII (*wēpan* 'weep'), with
weak presents. These too should be recognized on sight.

2. *Fēolan* 'press on' looks like class II strong, but belongs to
class III, as the 1st pret. *fealh* shows. (**Felhan* > **feolhan* by breaking (§97.2) > *fēolan* by loss of *h* + lengthening; see §38.)

3. A verb with *ǣ* + one cons. may be either strong or weak;
lǣtan 'let' is class VII strong, *lǣdan* 'lead' is class 1 weak.

4. For weak verbs with *ī* and *ēo*, see Appendix A.1 and 2.

5. Verbs with a short vowel + a double cons. are mostly weak
class 1, e.g. *fremman*. The recognition symbols of the strong verbs
of class III will enable us to distinguish *swimman* 'swim' and *winnan*
'fight' as class III strong; note *i* before the nasals compared with
the *e* of *fremman*. *Bannan* 'summon', *spannan* 'span', *feallan* 'fall',
and *weallan* 'boil', are class VII strong. On *bringan*, see §123.2.
On *hringan* and *ġeþingan*, see Appendix A.3.

§134   When you are reading Old English, your problem will often
be to find the infinitive from which a certain verb form is derived.
Let us take *bitt*, *stæl*, and *budon*, as examples.

For *bitt*, we note -*i*- and -*tt*. Together these suggest the synco-
pated 3rd sg. pres. ind. of a verb of class I. The ending -*tt* we know
to be a reduction of -*teþ* or -*deþ*. This gives us two possibilities—
bītan 'bite' or *bīdan* 'await'. The context should determine which
we have. In a text which does not mark long vowels, *bitt* could also
be from *biddan* V 'ask'.

For *stæl* we note -*æ*-. This suggests the 1st pret. of class IV or V.
Hence the inf. is *stelan* 'steal'. The medial *l* decides for class IV.

Budon is perhaps more difficult. Is it strong or (since it ends in
-*don*) weak? If it is strong, the medial *u* and the single cons. suggest
class II. Therefore the inf. could be *bēodan* or **būdan*. The glossary
decides for *bēodan* 'command'. If it were a weak pret., the inf. would
be *buan*. This would not fit *būan* 'dwell' with pret. pl. *būdon* unless
the text did not mark long vowels. If this were the case, the context
would again decide.

The verbs discussed in §122 present a problem, but you will soon
become familiar with their preterites.

x ADVERBS

Formation

§135   Characteristic endings of adverbs are -*e* (e.g. *hraþe* 'quickly'),
-*līċe* (e.g. *hrædlīċe* 'quickly'), and -*unga* (e.g. *eallunga* 'entirely'). The
ending -*an* means 'from', e.g. *norþ* 'north, northwards' but *norþan*
'from the north'.

The gen. and dat. can be used adverbially; see §§190 and 191.

The negative adverb is *ne*. For its use, see §184.4.

Comparison

Adverbs are normally compared by adding -*or*, -*ost*, e.g. *oft* 'often'
oftor oftost, and (dropping the -*e* of the positive) *swīþe* 'greatly'
swīþor swīþost.

Some have an *i*-mutated vowel in the comparative and superlative, e.g. *lange* 'long' *leng lengest* and *feorr* 'far' *fierr fierrest*.

A knowledge of the equivalent OE adjectives and MnE adverbs
will enable you to recognize in reading the irregular comparatives
and superlatives of the adverbs *wel* 'well', *yfle* 'evilly', *miċle* 'much',
and *lȳt* 'little'.

IV WORD FORMATION

INTRODUCTION

§136 Old English acquired new words in three ways—by borrowing from other languages (see §234), by making compounds of two words already existing in the language, e.g. *sǣ-weall* 'sea-wall', and by adding suffixes to existing words to change their function or meaning, e.g. *blōd* (neut.) 'blood' but *blōd-iġ* 'bloody, blood-stained', and *bēodan* 'command' but *for-bēodan* 'forbid'. A knowledge of these last two methods and of the formative elements used will help you to deduce the meaning of many words which may at first sight seem unfamiliar.

It is also important to realize that parts of speech wer e not inter changeable in OE as they often are in MnE. Thus the OE noun *drinc* has a corresponding verb *drincan* whereas today 'drink' is both a noun and a verb. Similarly the OE adjective *open* and the verb *openian* are both represented by MnE 'open'. Such correspondences are fairly obvious. But others are more difficult to spot because they are obscured by sound-changes. You may be able to deduce for yourself the change which causes the variations in the following pairs: *scrūd* (neut.) 'clothing' *scrȳdan* 'clothe'; *dōm* (masc.) 'judgement' *dēma* (masc.) 'a judge'; *hāl* 'whole, in good health' *hǣlan* 'heal, make whole'. If you cannot, see §§52-57. Other groups of related words have different vowels from the same gradation series (see §90), e.g. *beran* 'carry', *bǣr* (fem.) 'bier', and the ending *-bora* (masc.) 'bearer, carrier', which often occurs in compounds such as *sweord-bora* 'sword-bearer'. Both these sound-changes and Verner's Law (§§105-108) obscure the relationship between *ċēosan* 'choose' and *cyre* (masc.) 'choice', where *y* is an *i*-mutation of *u*.

Notes

1. On the gender and declension of nouns formed by compounding or by the addition of suffixes, see §§12, 13, and 41.
2. The work by Madden and Magoun mentioned in §253 adopts a 'packaging principle' by which parent words, their immediate derivatives, and those related by *i*-mutation and gradation, are grouped together. This makes for ease of learning, and is one of the reasons why the book is so useful.
3. Most of the examples in this chapter are taken from Sweet's *Anglo-Saxon Reader*.

COMPOUNDING

§137   The process of forming new words or compounds by joining
together two separate words which already exist was common in
OE. Some of the possible arrangements are exemplified below.
Nouns can be formed by combining:

1. Noun and noun, e.g. *hell-waran* (masc. pl.) 'inhabitants of hell',
niht-waco (fem.) 'night-watch', *scip-rāp* (masc.) 'ship-rope', *storm-sǣ*
(masc. or fem.) 'stormy sea';

2. Adjective and noun, e.g. *eall-wealda* (masc.) 'ruler of all', *hēah-
clif* (neut.) 'high cliff', *hēah-ġerēfa* (masc.) 'high reeve, chief officer',
wid-sǣ (masc. or fem.) '(open) sea';

3. Adverb and noun, e.g. *ǣr-dæġ* (masc.) 'early day, first dawn',
eft-siþ (masc.) 'return', *inn-faru* (fem.) 'expedition', *inn-gang* (masc.)
'entrance'.

Adjectives are found consisting of:

1. Noun and adjective, e.g. *ælmes-ġeorn* 'alms-eager, generous,
charitable', *ār-weorþ* 'honour-worthy, venerable', *dōm-ġeorn* 'eager
for glory', *mere-wēriġ* 'sea-weary';

2. Adjective and adjective, e.g. *hēah-þungen* 'of high rank', *hrēow-
ċeariġ* 'sad' (lit. 'sad-anxious'), *wid-cūþ* 'widely known', *wis-hycgende*
'wise-thinking';

3. Adverb and adjective, e.g. *ǣr-gōd* 'very good', *forþ-ġeorn* 'forth-
eager, eager to advance', *wel-þungen* 'well-thriven, excellent', *wel-
willende* 'well-wishing, benevolent';

4. Adjective and noun, e.g. *blanden-feax* 'having mixed hair, gray-
haired', *bliþe-mōd* 'of kindly mind, friendly', *hrēowiġ-mōd* 'gloomy-
minded, sad', *salu-pād* 'dark-coated'.

In all these words the first element is uninflected; cf. *folc-lagu*
(fem.) 'law of the people, public law' with *Godes* (gen.) *lagu* 'God's
law' and *win-druncen* 'wine-drunk' with *bēore* (dat.) *druncen* 'drunk
with beer'. But compounds do occur with an inflected first element,
e.g. *Engla-lond* 'land of the Angles, England' (but cf. *Fres-lond*
'Frisian land, Frisia') and *eġes-full* 'full of terror, terrible, wonderful'
(but cf. *synn-full* 'sinful').

Note

Compounds of three elements are sometimes found, e.g. *wulf-hēafod-
trēo* (neut.) 'wolf-head-tree, gallows, cross'.

Today, when we are faced with a new object or idea, we often
express it by a compound made up of foreign elements, e.g. 'telephone' and 'tele-vision'. But OE was less inclined to borrow words
than MnE and often 'translated' foreign words. Sometimes two
elements of a foreign word were represented by OE equivalents, e.g.

god-spel (neut.) 'good news', based on *evangelium*, for 'gospel',[1] *Þri-nes* (fem.) representing *Trini-tas* 'The Trinity', and Ælfric's grammatical terms *fore-set-nes* (fem.) for Lat. *prae-positio* 'preposition' and *betwux-āleǧed-nes* (fem.) 'between-laid-ness' for Lat. *interjectio* 'interjection'. Sometimes the word was analysed into its concepts and these were rendered into English, e.g. two words for 'Pharisees'—*sundor-halgan* (masc. pl.) 'apart-holies' and *ǣ-lāreowas* (masc. pl.) 'law-teachers'. That these processes are no longer natural for speakers of English can be seen in two ways. First, many native compounds such as *tungol-cræft* (masc.) 'star-craft' for 'astronomy' and *lār-hūs* (neut.) 'lore-house' for 'school' have disappeared from the language. Secondly, proposed replacements like the sixteenth-century 'hundreder' for 'centurion' or the nineteenth-century 'folk-wain' for 'bus' seem to us ridiculous, whereas to Germans *Fernsprecher* 'far-speaker' for our Greek-derived 'telephone' is not unnatural, though they do, of course, use *Telephon*.

To help provide the many synonyms beginning with different letters which were essential for the *scop* (poet) working in the alliterative measure, the Anglo-Saxon poets made great use of compounds. Of special interest is the kenning, a sort of condensed metaphor in which (a) is compared to (b) without (a) or the point of the comparison being made explicit; thus one might say of the camel 'The desert-ship lurched on'. So the sea is *hwæl-weǧ* (masc.) 'whale-way', a ship *ȳþ-hengest* (masc.) 'wave-horse', and a minstrel *hleahtor-smiþ* (masc.) 'laughter-smith'.

We find too that many set phrases inherited from the days when the poetry was composed orally survive in the lettered poetry. These 'oral-formulae' are set metrical combinations which could be varied according to the needs of alliteration. Thus the phrase 'on, over, across the sea' can be expressed by one of the prepositions *on*, *ofer*, *ǧeond*, followed by the appropriate case of one of the following words: *bæþ-weǧ* 'bath-way', *flōd-weǧ* 'flood-way', *flot-weǧ* 'sea-way', *hwæl-weǧ* 'whale-way' (all masc.), *hran-rād* 'whale-road', *swan-rād* 'swan-road', and *seǧl-rād* 'sail-road' (all fem.). References to further discussions on these points will be found in §§ 265-266.

THE ADDITION OF AFFIXES

§ 138 These can be divided into prefixes—elements placed at the beginning of words to qualify their meaning—and endings. The effect of many which survive today is obvious; we may cite the prefix *mis-* as in *mis-dǣd* (fem.) 'misdeed', prepositions or adverbs used as prefixes, e.g. *ofer-mæǧen* (neut.) 'superior force' and *ūt-gān*

---

[1] You should look up the noun 'gospel' in O.E.D. to find out why *godspel* has ǒ when the OE equivalent of 'good' is *gōd*.

'go out', adjectives ending in -*full*, -*isċ*, and -*lēas*, e.g. *synn-full* 'sinful', *ċild-isċ* 'childish', and *feoh-lēas* 'moneyless, destitute', and nouns ending in -*dōm*, -*ere*, -*scipe* (all masc.) and -*nes*, -*nis*, -*nys* (fem.), e.g. *wīs-dōm* 'wisdom', *fisc-ere* 'fisherman', *frēond-scipe* 'friendship', and *beorht-nes* 'brightness'. Others which occur frequently but are not so easily recognizable are set out below.

Prefixes

ā-	1. Sometimes it means 'away', as in *ā-fȳsan* 'drive forth'
	2. But sometimes it seems to have no effect on the meaning, e.g. *ā-galan* 'sing'.
ǣġ-	It generalizes prons. and advs., e.g. *ǣġ-hwā* 'everyone' and *ǣġ-hwǣr* 'everywhere'.
be-	1. In some words *be-* is the same as the prep. 'about', e.g. *be-gān* 'surround' and *be-rīdan* 'ride round, surround'.
	2. Sometimes it is a deprivative, e.g. *be-dǣlan* 'deprive' and *be-hēafdian* 'behead'.
	3. It can make an intransitive verb transitive, e.g. *be-penċan* 'think about' and *be-wēpan* 'bewail'.
for-	It is an intensifier, e.g. *for-bærnan* 'burn up, consume', *for-lorenness* (fem.) 'perdition', and *for-heard* 'very hard'.
ġe-	1. In some nouns it has the sense of 'together', e.g. *ġe-fēra* (masc.) 'companion' and *ġe-brōpru* (masc. pl.) 'brothers'.
	2. In verbs, it sometimes has a perfective sense, e.g. *ġe-āscian* 'find out' and *ġe-winnan* 'get by fighting, win'; hence its frequent use in past ptcs.
on-, an-	1. In verbs like *on-bindan* 'unbind' and *on-lūcan* 'unlock', it has a negative sense.
	2. Sometimes it means 'against', as in *on-rǣs* (masc.) 'attack'.
or-	This is a deprivative, as in *or-mōd* 'without courage, despairing' and *or-sorg* 'without care, careless'.
tō-	1. Sometimes it is the same as the prep. *tō*, e.g. *tō-cyme* (masc.) 'arrival' and *tō-weard* (prep.) 'towards'.
	2. But with verbs it frequently means separation, e.g. *tō-drīfan* (trans.) 'drive apart, disperse, scatter' and *tō-faran* (intrans.) 'go apart, disperse'.
un-	1. This is sometimes a negative prefix, e.g. *un-frip* (masc.) 'un-peace, war' and *un-hold* 'unfriendly'.
	2. Sometimes it is pejorative, as in *un-ġiefu* (fem.) 'evil gift' and *un-weder* (neut.) 'bad weather'.
wan-	This is a deprivative or negative prefix, e.g. *wan-hāl* 'not hale, ill' and *wan-hoga* (masc.) 'thoughtless man'.

ymb- This means 'around', e.g. *ymb-gang* (masc.) 'circuit, circumference' and *ymb-lǣdan* 'lead round'.

Endings

Nouns

-end This equals '-er', as in *Hǣl-end* (masc.) 'Healer, Saviour' and *wiġ-end* (masc.) 'fighter, warrior'. It derives from the pres. ptc. ending *-ende*.

-hād This introduces masc. nouns and equals MnE '-hood', as in *ċild-hād* 'childhood' and *woruld-hād* 'secular life'.

-ing 1. In masc. nouns it means 'son of', e.g. *Ælfred Æþelwulf-ing* 'Alfred son of Æthelwulf', or 'associated with', e.g. *earm-ing* 'wretch' and *hōr-ing* 'adulterer, fornicator'.
2. In fem. nouns, it equals *-ung*; see below.

-þ(o), -þ(u) This is used to form fem. abstract nouns, e.g. *fǣh-þ(o)* 'hostility' and *ierm-þ(u)* 'misery, poverty'. Note that *ġeogoþ* 'youth' is fem.

-aþ, -oþ This forms masc. nouns, e.g. *herg-aþ* 'plundering' and *fisc-oþ* 'fishing'.

-rǣden This forms fem. abstract nouns, e.g. *hierd-rǣden* 'guardianship, care, guard'.

-ung, -ing This is found in fem. abstract nouns formed from verbs, e.g. *bod-ung* 'preaching' and *rǣd-ing* 'reading'.

Adjectives

-en 1. This is the ending of past ptcs. of strong verbs.
2. It is also found in adjectives with an *i*-mutated vowel in the stem, e.g. *ǣttr-en* 'poisonous' and *gyld-en* 'golden'.

-iġ This equals MnE '-y', as in *cræft-iġ* 'powerful, mighty' and *hāl-iġ* 'holy'.

-liċ This, originally the same word as *līċ* (neut.) 'body', equals MnE '-ly, -like', e.g. *heofon-liċ* 'heavenly' and *ċild-liċ* 'child-like, childish'.

-sum This occurs in words like *wynn-sum* 'delightful, pleasant' (cf. 'winsome') and *hīer-sum* 'hear-some, obedient'.

Adverbs

See §135.

Verbs

-ettan   This is found in *lāp-ettan* 'hate, loathe' and *ōn-ettan* 'hasten'.

-lǣċan   This is seen in *ġe-ān-lǣċan* 'unite', *ġe-efen-lǣċan* 'be like, match', and *ġe-nēa-lǣċan* 'approach'.

V SYNTAX

INTRODUCTION

§139 Syntax has been described as the study of 'the traffic rules of language'. If this is so, you are offered here only a simplified Anglo-Saxon highway code, designed to deal with constructions likely to worry the beginner. OE syntax is recognizably English; in some passages the word-order at least is almost without exception that of MnE. At other times, we seem to be wrestling with a foreign language. Some of the difficulties arise from idiosyncrasies due to the Germanic ancestry of OE. Another reason, which obtains mostly in the early writings when OE prose was in a formative state, is that Alfred and his companions were struggling to develop the language as a vehicle for the expression of complicated narrative and abstract thought. They achieved no little success, but had their failures too. The breathless but vigorous account of the Battle of Ashdown (the annal for 871 in the Parker MS of the Anglo-Saxon Chronicle), which sweeps us along on a surging current of simple sentences joined by *ond*, is not untypical of the early efforts of prose writers who were not translating from Latin. There is only one complex sentence in the whole piece (the last but one). That the writer gets into trouble with it is symptomatic; cf. the account of the sea-battle of 897 in the same MS, where what has happened is not particularly clear on first reading. This inability to cope with complicated ideas is more apparent in the translated texts, where the influence of the Latin periodic structure often produces stilted prose, as in the story of Orpheus and Eurydice in King Alfred's translation of Boethius. Even Alfred's original prose is sometimes twisted in the same way, e.g. the sentences discussed in §172. Perhaps Latin, being the language of the Church, the language from which many works were translated, and the only model available, was accorded a status denied to it (or to any other original) today.

§140 Another source of difficulty becomes apparent from a study of the major differences between OE and MnE. It is sometimes said that OE is the period of full inflexions, ME the period of levelled inflexions (all with the vowel *e*, e.g. *-e*, *-es*, *-en*, as opposed to the endings of OE with their different vowels), and MnE the period of no inflexions. This statement points to the vital truth that MnE depends on word-order and prepositions to make distinctions which in an inflected language are made by the case endings. However, it

58

needs qualification. That there are still a few inflexions in MnE is of little importance. But it might be less misleading to say that OE is a 'half-inflected' language. Firstly, it has only four cases and remnants of a fifth left of the eight cases postulated for the original IE language. Secondly, as has been pointed out in §189 note, there is often no distinction in form between nominative and accusative. Hence word-order is often the only thing which enables us to tell which is subject and which is object; consider *Enoch gestrynde Irad and Irad gestrynde Mauiahel* (and so on) 'E. begat I. and I. begat M.' (cf. *Caesarem interfecit Brutus*) and *Hi hæfdon þa ofergan Eastengle and Eastsexe* 'They had then conquered the East Anglians and the East Saxons'. These and many similar examples support the view that the Anglo-Saxons already had the feeling that the subject came first. If we did not have evidence for this, we should have to hesitate instead of automatically following the modern rule and taking *Oswold and Ealdwold* as the subject in the following lines from *Maldon*, for the order object, subject, verb, is possible in OE (see §147):

> Oswold and Ealdwold ealle hwile,
> hegen þa gebroþru, beornas trymedon

'O. and E., the two brothers, all the time encouraged the warriors'. (More is said in §147 on the triumph of the order 'subject verb'.) Thirdly, prepositions followed by an oblique case are often used to express relationships which could be expressed by case alone; cf. *ond þa geascode he þone cyning lytle werode . . . on Merantune* 'and then he discovered the king [to be] at Merton with a small band (inst. case alone)' with *eode he in mid ane his preosta* 'he went in with one of his priests (*mid* +inst. case)'. All these things suggest a language in a state of transition. The implications of this for the future development of English are mentioned briefly in §231; here we are concerned with it as another source of difficulty.

§141 Important differences between OE and MnE are found in the following:

the position of the negative (§§144.1 and 184.4);
the use of the infinitives (§205);
the uses of moods and tenses of the verb (§§195 ff.);
the resolved tenses[1] and the function of the participles therein (§§199 ff.);
the meaning of 'modal' auxiliaries (§§206 ff.);
agreement (§187);
the meaning and use of prepositions (§§213-214).

[1] This term is explained in §199

§142　Features found in OE, but not in MnE, include:

strong and weak forms of the adjective (§§63 and 64);
some special uses of cases (§§188-192);
some special uses of articles, pronouns, and numerals (§§193-194);
the use of a single verb form where MnE would use a resolved tense or mood (§195);
idiomatic absence of the subject (§193.7).

But the main difficulty of OE syntax lies, not in these differences, but in the word-order of the simple sentence or clause, and in the syntax of the subordinate clauses. These fundamental topics are accordingly treated first; if any of the points mentioned in this or the preceding section cause immediate difficulty, see the Contents and read the appropriate section. The order of clauses within the complex sentence is very similar to that of MnE, and will cause little difficulty.

i　Word-Order[1]

§143　If we take subject and verb as the fundamental elements of a sentence, we shall find that the following arrangements are common in OE prose:

S.V., where the verb immediately follows the subject;
S. . . . V., where other elements of the sentence come between subject and verb;
V.S., where the subject follows the verb.

The same orders are also found in the poetry. But, like their successors, the Anglo-Saxon poets used the language much more freely than the prose writers did. Hence the comments made below apply to the prose only. But the word-order in the poetry will not cause you much difficulty if you understand what follows.

§144　As in MnE, the order S.V. can occur in both principal and subordinate clauses, e.g. *he hæfde an swiðe ænlic wif* 'he had a most excellent wife' and *þe getimbrode his hus ofer sand* 'who built his house on sand'. Therefore it cannot tell us whether a clause is principal or subordinate, except in the circumstances discussed in §§150ff. It is also found after *ond* 'and' and *ac* 'but', e.g. *ond his lic liþ æt Winburnan* 'and his body lies at W.'.

There are naturally variations of this order. Some are found in both OE and MnE. Thus an adverb precedes the verb in *Se Hælend*

---

[1] In these sections, the following abbreviations are used: S. (subject), V. (verb), O. (object), Adv. (adverb or adv. phrase). A MnE sentence such as 'Do you sing?' is characterized by v. (auxiliary verb) S.V. Brackets indicate that the feature in question is optional.

ða het þa ðeningmen afyllan six stænene fatu mid hluttrum wætere 'The Saviour then ordered the servants to fill six stone vessels with pure water'. The indirect object precedes the direct object in *Romane gesealdon Gaiuse Iuliuse seofon legan* 'The Romans gave Gaius Julius seven legions', but follows it in *ac he forgeaf eorðlice ðing mannum* 'but he gave earthly things to men'.

Arrangements not found in MnE are:

1. The position of the negative *ne* 'not' immediately before the verb. This is the rule in all three OE word-orders; see §184.4.

2. The placing of a pronoun O. between S. and V. when a noun O. would follow V. Thus *we hie ondredon* 'we feared them' is an idiomatic variation of the order S.V. rather than an example of S. . . . V.

3. The possibility that an infinitive or a participle may have final position, e.g. *he ne meahte ongemong oðrum monnum bion* 'he could not be among other men' and *Eastengle hæfdon Ælfrede cyninge aþas geseald* 'The East Angles had given King Alfred oaths'. On the order S.V. in non-dependent questions, see §160.

§145 The order S. . . . V. is most common in subordinate clauses, e.g. *se micla here, þe we gefyrn ymbe spræcon* 'the great army which we spoke about before' and *gif hie ænigne feld secan wolden* 'if they wished to seek any open country', and after *ond* 'and' and *ac* 'but', e.g. *Ac ic þa sona eft me selfum andwyrde* 'But again I immediately answered myself'. But it also occurs in principal clauses, e.g. *Ða reðan Iudei wedende þone halgan stændon* 'The cruel Jews in their rage stoned the saint' and *Stephanus soðlice gebigedum cneowum Drihten bæd . . .* 'Stephen however on bended knees besought the Lord . . .' Hence the order S. . . . V. does not certify that a clause is subordinate. With this order, the verb need not have final position, but may be followed by an adverbial extension, e.g. *ær he acenned wæs of Marian . . .* 'before He was born of Mary' and *. . . þæt hi wel wyrðe beoð þære deoflican ehtnysse . . .* 'that they will be very worthy of devilish persecution'. On this order in non-dependent questions, see §160.

§146 The order V.S. occurs in MnE in questions with the verbs 'to have' and 'to be', e.g. 'Have you the book?' and 'Are you there?', and in a few other set phrases or constructions, e.g. 'said he', 'Long live the King!', 'be he alive or be he dead', and 'Had I but plenty of money, I would be in Bermuda'. It must not be confused with the normal interrogative word-order of MnE, which is v.S.V., e.g. 'Have you found him?', 'Is he coming?', and 'Do you see him?' In OE the order V.S. is found in:

1. Positive non-dependent questions either with or without inter-

rogative words, e.g. *Hwær eart þu nu, gefera?* 'Where are you now, comrade?' and *Gehyrst þu, sælida?* 'Do you hear, sailor?'

2. Negative non-dependent questions, e.g. *ne seowe þu god sæd on þinum æcere?* 'Did you not sow good seed in your field?'

3. Positive statements, e.g. *Hæfde se cyning his fierd on tu tonumen* 'The king had divided his army in two'.

4. Negative statements, e.g. *Ne com se here* 'The army did not come'.

5. In subordinate clauses of concession and condition, e.g. *swelte ic, libbe ic* 'live I, die I' i.e. 'whether I live or die'.

6. In principal clauses introduced by certain adverbs; cf. MnE 'Then came the dawn'. On the value of this word-order for distinguishing principal from subordinate clauses, see §§ 150 ff.

Notes

1. The orders described in 3 and 4 above are NOT necessarily emphatic.
2. In *Matthew* 20:13, we read: *Eala þu freond, ne do ic þe nænne teonan: hu, ne come þu to me to wyrcenne wið anum peninge?* 'Friend, I do thee no wrong; lo, didst thou not come to me to work for one penny?' Here exactly the same word-order is used first in a statement (order 4 above) and then in a question (order 2 above).

§147 Other word-orders may, of course, occur. Some which are used for emphasis are also found in MnE, e.g. *Gesælige hi wurdon geborene* . . . 'Blessed they were born', *Micelne geleafan he hæfde* . . . 'Great faith he had', and (with a MnE preposition replacing the OE dative case) *þam acennedan Cyninge we bringað gold* . . . 'To the new-born King we bring gold' and *Gode ælmightigum sie ðonc* 'To God Almighty be thanks'. But the order O.V.S. found in *deman gedafenað setl* 'a seat is the proper place for a judge' would be impossible today because, in a MnE sentence of the pattern 'Man flees dog', what precedes the verb must be the subject. Consider what happens to the meaning of the spoken sentence if the word-order is altered. 'Dog flees man', 'Fleas dog man', and even 'Fleas man dog', all mean something different. The absence of endings and the interchangeability of MnE parts of speech have left word-order the only guide and the absolute master. The gradual triumph of this order S.V.O. is one of the most important syntactical developments in English. Its beginnings can be seen in OE. Thus in *Matthew* 7:24 *ælc þæra þe þas min word gehyrð and þa wyrcð, bið gelic þæm wisan were, se his hus ofer stan getimbrode*, the two subordinate clauses have S. . . . V. But in *Matthew* 7:26 *And ælc þæra þe gehyrð þas min word, and þa ne wyrcð, se bið gelic þam dysigan men, þe getimbrode his hus ofer sand-*

ceosel, they both have S.V. This suggests that any difference there may have been between these orders was disappearing. Again, the old preference for V.S. after an adverb (compare modern German) is at times conquered by the new preference for S.V., e.g. *Her cuomon twegen aldormenn* 'In this year two chiefs came' but *Her Hengest 7 Æsc fuhton wiþ Brettas*[1] 'In this year H. and A. fought against the Britons'. Of course, in OE, where the distinction between the nominative and accusative is not always preserved, freedom sometimes leads to ambiguity, e.g. *Ðas seofon hi gecuron . . .*, where only the context tells us that *hi* is the subject. In MnE 'these seven they chose' is unambiguous because of 'they' and because, while the order O.S.V. is possible, the order S.O.V. is not.

ii SENTENCE STRUCTURE

Three difficulties in sentence structure must now be discussed.

Recapitulation and Anticipation

§148 The first is this. In their attempts to explain complicated ideas, Anglo-Saxon writers often had recourse to a device similar to that used by some modern politician who has the desire but not the ability to be an orator, viz. the device of pausing in mid-sentence and starting afresh with a pronoun or some group of words which sums up what has gone before. A simple example will be found in Alfred's Preface to the translation of the *Cura Pastoralis*. Alfred, having written (or dictated) *Ure ieldran, ða ðe ðas stowa ær hioldon* 'Our ancestors who previously occupied these places' pauses as it were for thought and then goes on *hie lufodon wisdom* 'they loved wisdom', where *hie* sums up what has gone before and enables him to control the sentence. Compare with this the orator's gesture-accompanied 'all these things' with which he attempts to regain control of a sentence which has run away from him. Other examples of recapitulatory pronouns will be found in *7 þæt unstille hweol ðe Ixion wæs to gebunden, Leuita cyning, for his scylde, ðæt oðstod for his hearpunga. 7 Tantulus se cyning ðe on ðiosc worulde ungemetlice gifre wæs, 7 him ðær ðæt ilce yfel filgde ðære gifernesse, he gestilde* 'And the ever-moving wheel to which Ixion, King of the Lapithae, was bound for his sin, [that] stood still for his (Orpheus's) harping. And King Tantalus, who in this world was greedy beyond measure and whom that same sin of greed followed there, [he] had rest'. More complicated examples will be found in *hergode he his rice, þone ilcan ende þe Æþered his cumpæder healdan sceolde* 'He (Hæsten) ravaged his (Alfred's) kingdom, that same province which Æthered, his son's godfather,

[1] 7 is a common MS abbreviation for *ond* which is often reproduced by editors.

had the duty of holding', where *his rīċe* is qualified by the rest of the
sentence, and in the second passage discussed in §172.

The common use of a pronoun to anticipate a noun clause may
be compared with this. A simple example is

> Þa þæt Offan mæg   ærest onfunde,
> þæt se eorl nolde   yrhðo geþolian

lit. 'Then the kinsman of Offa first learned that thing (the first *þæt*),
that the leader would not tolerate slackness'. We have perhaps all
had this experience at the hand of some leader, but MnE would dis-
pense with the tautologic *þæt* in giving it expression. In *þæs ic
gewilnige and gewysce mid mode, þæt ic ana ne belife æfter minum
leofum þegnum* lit. 'That thing I desire and wish in my mind, that I
should not remain alone after my beloved thanes', the pronoun *þæs*
anticipates the following *þæt* clause. It is in the genitive after the
verbs *gewilnian* and *gewyscan*. The pronoun *hit* is sometimes found
similarly used, e.g.

> Þæt is micel wundor
> þæt hit ece God   æfre wolde
> Þeoden þolian,   þæt wurde þegn swa monig
> forlædd be þam lygenum. . . .

Here the first *þæt* is in apposition with the *þæt* clause in 1.2 while *hit*
anticipates the *þæt* clause in 1.3: lit. 'That is a great wonder that
eternal God the Lord would ever permit it, that so many a thane
should be deceived by those lies'. Dependent questions may be
similarly anticipated, e.g. *Men þa þæs wundrodon, hu þa weargas
hangodon* lit. 'Men then wondered at that, how the criminals hung'
(where *þæs* is genitive after *wundrodon*) and

> Hycgað his ealle,
> hu ge hi beswicen

lit. 'All [of you] take thought about it, how you may deceive them'
(where *his* is genitive after *hycgað*).

Note

It is possible that in the sentence 'He said that he was ill', 'that'
was originally a demonstrative—'He said that: he was ill'—which
gradually became a part of the noun clause. If so, the introduction
of the second *þæt* or of *hit* illustrates clearly the difficulty our ancestors
seem to have had in collecting and expressing complicated thoughts.

The Splitting of Heavy Groups

§149   The second thing which sometimes helps to make OE seem
a foreign language is a tendency to split up heavy groups. Thus we

say today 'The President and his wife are going to Washington'. But the more common OE arrangement was 'The President is going to Washington, and his wife'. Examples of this tendency are common. We find

1. A divided subject in *eower mod is awend, and eower andwlita* 'your mind and your countenance are changed'. Note here the word-order S.V. and the singular verb; cf. MnE 'Tom was there and Jack and Bill and all the boys'.

2. A divided object in *þa he þone cniht agef 7 þæt wif* 'when he returned the child and the woman'.

3. A divided genitive group in *Inwæres broþur 7 Healfdenes* 'the brother of I. and H.'.

4. Divided phrases in *þa þe in Norþhymbrum bugeað ond on East Englum* 'those who dwell in Northumbria and East Anglia'.

5. Separation of adjectives governing the same noun in *þæt hi næfre ær swa clæne gold, ne swa read ne gesawon* 'that they never before saw such pure, red gold'.

But such groups are not always divided, e.g. *Her Hengest 7 Horsa fuhton wiþ Wyrtgeorne þam cyninge* 'In this year, H. and H. fought against King W.'.

Correlation

§ 150 The third thing which makes us feel that OE is a foreign language is its marked fondness for correlation. This may have its origin in, and so be a more sophisticated manifestation of, the same feeling of insecurity in the face of the complicated sentence which produced the awkward repetitions already discussed. But it later becomes a very important stylistic device which such an outstanding writer as Ælfric exploited to the full. Consider the following sentence from his Homily on the Passion of St. Stephen: *Þider ðe Stephanus forestop, mid Saules stanum oftorfod, þider folgode Paulus, gefultumod þurh Stephanes gebedu* 'Where Stephen went in front, stoned by the stones of Saul, there Paul followed, helped by the prayers of Stephen'. Note:

1. that both the principal and subordinate clause contain the same elements;

2. the word-order S.V. in the subordinate clause *þider ðe Stephanus forestop* and V.S. in the principal clause *þider folgode Paulus*. This is regular OE (see § 151) but produces a chiasmus;

3. that the word-order 'prepositional phrase + participle' in the first clause is reversed in the second. Again, both are good OE, but the change produces another chiasmus;

4. the change from *Saules* to *Paulus*—a sermon in itself.

GOE F

It is (we can say) certain beyond all doubt that Ælfric was influenced by Latin prose style; I cannot see how it could have been otherwise. But it is equally important to realize that this powerful and moving sentence—parallel yet doubly chiastic and with the effective contrast between Saul and Paul—contains nothing which is not 'good Old English'. It follows therefore that we must avoid the tendency (often found in critics of Milton's *Paradise Lost*) to rush around slapping the label 'Latinism' on anything which deviates in the slightest from our preconceived notions of the norms of ordinary speech.

§151 Much of the difficulty with correlative pairs arises from the fact that (with a few exceptions such as *ġif . . . þonne* 'if . . . then') the conjunction and the adverb have the same form, e.g. *þā* can mean both 'when' and 'then'. For the interrogatives (with the possible exception of *hwonne* 'when, until') were not used to introduce adjective or adverb clauses in OE; see §159 n. 2. Sometimes the indeclinable particle *þe* is added to the conjunction, e.g. in the passage discussed in §150 *þider ðe* means 'whither' and *þider* 'thither'. But this is by no means the rule. Sometimes the context helps, e.g. we can safely translate *Þa se cyng þæt hierde, þa wende he hine west* as 'When the king heard that, then he turned (reflexive) west'. But the word-order is an even more useful and reliable guide, for it may be taken as a pretty safe rule for prose that, when one of two correlative *þā* clauses has the word-order V.S., it must be the principal clause and *þā* must mean 'then'. The temporal clause introduced by *þā* 'when' may have the order S. . . . V., e.g. *þa he on lichoman wæs* 'when he was in the flesh', or S.V., e.g. *þa þunor ofslog XXIIII heora fodrera* 'when thunder killed twenty-four of their foragers'. The adverb *þā* may be repeated within the subordinate clause, e.g. *þa he þæt þa sumre tide dyde* 'when he did that on one particular occasion', where it need not of course be translated. Doubled *þā*, as in *ða þa seo boc com to us* 'when the book came to us' and *þa þa Dunstan geong man wæs* 'when Dunstan was a young man' usually introduces a subordinate clause, as the word-order in these examples testifies. Ælfric is very fond of this device.

§152 Other correlative pairs with which we can use word-order to determine which of the clauses is principal are

> *þonne . . . þonne* 'when . . . then'
> *þǣr . . . þǣr* 'where . . . there'
> *þider . . . þider* 'whither . . . thither'.

On the distinction between *þā* and *þonne*, see §168, s.v. *þonne*.

Note

Correlative pairs to which this rule does not regularly apply include:

ǣr ... *ǣr, nū* ... *nū, sippan* ... *sippan, swā* ... *swā, þanon* ... *þanon, þēah* ... *þēah*; on these, see §168. *Þēah* ... *hwæþre* 'though ... yet' and *ġif* ... *þonne* 'if ... then' present no problems. It should also be noted that the word-order S.V. often occurs after adverbs other than those discussed above; see §147 for an example after *Hēr*, and note *nu todæg hi underfengon Stephanum* 'now today they received Stephen' and *On deaðe he wæs gesett* ... 'he was placed in death ...'

Exceptions to the rule do exist. But you should view with suspicion any you meet, for the punctuation of some modern editions is sometimes at fault. Remember, however, that the rule does not apply to the poetry and that correlation is not essential, e.g.

Þa he þa wið þone here þær wæst abisgod wæs, 7 þa hergas wæron þa gegaderode begen to Sceobyrig on Eastseaxum, 7 þær geweorc worhtun, foron begen ætgædere up be Temese

'When he was occupied against the army there in the west, and the [other] Danish armies were assembled at Shoebury in Essex, and had made a fortress there, they both went together up along the Thames'.

§153 The value of this rule can be demonstrated from the following complicated passage in the Old English version of Bede's account of the poet Cædmon, quoted here with the emendations of *Sweet's Anglo-Saxon Reader*:

and he for þon oft in gebeorscipe, þonne þær wæs blisse intinga gedemed þæt hie ealle sceolden þurh endebyrdnesse be hearpan singan, þonne he geseah þa hearpan him nealæcan, þonne aras he for scome from þæm symble, and ham eode to his huse. Þa he þæt þa sumre tide dyde, þæt he forlet þæt hus þæs gebeorscipes, and ut wæs gongende to neata scypene, þara heord him wæs þære nihte bebodon, ða he þa þær in gelimplicre tide his limu on reste gesette and onslæpte, þa stod him sum mon æt þurh swefn, and hine halette and grette, and hine be his naman nemde.

We can begin by underlining the verbs in the second sentence: *dyde, forlēt* ... *and ūt wæs gongende, wæs* ... *beboden, gesette and onslǣpte, stōd* ... *and* ... *hālette* ... *and grētte* ... *and nemde*. Now the corresponding conjunctions for these five verbs or groups of verbs are *þā* ... *þā, þæt, þāra, ðā* ... *þā,* and *þā. Þæt* introduces a noun clause (§155) and *þāra* an adjective clause (§162). From our word-order rule, we know that '*þā* subject *þā*' introduces a subordinate clause, '*þā* V.S.' a principal clause. Hence the last *þā* means 'then', the syntax of the sentence is clear, and we can translate fairly literally: 'When he did that on one particular occasion, namely left the feast-hall and went out to the stall of the cattle, the care of which had been entrusted to him for that night [and] when in due time he stretched

his limbs on the bed there and fell asleep, then a certain man appeared to him in a dream and saluted him and greeted him and
called upon him by name'.

Similarly, in the first sentence, we have three *þonne* clauses, viz.
þonne þǣr wæs . . . , þonne hē geseah . . . þonne ārās hē. . . . The rule
instantly tells us that the last is the principal clause 'then he arose . . .'

iii NOUN CLAUSES

Introduction

§ 154   This heading traditionally comprehends dependent statements, desires (commands, wishes, etc.), questions, and exclamations.
The OE patterns conform very closely to those of MnE, apart from
the use of *þæt* and *hit* to anticipate a noun clause (see § 148).

Dependent Statements and Desires

§ 155   Dependent statements are introduced by *þæt*, e.g. *ða ðohte
he ðæt he wolde gesecan helle godu* 'then he thought that he would seek
the gods of hell', or *þætte* (= *þæt þe*), e.g. *ic wene ðætte noht monige
begiondan Humbre næren* 'I believe that there were not many beyond
the Humber'. *Þæt(te)* is sometimes repeated, as in the second sentence discussed in § 172, and is sometimes not expressed, e.g. *Swa ic
wat he minne hige cuðe* 'So I know he perceived my intention'.

Dependent desires are also introduced by *þæt*, e.g. *bæd þæt hyra
randas rihte heoldon* 'requested that they should hold their shields
properly', or *þætte*.

Þæt clauses are, however, more common in OE than their equivalent in MnE, for they are often found where we should use an
accusative and infinitive (as in the last example, where we should
say 'requested them to hold their shields properly') or some other
construction.

§ 156   The verb of the *þæt* clause may be indicative or subjunctive.
Two questions arise—first, 'What is the significance of the two
moods?' and second 'When must the subjunctive be represented in
translation?' The first is usually answered in some such way as this:

The *indicative* is used when the content of the noun clause is presented as a fact, as certain, as true, or as a result which has actually
followed or will follow.

When the *subjunctive* occurs, some mental attitude towards the
content of the noun clause is usually implied; one of the following
ideas may be present—condition, desire, obligation, supposition,
perplexity, doubt, uncertainty, or unreality.

There is some truth in this. Thus the subjunctive is the natural
mood in dependent desires, e.g. *ic ðe bebiode ðæt ðu do . . .* 'I com-

mand that you do . . .' But the indicative sometimes occurs after verbs of commanding, compelling, and the like, e.g. *he bebead Tituse his suna þæt he towearp þæt templ* and *and ðurh ðine halige miht tunglu genedest þæt hi ðe to hera*ð. Here the indicative emphasizes that the action desired actually took place; hence the translations might read 'Titus carried out his father's command and destroyed the temple' and 'through your holy power you compel the stars to worship you'. These and similar clauses could be called result clauses or noun clauses with the indicative showing that the event actually took place. But 'a rose by any other name . . .'

Similarly, in dependent statements, the indicative shows that the speaker is certain of the factuality of what he says and is vouching for its truth, e.g. *ic wat þæt þu eart heard mann* 'I know that you are a hard man', . . . *ðe cyðan . . . ðæt me com swiðe oft on gemynd* . . . 'to make known to you that it has often come into my mind . . .', and *þonne wite he þæt God gesceop to mæran engle þone þe nu is deofol* 'let him know therefore that God created as a great angel the creature who is now the devil'. But the subjunctive appears when no certainty is implied about a happening in the future, e.g. *Hit wæs gewitegod þæt he on ðære byrig Bethleem acenned wurde* 'It was prophesied that He should be born in the city of Bethlehem', when the truth of another's statement is not vouched for, e.g. *Be þæm Theuhaleon wæs gecweden . . . þæt he wære moncynnes tydriend, swa swa Noe wæs* 'About that Deucalion it was said that he was the father of mankind, as Noah was', or when it is denied, e.g. *Nu cwædon gedwolmen þæt deofol gesceope sume gesceafta, ac hi leogað* 'Now heretics said that some creations were the work of the devil but they lie'. This distinction between the indicative and the subjunctive is seen clearly in *Ne sæde þæt halige godspel þæt se rica reafere wære, ac wæs uncystig and modegode on his welum* 'The holy gospel did not say that the rich man was a robber, but that he was mean and exulted in his wealth'.

However, the rule does not tell the whole truth. The indicative does not always state a fact, e.g. *And gif hit gelimpþ þæt he hit fint* 'And if it happens that he finds it', nor does the subjunctive always imply uncertainty, doubt, or the like, e.g. *Mine gebroðra, uton we geoffrian urum Drihtne gold, þæt we andettan þæt he soð Cyning sy, and æghwær rixige* 'My brothers, let us offer our Lord gold, that we may confess that He is [the] true King and rules everywhere'; they all believe this. Again, in *Se wisa Augustinus . . . smeade hwi se halga cyðere Stephanus cwæde þæt he gesawe mannes bearn standan æt Godes swyðran* 'The wise Augustine . . . enquired why the holy martyr Stephen said that he saw the Son of Man standing at God's right hand', the subjunctive *gesāwe* does not mean that Augustine is casting doubt on Stephen's statement; it is probably due in part to the 'attraction' of the subjunctive form *cwæde* and in part to the influence of the verb *cweðan* itself. For, when introducing a dependent statement, *cweðan* prefers the subjunctive, *cȳðan* the indicative. This may reflect some original difference in meaning such as 'I (think and) give it as my opinion' as against a more objective 'I (know and) make it known'. Perhaps originally *cweðan* always had the subjunctive and *cȳðan* the indicative, and perhaps this situation would have continued if language were always a strictly logical activity in which verbs of thinking took the subjunctive and verbs of knowing the indicative. But it is not. We tend to say 'I think he may come' and 'I know he will come'. But 'I know he may be here in ten minutes, but I can't wait' and 'I think that he is without doubt the cleverest boy in the school' show that no hard and fast rules can be laid down. Each situation must be judged on its merits.

Hence we may say that, while the rule set out above often works, fluctuation between the subjunctive and the indicative in OE noun clauses is often of little significance. It is just as dangerous to place too much reliance on the presence of a subjunctive in OE as it would be to draw firm conclusions about a modern speaker's attitude from the fact that he started his sentence with 'I know that . . .' rather than 'I think that . . .'

So the answer to our second question 'When must the subjunctive be represented in translation?' can only be something indefinite like 'When the situation demands it'. It is, for example, unnecessary to bring out the fact that a verb of denying or supposing is followed by a subjunctive referring to some past act, for the verb 'to deny' or 'to suppose' is in itself enough to give a modern reader the necessary information. The subjunctive which will be most frequently represented in MnE is that in which some doubt or uncertainty arises over an action which, at the time of speaking, is still in the future. Such a subjunctive, of course, occurs most commonly in dependent desires.

Dependent Questions

§157 Questions fall into two main divisions—those in which the questioner seeks new information, e.g. *Hwær eart þu?* 'Where are you?' and *Hwy stande ge ealne dæg idele?* 'Why do you stand here all day idle?', and those in which he asks his hearer to choose between alternatives expressed or implied in the question, e.g. '*Wilt þu we gað and gadriað hie?* Ða cwæð he: '*Nese*' ' "Do you wish us to go and gather them?" And he answered "No".' [But he could have answered 'Yes'.] Rhetorical questions may, of course, be of either type.

§158 Those questions which seek new information present little difficulty. The dependent question will include the interrogative word of the non-dependent question. This may be a pronoun (e.g. *hwā* 'who' and *hwæt* 'what'), an adjective (e.g. *hwelċ* 'which, what sort of'), or an adverb (e.g. *hū* 'how' and *hwǣr* 'where'). Other common adverbs are *hwider* 'whither', *hwanon* 'whence', *hwonne* 'when' (see §159 n. 2), *hwȳ* and *hwæt* 'why', and combinations of a preposition + an oblique case of *hwæt*, e.g. *tō hwæs* 'whither', *for hwon* and *for hwȳ* 'why'. These questions may be anticipated by a demonstrative or personal pronoun; see §148.

Note

Some of these interrogative words can also be used indefinitely, e.g. *hwā* can mean 'someone, anyone' and *hwǣr* 'somewhere, anywhere'.

§159 In MnE many of these interrogative words can also be used as relative pronouns, e.g. 'The man who . . .', 'The place where . . .', and so on. This use seems to stem (in part at least) from OE sentences of the type 'I know you, what you are' and 'Consider the lilies of the field, how they flourish', in which the main verb has as objects both a noun (or pronoun) and a clause containing a dependent question. A convenient OE example is

> ond ic hean þonan
> wod wintorcearig   ofer waþoma gebind,
> sohte sele dreorig   sinces bryttan,
> hwær ic feor oþþe neah   findan meahte
> þone þe in meoduhealle   min mine wisse

'and I, miserable, with winter in my heart, made my way thence over the frozen expanse of the waves, sadly seeking the hall of a giver of treasure, [sadly seeking] far and near where I might find one who would show regard for me in the mead-hall'.

Here the two objects of *sōhte* are *sele* and the *hwǣr* clause.

Note 1

The first object of *sōhte* is *sinces bryttan* if the attractive compound *seledrēorig* 'sad for a hall' is accepted. But the fact that this interpretation is possible emphasizes that the *hwǣr* clause is interrogative, not adjective. It could not qualify *bryttan*.

Similarly in

> Ne meahte hire Iudas . . .
> sweotole gecyþan   be ðam sigebeame
> on hwylcne se hælend   ahafen wære

hwylcne is strictly an interrogative introducing a noun clause, object of *gecȳþan*, and the literal sense is 'Nor could Judas . . . tell her

beyond doubt about the victorious tree, [tell her] on which tree the
Saviour was raised up'.[1] It is easy to see how such juxtaposition of
noun and interrogative would lead to the use of the interrogative as
a relative. But this stage has not been reached in OE.

Note 2

   Hwonne 'when, until' is perhaps furthest advanced of all the OE
interrogatives on the way to becoming a word which could introduce
adverb and adjective clauses. Those who are interested may care to
look at the ways in which *hwonne* is used in the following examples:
Andreas l. 136 (noun clause); *Riddle* 31 l. 13 (adjective clause); *Maxims*
I l. 104 (adverb clause of time 'when'); *Genesis* l. 1028 (adverb clause
of time 'whenever'); and *Andreas* l. 400 (adverb clause of time 'until').
I have put in brackets the interpretation which seems to offer the
most convenient translation. But careful consideration will show
that an Anglo-Saxon might have regarded all these as noun clauses
—if he ever thought about it.

   §160   Non-dependent questions inviting a choice between alternatives can be asked in two ways in OE:

   1. by the word-order V.S. (as in MnE)—for examples see §§146.1
and 146.2;

   2. with *hwæþer* (*þe*) and the word-order S. . . . V., e.g. *Hwæþer þe
þin eage manful is?* 'Is your eye evil?', or S.V., e.g. *Hwæðer ic mote
lybban oðþæt ic hine geseo?* 'May I live until I see him?'

   As in MnE, dependent questions of this type are normally introduced by an interrogative word—either *hwæþer* 'whether', e.g. *Lætaþ
þæt we geseon hwæðer Elias cume* 'Let us see whether E. comes', or
ġif 'if', e.g. *frægn gif him wære niht getæse* 'asked if the night had been
pleasant to him'. An occasional example like 'He asked was any-
body there', occurs (e.g. *Elene* ll. 157 ff.); in these the original
word-order is retained but the tense has been changed.

   In the examples cited above, the alternative 'or not' is implied.
But it is occasionally expressed, e.g. *Anra gehwylc wat gif he be-
swuncgen wæs oððe na* 'Each man knows whether he was beaten, or
not'. An unusual example of the type of question under discussion
here occurs in *Genesis* ll. 531 ff., where the conjunctions are *þēah . . .
þe* 'whether . . . or'.

   The remarks made about mood in dependent statements also apply
in general to dependent questions.

   [1] The OE relative construction occurs in
                              . . . ond geflitu ræran
        be ðam sigebeame   on þam soðcyning
             ahangen wæs . . .
'to stir up controversy about the victorious tree on which the true King was
crucified . . .' Note the difference in mood—*wære* above but *wæs* here.

The Accusative and Infinitive

§161 This construction, well known in Latin, e.g. *Solon furere se simulavit* 'Solon pretended to be mad', and in MnE, e.g. 'I know him to be dead', is also an OE idiom. The subject accusative may be expressed, as in

>Het þa hyssa hwæne   hors forlætan,
>feor afysan,   and forð gangan

'He ordered each of the warriors to release his horse and drive it away, and to go forth', but is often left unexpressed, as in *& ðe cyðan hate* lit. 'I order [someone] to make known to you . . .', and *he het hie hon on heam gealgum* lit. 'he ordered [someone] to hang them on the high gallows' (where *hie* is the object of *hōn*). In the last two examples, the subject accusative is not expressed, either because everybody knows or because nobody cares who is to perform the action. In these, it is very convenient to translate the infinitives *cyðan* and *hōn* as if they were passive—'I order you to be told' (or '. . . that you be told . . .') and 'he ordered them to be hanged'. Much time has been spent in idle controversy over the question whether those infinitives were actually passive; what is important is that, when the subject accusative of the accusative and infinitive is not expressed, the active infinitive can usually be *translated* as a passive.

iv ADJECTIVE CLAUSES

Definite Adjective Clauses

§162 Definite adjective clauses are those which refer to one particular antecedent, e.g. 'This is the man who did it' as opposed to indefinite clauses whose antecedent is unspecified, e.g. 'Whoever did it will be caught'. As in Latin, the relative pronoun agrees with its antecedent (expressed or implied) in number and gender, but takes its case from the adjective clause. There are various ways of expressing it in OE.

1. The indeclinable particle *þe* is very common when the relative is the subject, e.g. *Ic geseah þa englas þe eower gymdon* 'I saw the angels who took care of you', *ælc þæra þe ðas min word gehyrð* 'each of those who hears these my words', and *swa swa hit gewunelic is þæm ðe on wuda gað oft* 'as is customary among those who frequently go in the wood'. It occurs fairly often when the relative is the object, e.g. *her onginneð seo boc þe man Orosius nemneð* 'here begins the book which one calls Orosius'. It very occasionally functions as a relative in the genitive or dative. Examples are *of ðæm mere ðe Truso standeð in staðe* 'from the sea on whose shore Truso stands' and *oð ðone dæg þe hi hine forbærnað* 'until the day on which they burn him'.

74 Syntax

2. In these last two examples, however, the case of the relative pronoun is not immediately clear because *þe* is indeclinable. So the appropriate case of the third person pronoun was sometimes added. Thus there is no ambiguity in *Eadig bið se wer, þe his tohopa bið to Drihtne* 'Blessed is the man whose hope is in the Lord' or in

> Þæt se mon ne wat
> þe him on foldan   fægrost limpeð

'The man for whom things go very pleasantly on the earth does not know that'.

Note

This combination sometimes occurs when the relative is nominative, e.g. *Paris Psalter* 67 l. 4 (*þe hē*) and, with first person pronouns, *Riddle* 12 l. 14 (*þe iċ*) and *Christ* l. 25 (*þe wē*). With the second person pronoun the regular combination is *þū þe* and *ġē þe*; see *The Review of English Studies* XV (1964), 135-137.

3. The appropriate case of the demonstrative *se, sēo, þæt* is often used as a relative, e.g. *se hearpere, ðæs nama wæs Orfeus, hæfde an wif, seo wæs haten Eurydice* 'the harper, whose name was Orpheus, had a wife called Eurydice', *eall þæt ic geman* 'all that I remember', and *fif Moyses boca, ðam seo godcunde æ awriten is* 'five (of the) books of Moses in which the divine law is written'. Here there is no ambiguity about case and number, but we cannot always be sure whether the pronoun is demonstrative or relative.

4. But there is no ambiguity at all for us in sentences like *Þa com he on morgenne to þam tungerefan, se þe his ealdormon wæs* 'Then he came in the morning to the steward, who was his superior' and *þystre genip, þam þe se þeoden self sceop nihte naman* 'the cloud of darkness, for which the Lord Himself made the name "night"', for the presence of the particle *þe* after *se* and *þām* makes it clear that we have to do with a relative pronoun, while *se* and *þām* tell us its case. This can be called the *seþe* relative (or the *se þe* relative: the elements are sometimes written together, sometimes separately, by the scribes).

Note

In the nominative, this combination can mean 'he who' or 'the one who'; cf. §164.

5. In short, the OE relatives are the indeclinable particle *þe*, to which the personal pronoun can be added to remove ambiguities of case, and the demonstrative pronoun *se, sēo, þæt* in the case required by the adjective clause, either alone or followed by the indeclinable particle *þe* to make clear that we have a relative and not a demonstrative pronoun.

§163 The comments which follow may be useful when you have mastered §162.

1. Another example like those in §162.4 is

Se wæs Hroþgare hæleþa leofost
rice randwiga, þone ðe heo on ræste abreat

'He whom she (the monster) killed in his resting-place was the most beloved of heroes to Hrothgar, a mighty shield-warrior'. But a word of warning is necessary here, because you are likely to meet sentences which seem to contain this combination, but do not. Thus in *gedo grenne finul XXX nihta on ænne croccan þone þe sie gepicod utan* 'put green fennel for thirty nights into a jar which is covered with pitch on the outside' and in

syððan hie gefricgeað frean userne
ealdorleasne, þone ðe ær gehcold
wið hettendum hord ond rice

'when they learn our lord to be dead, he who in the past guarded our treasure and kingdom against enemies' *þone þe* is not an accusative relative, for *þone* has the case of the *principal* clause agreeing with its antecedent. Formally, *þone* belongs to the principal clause and we can therefore say that the relative in these examples is *þe*. But they differ from the second and third sentences quoted in §162.1 (where the demonstrative is the only antecedent) in that there is already an antecedent and the demonstrative is therefore superfluous. In earlier times *þone* was no doubt stressed in such sentences—'our lord . . . that one . . . he'. But there may be some truth in the view that in our sentences *þone* belonged rhythmically to the adjective clause and was felt as part of the relative; hence we can (if we wish) distinguish examples in which the demonstrative has the case of the principal clause as the *se'þe* relative. In sentences like *sægde se þe cuþe* 'he who knew said . . .', where both clauses have the same case, there is no difficulty; cf. the *ðā ðe* clause in example B in §172, where the two clauses require different cases (acc./nom.) but where *ðā* can be either nominative or accusative. But you should be on the alert for examples of what I have called the *se'þe* type.

Notes

1. Examples in which real ambiguity occurs are rare. But there is one in *Beowulf* ll. 2291-93:

Swa mæg unfæge eaðe gedigan
wean and wræcsið se ðe Wealdendes
hyldo gehealdeþ.

If the relative pronoun is *se'þe*, *hyldo* (indeclinable feminine) is the

subject of the adjective clause, *ðe* is accusative, and the translation
would read 'So may an undoomed man whom the favour of the
Almighty protects easily survive both woe and banishment'. If the
relative pronoun is *sepe*, it is nominative, *hyldo* is accusative, and
the translation would read 'So may an undoomed man who retains
the favour of the Almighty . . .'

2. Sometimes, when the relative pronoun is in a case other than
the nominative, the personal pronoun follows a relative of the *se'pe*
type. This enables us to tell immediately the case of the relative
pronoun, e.g.

se biþ leofast   londbuendum
se þe him God syleð   gumena rice

'that one is most beloved by land-dwellers to whom God gives the
kingdom of men' and *se, se þe him ær gepuhte þæt him nan sæ wiþ-
habban ne mehte þæt he hine mid scipum afyllan ne mehte, eft wæs
biddende anes lytles troges æt anum earman men, þæt he mehte his feorh
generian* 'he to whom it once had seemed that no sea was so great (lit.
could stop him) that he could not fill it with ships, finally asked a
wretched man for one little boat so that he could save his life'. See
also *Dream of the Rood* ll. 85-86.

2. A not uncommon idiom is found in the sentence about Tantalus
quoted in § 148. The antecedent *Tantulus* is followed by two adjective clauses joined by *ond*. In the first, *ðe . . . gifre wæs*, the relative
pronoun is nominative. The second is *him . . . ðære gifernesse*. Here
the relative pronoun is [*þe*] *him* 'whom'. But it is idiomatic not to
repeat the *þe*; *him* warns us of the change of case from nominative
to dative.

Another idiom is found in

Nis nu cwicra nan
þe ic him modsefan   minne durre
sweotule asecgan.

Here the antecedent is *nān cwicra*. The relative pronoun is *þe him*.
Iċ is the subject of the adjective clause. So we have 'There is no one
alive to whom I dare reveal my thoughts'. When the relative pronoun is *þe* + personal pronoun and another pronoun is the subject
of the adjective clause, the latter comes between the two elements
of the relative. So *þe iċ him*.

3. The indeclinable relative *þe* always precedes any preposition
which governs it; see the sentence about Ixion quoted in § 148.

4. The adjective clause need not immediately follow the antecedent.

5. *Þæt* often combines antecedent and relative pronoun. It must
then be translated 'what', e.g. *he hæfde ðeah geforþod þæt he his frean
gehet* 'he had, however, done what he promised his lord'. This sur-

vived into eMnE, e.g. in the Authorized Version *John* 13:27 'That thou doest, do quickly'. In

<blockquote>
Gode þancode

mihtigan Drihtne,   þæs se man gespræc,
</blockquote>

þæs is genitive after *þancode* and we might expect *þe*: '... thanked God for that which the man spoke'. But this is probably an example of *þæt* 'what'—'thanked God, the mighty Lord, for what the man spoke'.

6. In MnE the difficulty of combining an adjective clause and a verb of saying or thinking often produces a 'grammatical error', e.g. 'This is the man whom they thought would revolutionize the teaching of English' where we should have '... who, they thought, ...' The same problem arises in OE and often results in what seems to us a somewhat incoherent arrangement, e.g. *Đa eode he furður oð he gemette ða graman gydena ðe folcisce men hata ð Parcas, ða hi secgað ðæt on nanum men nyton nane are, ac ælcum men wrecen be his gewyrhtum; þa hi secgað ðæt walden ælces mannes wyrde* 'Then he went on further until he met the terrible goddesses whom the people of that land call the Parcae, who (they say) show no mercy to any man, but punish each man according to his deserts; these (they say) control each man's fate'. A result acceptable in MnE can be obtained in these examples by omitting the *ðæt*. Sometimes, however, the subject is expressed twice, e.g. *in þære cirican seo cwen gewunade hire gebiddan, þe we ær cwædon þæt heo Cristen wære*. Here we need to omit *þæt hēo* to get the sense: 'in that church the queen who, we said formerly, was Christian, was wont to say her prayers'. But even this is clumsy and needs polishing.

7. Attempts have been made to lay down the rules which governed the use of the various relative pronouns in OE. They have not succeeded, largely (I think) because the vital clue of intonation is denied to us.

Indefinite Adjective Clauses

§164 The relative pronouns used in definite adjective clauses also appear in the indefinite ones, e.g.

<blockquote>
Þa wæs eaðfynde   þe him elles hwær

gerumlicor   ræste sohte
</blockquote>

'Then it was easy to find whoever (=the man who) sought a bed elsewhere, further away', and

<blockquote>
heold hyne syðþan

fyr ond fæstor   se þæm feonde ætwand
</blockquote>

'whoever escaped the enemy thereafter kept himself further away and in greater safety'.

As has already been noted, the interrogatives *hwā* 'who', *hwǣr* 'where', and the like, are not used alone in OE as relatives; see §159. But they are used in the indefinite relatives *swā hwā swā* 'whoever', *swā hwæt swā* 'whatever', *swā hwǣr swā* 'wherever', and so on. One example will suffice—*swa hwa swa þe genyt þusend stapa, ga mid him oðre twa þusend* 'whoever compels thee [to go] one mile, go with him two'.

Mood

§165   The adjective clause usually has its verb in the indicative, even when it is in dependent speech. But the subjunctive may occur in the following situations:

1. When the principal clause contains an imperative or a subjunctive expressing a wish, e.g. *Matthew* 5:42 *syle þam ðe þe bidde* Authorized Version 'Give to him that asketh thee'. However, the fact that the indicative is found in such circumstances, e.g. *Matthew* 19:21 *becyp eall þæt þu ahst* Authorized Version 'sell that thou hast', shows that the mood varies with the speaker's attitude and not with any automatic 'law of symmetry'. In the first example, there is uncertainty because the asker is as yet unknown and indeed may not exist; we could translate 'Give to anyone who may ask'. In the second, the young man's possessions exist and are known to him. For, as the story tells us, 'he went away sorrowful, for he had great possessions'.

2. When the principal clause contains a negative, e.g. the second sentence discussed in §163.2. But this again is no automatic rule. The subjunctive is found only when the content of the adjective clause is put forward as unreal; in the example, there is no such person in existence nor probably could there be. But in *Beowulf* ll. 1465-7

Huru ne gemunde   mago Ecglafes
eafoþes cræftig,   þæt he ær gespræc
wine druncen

'However, the son of Ecglaf, powerful in his might, did not remember what he had said before, when drunk with wine', Unferth (*mago Ecglāfes*) actually had spoken the words, but he did not now remember them; the poet could have said that he had forgotten them. In this example, the *ne* negates merely the verb of the principal clause, not the whole idea which follows; hence th indicative in the adjective clause.

3. When the principal clause contains a rhetorical question, e.g.

> Hwa is on eorðan   nu unlærdra
> þe ne wundrige   wolcna færeldes . . . ?

'Who is there on earth among the unlearned who does not wonder at the motion of the clouds . . . ?' The answer demanded is, of course, 'No-one'. Such examples are exactly parallel to those discussed in 2 above, for the poet could easily have said 'There is no-one on earth . . .'

4. When a limiting adjective clause[1] has as antecedent a genitive depending on a superlative, e.g.

> Niwe flodas   Noe oferlað,
> . . .
> þone deopestan   drencefloda
> þara ðe gewurde   on woruldrice.

Here the poet is saying that Noah sailed over the deepest deluge that could ever be or have been. Similar examples occur in *Beowulf* ll. 2129 ff., *Genesis* ll. 626 ff., and *Daniel* ll. 691 ff. In these the subjunctive is used to imply that all the possible examples of floods, griefs, women, and cities, respectively are being considered—those which the writer knows about, those which have happened without his knowledge, and those which may yet happen. That the 'superlative + genitive' does not automatically cause the subjunctive is shown by examples like

> . . . ond hi þa gesette   on þone selestan
> foldan sceata,   þone fira bearn
> nemnað neorxnawong . . .

'and then he placed them in the best regions of the earth, which the sons of men call Paradise', where the non-limiting adjective clause has the indicative.

v   ADVERB CLAUSES

Introduction

§166 The conventional classification will serve us here. It distinguishes eight types—place, time, purpose, result, cause, comparison, concession, condition. On the whole, you will find that these clauses are fundamentally very similar to their counterparts in MnE. The main differences to be noted are:

---

[1] In the sentence 'The soldiers who (that) were tired lay down' the adjective clause does not merely describe the soldiers; it limits the action of lying down to a particular group—those who were tired. Hence it is a 'limiting' clause. But in 'The soldiers, who were tired, lay down' the adjective clause merely tells us something more about all the soldiers. Hence it is 'non-limiting'.

1. the conjunctions themselves;
2. the methods of correlation, linked with
3. the word-order within the clauses. On these two points, see §§150-153;
4. a more frequent use of the subjunctive mood. Sometimes it is used by rule and is of little significance for us, sometimes it makes an important distinction. On this, see §§173-180.

§§167-171 contain a discussion of the conjunctions and alphabetical lists of non-prepositional and prepositional formulae with their main uses. §§173-180 discuss each type of clause in turn, outlining briefly the conjunctions and moods used in them and any other points of special interest.

§167 If we adopt a purely formal classification, we can detect in MnE at least five types of conjunction. Consider the following series of clauses:

1. Christ died, *that* we may live.
2. Christ died, *so that* we may live.
3. *So* boldly did Christ speak, *that* all men listened.
4.
5.
6. Christ died, *to the end that* we may live.
7. *To this end* Christ died, *that* we may live.

In OE, we can find comparable examples to these and can fill in the missing items 4 and 5:

1. ... *he biþ geseald hæþnum mannum þæt hie hine bysmrian* ' ... he will be given to heathen men that they may mock him'.
2. *Hæfde se cyning his fierd on tu tonumen, swa þæt hie wæron simle healfe æt ham, healfe ute* 'The king had divided his army into two, so that at any one time half were at home, half in the field'.
3. *He ... swa anræd þurhwunode þæt he nolde abugan to bismorfullum leahtrum* 'he ... remained so resolute that he was unwilling to turn aside to shameful sins'.
4. ... *ond ðæs ðe ðu gearo forwite hwam ðu gemiltsige, ic eom Apollonius, se Tyrisca ealdormann* ' ... and, so that you may know who is receiving your mercy, I am Apollonius, Prince of Tyre'.
   Note: This use of *ðæs ðe* is a rare one, but it is included to complete the series.
5. *Ic wat þæt nan nis þæs welig þæt he sumes eacan ne þyrfe* 'I know that there is no man so wealthy that he does not need more of something'.

6. *And ic hyne nyste, ac ic com and fullode on wætere, to þam þæt he wære geswutelod on Israhela folce* 'And I knew him not, but I came and baptized [him] in water, to the end that he might be manifested to the people of Israel'.

7. [the Heavenly King] *þe to ði com on middangeard þæt he of eallum ðeodum his gecorenan gegaderode* ... '[the Heavenly King] who to this end came into the world that he might gather his chosen from all nations'.

So we find

	MnE	OE
1.	'that'	*þæt*
2.	'so that'	*swā þæt*
3.	'so . . . that'	*swā . . .þæt*
4.		*þæs þe*
5.		*þæs . . .þæt*
6.	'to the end that'	*tō þām þæt*
7.	'to this end . . . that'	*tō þī . . . þæt*

On the variations *þe/þæt* in 4 and 5 and *þām/þī* in 6 and 7, see §169.

We can therefore speak of prepositional conjunctions (6 and 7) and non-prepositional conjunctions (1-5). We can speak of simple conjunctions (1), grouped conjunctions (2, 4, and 6), and divided conjunctions (3, 5, and 7). MnE has no exact equivalent for types 4 and 5. Their real force cannot be brought out literally today because *þæs* is the genitive of *þæt* used adverbially and we no longer have a genitive of 'that' to use in this way. So we must translate them either 'so that' and 'so . . . that', which brings out the adverbial force only, or 'to the end that' and 'to the end . . . that', which brings out the adverbial force and at the same time demonstrates the important truth that a good many functions of the OE cases have been taken over by MnE prepositions. Other examples of this type in OE include:

(a) *þȳ . . . þȳ* (the instrumental of *þæt*) in comparisons, the ancestor of MnE *'the* more, *the* merrier' (lit. 'by that much . . . by that much');

(b) *þā hwīle þe* 'while', where we have an accusative of duration of time turned into a conjunction by the addition of the indeclinable particle *þe*;

(c) *þȳ lǣs (þe)* MnE 'lest'. On the use of *þe* in (b) and (c), see §169.

For practical purposes, the best grouping is a twofold one—non-prepositional conjunctions, simple, grouped and divided (i.e. items 1-5), and prepositional conjunctions or formulae, grouped and divided (items 6-7). The following sections contain separate alpha-

betical lists of the most important OE conjunctions in these two
groups, with any comments necessary on their use. Examples are
often given from poems you are likely to read.

Non-Prepositional Conjunctions

§168 (Note: The list mentions any adverbial and prepositional
uses of the conjunctions discussed and any pronominal forms with
which they may be confused.)

ǣr

1. Prep. 'before'. As prep. it also introduces prep. conjs. of time;
   see §171.
2. Adv. 'formerly'. Often a sign of the pluperfect; see §197.4.
3. Temporal conj. 'before'. Often takes the subj. But this need
   not be brought out in translation.

būtan, būton

1. Prep. 'without'.
2. Conj. 'except that, but' + ind.
3. Conj. 'unless, if not' + subj.

ġif

1. Conj. 'if, whether' introducing dependent questions.
2. Conj. 'if' introducing conditional clauses.

hwonne

Conj. 'when'. Originally an interrogative introducing questions,
it shades into a temporal conj. 'when, until'; see §159 n. 2.

nefne, nemne, nymþe

The Anglian equivalent of *būton*; you will meet it mostly in the
poetry, e.g. *Beowulf* l. 1552.

nō ðȳ ǣr

Adv. 'none the sooner, yet . . . not, not yet'.

nū

1. Adv. 'now'.
2. Conj. 'now that, because', often combining the ideas of time
   and cause; it takes the ind. and is not used when a false reason
   is given. It usually refers to a state in the present, e.g. (with
   present tense) *Maldon* l. 222 and (with preterite tense to be
   translated as perfect) *Maldon* l. 250. In the latter example,
   the state in the present is the result of an action completed in
   the past.

oð

1. Prep. 'until, up to' of time or place. As a prep. it also introduces prep. conjs. of time; see §171.
2. Conj. 'until' marking temporal and/or local limit.

sam . . . sam
'Whether . . . or' in concessive clauses.

sippan
1. Adv. 'after'.
2. Conj. meaning
  (*a*) *ex quo* 'since'.
  (*b*) *postquam* 'after'.
  (*c*) sometimes 'when, as soon as'.

swā
1. Adv. 'so, thus'. It usually refers back, but may anticipate what is to come.
2. Conj. alone and in combination. The following main uses can be distinguished:
 (*a*) In indefinite combinations
    In adjective clauses; see §164.
    In clauses of place, e.g. *swā hwǣr swā* 'wherever' and *swā wīde swā* 'as widely as'.
    In clauses of time, e.g. *swā hraþe swā* 'as quickly as', *swā lange swā* 'as long as', *swā oft swā* 'as often as', and (*swā*) *sōna swā* 'as soon as'.
 (*b*) With the superlative
    e.g. *swa ðu oftost mæge* 'as often as you can' and *swa hie selest mihton* 'as well as they could'.
 (*c*) In clauses of comparison
    swā 'as'.
    swā swā 'as, just as'.
    swā . . . swā 'so . . . as, as . . . as'.
    swā . . . swā swā 'so . . . as'.
 (*d*) Other uses
    swā + subj. often means 'as if', e.g. *Wanderer* l. 96.
    swā can sometimes be translated 'as far as', e.g. *Elene* l. 971, or 'wherever', e.g. *Andreas* l. 1582.
    swā can sometimes be translated 'because'.
    swā sometimes means 'so that'.
    Frequently it is 'a rather characterless connective, shading into concession, result, or manner, as the case may be, and, with the negative, corresponding to Modern English "without", "not being" ' (Burnham), e.g. *Hi fuhton fif dagas, swa hyra nan ne feol* 'They fought for five days without any of them falling'.

    For *swā . . . swā* 'either . . . or', see §184.3.
    With a comparative, *swā . . . swā* means 'the . . . the', e.g. *swa norðor swa smælre* 'the further north, the narrower'.

Note

swā is sometimes translated as a relative pronoun. On this point
see *The Review of English Studies* XV (1964), 140.

swā þæt

Conj. 'so that' introducing result clauses. No unambiguous examples of purpose clauses after *swā þæt* have been noted. But the
distinction is often a very fine one, e.g. *swa þæt he mehte ægþerne
geræcan*, which might mean either 'was able to reach' or 'might
reach'; see § 207.

swā . . . þæt

Conj. 'so . . . that'. Like its MnE equivalent, it usually introduces
result clauses.

swelċe, swilċe, swylċe

  1. It can be a form of the pron. *swelċ* 'such, such a one, such as,
     which'.
  2. Conj. 'such as', e.g. *Beowulf* l. 757, where it would be *swylċne*
     if it were the pronoun. In *Dream of the Rood* l. 92 *swylċe swā*
     may be translated 'just as'.

Frequently we can not tell whether we have 1 or 2, e.g. *Seafarer*
l. 83. This does not matter.

  3. Adv. 'likewise, also'.
  4. Conj. 'as if' with subj. or without verb, e.g. *swelce to gamenes*
     'as if in fun'.

þā

  1. Acc. sg. fem. and nom. acc. pl. of *se*.
  2. Adv. 'then'.
  3. Conj. 'when'. Used only with pret. ind. of a single completed
     act in the past. For further explanation, see under *þonne*.
  4. *þā . . . furþum* = Lat. *cum . . . primum*, e.g. *Beowulf* l. 465.
  5. In *Maldon* l. 5 (quoted in § 148) *þā . . . ærest* may mean 'as
     soon as'.

þā hwīle þe

Conj. 'as long as, while' (lit. 'during that time in which', i.e. acc. of
duration of time + particle *þe*). It is found only eight times in the
poetry, where *þenden* (an older word) is preferred for metrical
reasons. *The Battle of Maldon* contains four of these eight examples.

þanon

  1. Adv. 'thence'.
  2. Conj. 'whence'.

þær

  1. Adv. of place 'there'. Sometimes it can be translated 'then'.

2. With *wæs*, equals MnE 'there was . . .', e.g. *Beowulf* l. 2105.
3. Conj. 'where', alone, doubled *þǣr þǣr*, or correlative *þǣr* . . . *þǣr*.
   (Sometimes it can be translated 'when' or 'because'.)
4. Conj. 'whither, to the place where', e.g. *Dream of the Rood* l. 139.
5. Conj. 'wherever', e.g. *Beowulf* l. 1394.
6. Conj. 'if', especially with pret. subj. of impossible wishes, e.g. *Beowulf* l. 2730.
7. Introducing a wish with subj. 'if only', e.g. *Metres of Boethius* 8 l. 39.

þæs
Gen. sg. neut. of *þæt* used as an adv.
1. of time 'from that, after'.
2. of extent or comparison 'to that extent, so'; see under *þæs* (*þe*), *þæs* . . . *þe*, *þæs* . . . *þæt*.

þæs (*þe*)
1. Gen. sg. masc. or neut. of the relative pronoun; see §162.
2. Conj. of time 'when, after, since', sometimes shading into 'because'.
3. Comparative conj. 'as'.
4. After verbs like *þancian*, see §163.5.

þæs . . . *þæt*
Conj. 'so . . . that' introducing consecutive clauses, e.g. *Beowulf* ll. 1366-7 and *Seafarer* ll. 39 ff. *Þæs* . . . *þæt* is commoner in the poetry; prose writers prefer *swa* . . . *þæt*.

Notes
1. The subject for the *þæt* clause in *Beowulf* l. 1367 is absent. Some take *þæt* as rel. pron. 'who'; this would be an early example of the use of *þæt* without regard to gender. Such absence of a subject is, however, idiomatic; see §193.7 and *Christ* ll. 241 ff. where *þæs* . . . *þæs* is followed by *þe* in what may be an adjective or a consecutive clause. *Metres of Boethius* 28 contains examples of *þæt* and *þe* in clauses which seem the same. It is dangerous to say dogmatically that the former are consecutive clauses with unexpressed subjects, the latter adjective clauses. But this may have been the original situation.
2. In *Seafarer* ll. 39 ff. *þæs* . . . *þæs* . . . is paralleled by *tō þæs* (3 times); see §171.

þæs . . . *þe*   See *þæs* . . . *þæt*.
þæt
1. Neut. dem. and rel. pron. 'that, which, what'; see §§162 and 163.5.
2. Conj. introducing noun clauses; see §155.

3. Conj. 'so that' introducing:

(a) clauses of purpose with subj.

(b) clauses of result with ind. After verbs of motion, it can be translated 'until'.

(c) with ambiguous verb forms, clauses which may be either purpose or result. Often the context makes clear which it is.

4. Conj. introducing some local and temporal clauses where its use is idiomatic, as in MnE, e.g. *Beowulf* l. 1362 and *Maldon* l. 105.

þe

1. In texts which do not mark long vowels, *þe* = *þē* can be a spelling for *þȳ*.

2. Indeclinable rel. pron.; see §162.

3. Subordinating particle turning an adv. into a conj.; see §169.

4. *þēah . . .þe* in *Genesis* ll. 531-2 = 'whether . . . or'.

5. Conj. of time 'when', e.g. *Beowulf* l. 1000. This is not a common use.

6. Sometimes a comparative conj. 'as'; *Maldon* l. 190 is a possible example.

þēah, þēh

1. Adv. 'yet, however'.

2. Alone, or with *þe*, concessive conj. 'although', nearly always with the subj.

3. On *Genesis* l. 531 see s.v. *þe* 4.

þenden

1. Adv. 'meanwhile'.

2. Temporal conj. 'as long as, while'. See *þā hwīle þe* above.

þider

1. Adv. of place 'thither'.

2. Conj. of place 'whither'.

þon mā þe

Conj. 'more than', a rare alternative to a comparative + *þonne* in negative sentences. Its literal meaning is *mā* 'more' *þon* (inst. of *þæt* expressing comparison) 'than this' *þe* 'namely' (see §169).

þonne

1. Adv. of time 'then', frequently correlative with *ġif*.

2. Conj. of time 'when':

(a) with preterite tense, frequentative 'whenever'.

The difference between *þā* and *þonne* in the past is made clear by a study of the second paragraph of Bede's account of the poet Cædmon, which is quoted in §153. *Þā* is used only of a single completed act in the past; note *þa he þæt sumre tide dyde* 'when he did that on one particular occasion'. *Þonne* is frequentative 'whenever'; note *oft . . . þonne* 'often . . . whenever'. Cf. Modern German *als* and *wenn*.

(b) in the present and future 'whenever' in both senses:
    (i) of a single act to be performed at some unknown time, e.g. *Beowulf* l. 3106.
    (ii) 'whenever' frequentative of repeated acts, e.g. *Riddle* 7 l. 1.

As in MnE, the distinction is not always clear; cf. 'I'll see him whenever he comes' with *Beowulf* l. 23.

3. Comparative conj. 'than':
    (a) with full clause following, e.g. *Maldon* l. 195.
    (b) with contracted clause following, e.g. *Beowulf* l. 469.
    (c) sometimes = 'than that' when two clauses are compared, e.g. *Maldon* ll. 31-33.

þȳ
1. Inst. of *þæt* in the combination *þȳ . . . þȳ* (lit. 'by that much . . . by that much') MnE 'the . . . the', e.g. *Maldon* ll. 312-3.
2. Alone, or in the combination *þȳ þe*, 'because', e.g. *Genesis* l. 2626 and *Daniel* l. 85.

þȳ lǣs (þe)
Conj. 'lest' introducing negative clauses of purpose, almost always with the subj.

Prepositional Conjunctions

§169   Basically these consist of
    a preposition + an oblique case of *þæt* (+ *þæt* or *þe*).

Note

    The case used depends on the preposition. Thus, since *for* governs the dat. or inst., we find in the MSS *for þæm, for þam, for þan, for þon, for þy, for þi*—all variant spellings of the dat. or inst. (*ð* may appear instead of *þ* in any of these spellings.) The formulae are sometimes written together, e.g. *forþon*. In the discussions which follow, one particular form of the prepositional formula (such as *for þæm*) includes all these variant spellings unless the contrary is specifically stated. *To* sometimes governs the gen. instead of the dat. or inst.; so we find *to þæs* in addition to *to þæm* etc.

    These conjunctions probably grew out of an originally adverbial use of a prepositional phrase such as occurs in *ond for ðon ic ðe bebiode ðæt ðu . . .* 'and for that (='therefore') I command you that you . . .' and in *for þan wearð her on felda folc totwæmed . . .* 'because

of that the army here in the field was divided . . .' Such phrases
were then used as conjunctions by the addition of *þe* or *þæt* to
indicate the new function, e.g. . . . *ond he hi him eft ageaf, for þæm
þe hiora wæs oþer his godsunu* . . . 'and he afterwards returned them
to him, because one of them was his godson . . .' Here *þe* warns us
that the combination is a conjunction. We can call *þe* (if we wish)
a subordinating particle. This is the general function of *þe* and its
use as a relative pronoun is probably a special adaptation; see §162.
We can perhaps get nearest to its original force by translating it as
'namely'. So, in the example above, we have 'and he afterwards
returned them to him, for that [reason], namely, one of them was
his godson'.

These formulae can be used in two ways. Thus *for þæm* sometimes
refers *back* to a reason already given as in the second example above
—'Some fled. Therefore the army was defeated'. Here it is equivalent to MnE 'therefore'. But sometimes it refers *forward* to a
reason yet to be given, as in the third example above, where the *þe*
warns us not to relax because something—the reason—is still to
come, and so tells us that *for þæm* means 'because' and not 'therefore'.

Sometimes *þæt* is used instead of *þe*, e.g. *forþan þæt he wolde Godes
hyrde forlætan* 'because he wished to desert God's flock'. This use of
þæt becomes more common as we move from OE to ME and still
survives in Chaucer's metrically useful 'if that', 'when that', and
the like.

So far we have distinguished *for þæm* adverb 'therefore' from *for
þæm þe* conjunction 'because'. But this distinction was not long
preserved by the Anglo-Saxons. They could distinguish adverb and
conjunction by the context, word-order, and intonation, just as we
can distinguish the use of 'who' in 'The man who did that is a fool'
from its use in 'The soldiers, who were tired, lay down'. So they
sometimes dispensed with the subordinating particle and used the
formula as a conjunction without *þe* or *þæt*, e.g. *Wuton agifan ðæm
esne his wif, forðæm he hi hæfð geearnad mid his hearpunga* 'let us
give the man back his wife, because he has earned her with his
harping'.

Like other adverbs and conjunctions such as *þā* (see §§150 ff.),
prepositional conjunctions may be used correlatively. Examples are
*forðæm we habbað nu ægðer forlæten ge ðone welan ge ðone wisdom
forðæmðe we noldon to ðæm spore mid ure mode onlutan* 'and for that
reason we have now lost both the wealth and the wisdom, because
we would not bend to the track with our minds', and, without *þe* in
the conjunction, *For þon nis me þæs þearf . . . to secgenne, for þon hit
longsum is, ond eac monegum cuð* 'For this reason, there is no need
for me . . . to speak of it, because it is long and also known to many'.

So now we have

> *for þǣm* adv. 'therefore'
> *for þǣm þe* conj. 'because'
> *for þǣm* conj. 'because'

and the correlative combination *for þǣm . . . for þǣm (þe)*, 'for this reason . . . because'.

One further variation needs to be recorded. We have already seen that conjunctions can be divided. An OE example of a divided prepositional conjunction is *þa comon for ðy on weg ðe ðara oðerra scipu asǣton* lit. 'those (men) got for that away, namely, the ships of the others had gone aground' and so 'those escaped because the others' ships were aground'. The causal conjunction is *for ðȳ . . . ðe*, divided by *on weg*.

§170   Since all these arrangements are possible with the prepositional conjunctions, it follows that, when in your reading you meet *for þǣm* or some such combination, it may be

1. an adverb used alone;
2. a conjunction used alone;
3. an adverb used correlatively with a prepositional conjunction;
4. the first part of a divided prepositional conjunction. If it is this, you will need to find the following *þe* or *þæt*.

The combination *for þǣm þe* is almost always a conjunction. But sometimes MnE 'for' will be a better translation than 'because'.

§171   The remarks made in §170 about *for þǣm* and *for þǣm þe* apply to all the prepositional conjunctions set out in the list which follows. It contains all that you are likely to meet. You should note, however, that these combinations may occur 'in their own right' and may not be true prepositional conjunctions. Thus *mid þǣm þæt* does not mean 'while' or 'when' in *ealles swiþost mid þǣm þæt manige þara selestena cynges þegna forðferdon*; we must translate 'most of all by the fact that (lit. 'with that, namely') many of the king's best thanes died'.

æfter + dat., inst.
  Adv. and conj. 'after'.

Note
  æfter is never used alone in OE as a conj. But it does occur as an adv.

ǣr + dat., inst.
  Adv. and conj. 'before'.

Note
  ǣr is used alone as a conj. and adv.; see §168.

betwix + dat., inst.
Conj. 'while'.

for + dat., inst.
See §§169-170 above.

mid + dat., inst.
Conj. 'while, when'.

oþ + acc.
Conj. 'up to, until, as far as' defining the temporal or local limit.
It appears as *oþþe, oþþæt*, and *oð ðone fyrst ðe* 'up to the time at which' (a good example of how *þe* can turn a phrase into a conj.).

Note
  oþ can be used alone as a conj.; see §168.

tō + dat., inst.
Conj. 'to this end, that' introducing clauses of purpose with subj. and of result with ind.

tō + gen.
Conj. 'to the extent that, so that'.

wiþ + dat., inst.
Conj. lit. 'against this, that'. It can be translated 'so that', 'provided that', or 'on condition that'.

An Exercise in Analysis

§172 Now you are in a position to 'try your strength' by analysing and translating the following sentences *before* consulting the key given below:

A. Forðon ic ðe bebiode ðæt ðu do swæ ic geliefe ðæt ðu wille, ðæt ðu ðe ðissa woruldðinga to ðæm geæmetige, swæ ðu oftost mæge, ðæt ðu ðone wisdom ðe ðe God sealde, ðær ðær ðu hiene befæstan mæge, befæste.

B. Forðy me ðyncð betre, gif iow swæ ðyncð, ðæt we eac sume bec, ða ðe niedbeðearfosta sien eallum monnum to wiotonne, ðæt we ða on ðæt geðiode wenden ðe we ealle gecnawan mægen, & gedon, swæ we swiðe eaðe magon mid Godes fultume, gif we ða stilnesse habbað, ðætte eall sio gioguð ðe nu is on Angelcynne friora monna, ðara ðe ða speda hæbben ðæt hie ðæm befeolan mægen, sien to liornunga oðfæste, ða hwile ðe hie to nanre oðerre note ne mægen, oð ðone first ðe hie wel cunnen Englisc gewrit arædan.

In A, we have

1. three noun clauses introduced by *ðæt*—one the object of *bebiode*,

one the object of *ġelīefe*, and one which is perhaps most simply explained as being in explanatory apposition to the clause *ðæt ðū dō*.

2. an adjective clause introduced by *ðe*.

3. two prepositional formulae—
for ðon adverb used alone 'therefore' and
tō ðǣm . . . ðæt used as a divided prepositional conjunction.

4. two *swā* clauses, one of comparison (*swǣ iċ ġelīefe*) and the other of time (*swǣ ðū oftost mæġe*).

5. an adverb clause of place introduced by *ðǣr ðǣr*.

In B, we have

1. two noun clauses—
the *ðæt* clause subject of *ðynċð* 'seems', which begins after *ðynċð* and has *ðæt*, the subject, and the object, repeated after *wiotonne*. It has two verbs—*wenden* and *ġedōn*;
the *ðætte* clause object of *ġedōn*.

2. four adjective clauses—
the *ðā ðe* clause, where the relative pronoun does not clearly tell us its case (see §163.1);
two *ðe* clauses, excluding that mentioned in 7;
the *ðāra ðe* clause.

3. two conditional clauses introduced by *ġif*.

4. a *swā* clause of comparison.

5. a clause of purpose or result introduced by *ðæt* (following *hæbben*).

6. a clause of time introduced by *ðā hwīle ðe*. Here we must understand *oðfæste wesan*.

7. two prepositional formulae—
for ðȳ adverb 'therefore';
the temporal conjunction *oð ðone first ðe*, where *ðe* can be described as a relative pronoun 'until the time at which'.

These and similarly complicated sentences in Alfred's Preface to the *Cura Pastoralis* show the problems which faced the first men to write in English prose about difficult and complicated subjects. But they and later writers overcame them, often triumphantly.

Clauses of Place

§173 The main conjunctions are:

1. *þǣr* 'where', 'whither', *þider* 'whither', and *þanon* 'whence'. These may introduce definite and indefinite clauses.

2. *swā hwǣr swā* 'wherever' and *swā hwider swā* 'wherever, whithersoever'.

The prevailing mood is the indicative. In examples like *Beowulf*

l. 1394 *ga þær he wille*, the subjunctive reflects the subjunctive in the principal clause, the indefiniteness of the abverd clause, and probably also the fact that the whole expression means 'no matter where he goes' and therefore has a concessive force. For other examples see *Genesis* ll. 2723-4 and a passage from Gregory's *Dialogues* where MS C reads *Far þu þider þe þu wille* and MS H *Far þu nu swa hwider swa þu wille* 'Go wherever you wish'.

Clauses of Time

§ 174   1. Conjunctions whose primary meaning is 'when' or 'while' are: *þā, þonne, mid þām (þe), þā hwīle (þe), þenden*, and *swā lange swā*.

2. Conjunctions whose primary meaning is 'after' are: *siððan* and *þæs þe*. *Æfter* is not used alone as a conjunction in OE.

3. 'Before' is rendered by *ær* either alone or introducing a prepositional formula.

4. Conjunctions whose primary meaning is 'until' are: *oð, oð þe, oð þæt*, and *hwonne*; on the last, see § 159 n. 2.

All these conjunctions usually take the indicative with the exception of *ær*, which prefers the subjunctive, and *hwonne*, which always seems to take the subjunctive (except in *Exodus* l. 251, which is therefore suspect).

Note

Doubtless the fact that both *ær* and *hwonne* clauses refer to a time AFTER the action of the verb of the main clause has something to do with the subjunctive, but the same is true of *oð þæt* which prefers the indicative. The interrogative origin of *hwonne* is also relevant. There are other factors too, but when they have all been investigated, we have to fall back on 'the attitude of the speaker' to explain some variations in mood.

The conjunctions which prefer the indicative may take the subjunctive if circumstances demand. Thus cf. *Beowulf* l. 1374 and l. 1485, in both of which *þonne*, while frequentative and/or indefinite and referring to the future, has the indicative after an indicative principal clause, with *Luke* 14:13 *Ac þonne þu gebeorscype do, clypa þearfan* 'When you make a feast, call the poor', where the imperative *clypa* imparts to the sentence a further element of wishing and uncertainty which is reflected in the subjunctive *dō*. Again, while *þonne* frequentative in the past is followed by the preterite indicative, e.g. *Beowulf* ll. 1580 ff., it has the subjunctive when the time reference was to the future at the time of speaking. (We may call this the 'future-in-the-past'.) In these circumstances, the reference may be to a single act, e.g. *þa bæd he hine þæt he him þæs arwyrþan treos hwylcne hwego dæl brohte, þonne he eft ham come* 'he asked him to

bring a little bit of that precious tree when he came home again'—
þonne, the conjunction appropriate to a single act in the future, is
retained for the future-in-the-past—or to a series of acts, e.g. *He þa*
... geworhte anes fearres anlicnesse of are, to ðon, þonne hit hat wære,
7 mon þa earman men oninnan don wolde, hu se hlynn mæst wære
þonne hie þæt susl þæron prowicnde wæron 'He then made the like-
ness of a boar in brass with the object [of showing] how, when it was
hot and the wretches had been put inside it, the noise would be
greatest when they were undergoing the torture'.

Clauses of Purpose and Result

§ 175 Since a result is often a fulfilled purpose and a purpose a
yet-to-be-completed result, these two have much in common. Both
can be introduced by the following conjunctions: *þæt*, *þætte*, *swā*
þæt, and *swā ... þæt*, though the last two are rare in purpose clauses.
Þæs ... þæt and *tō þæs ... þæt* occasionally introduce result clauses,
more commonly in the poetry than in the prose. *Þȳ lǣs (þe)* 'lest' is
found only in negative clauses of purpose.

It is generally agreed that purpose clauses take the subjunctive,
result clauses the indicative. This proposition cannot be proved, for
it is only by classifying all clauses with the subjunctive as purpose
and all clauses with the indicative as result that we can deduce the
rule. This is clearly a circular argument. But it seems likely enough
when we think of MnE usage.

Note

Much time has been spent on arguing whether a clause with the
indicative can be purpose. This seems to me a pointless terminological controversy. A much-discussed example is *Elene* ll. 930 ff.,
where the indicative *widsæcest* is used of an event which has yet to
take place. Some describe the *þæt* clause as purpose, some as result.
The indicative clearly reflects the speaker's belief that a future event
is sure to take place. In one sense it is therefore a probable result
regarded by the speaker as certain. But it does not seem to have
taken place. So in another sense it is an unfulfilled purpose which
someone once thought certain to be fulfilled. Hence the indicative
reflects the certainty of the speaker, when he spoke, that the event
would take place. And that seems to me all that we can usefully say.
Cf. *Husband's Message* ll. 26 ff.

The subjunctive occurs in result clauses under much the same
conditions as in adjective clauses (see § 165). They are:

1. When the principal clause contains an imperative or a subjunctive expressing a wish, e.g. *alswa litel þu gewurþe þet þu nawiht*
gewurþe 'may you become so small, that you become nothing'. Here

the result is expressed as a tendency. A more difficult example is

> ... ne huru on weg aber   þone halgan gast,
> þæt he me færinga   fremde wyrðe

'... nor take away thy Holy Spirit so that he quickly becomes a stranger to me'.

Here the result has not actually taken place. It is a possible future result of an action not yet performed. It is not the purpose or wish of the speaker that the Holy Spirit should depart from him. His purpose would require a *þæt ... ne* or *þȳ lǣs* 'lest' clause. It may be a purpose attributed by the speaker to God. But from the speaker's point of view it is a result he is anxious to avoid.

Sometimes, it is impossible to decide whether a clause with a subjunctive after an imperative should be classified as purpose or result, e.g. *Andreas* ll. 1182-3 and *Andreas* ll. 1332-3

> Gað fromlice,
> ðæt ge guðfrecan   gylp forbegan

'Go quickly to humble the warrior's pride'. But this is probably a distinction without a difference; cf. *Elene* ll. 930 ff. discussed above.

2. When the principal clause contains a negative which implies that the content of the result clause is doubtful or unreal, e.g. *Beowulf* ll. 1366-7, where the poet means that no human being could possibly know. This should be compared with *Beowulf* ll. 1520-1 and *Maldon* ll. 117-19, where we have examples of litotes in which the negatives refer only to the verbs immediately following them. Hence 'He did not withhold the blow' means 'He gave him a very severe blow'. Thus a result which has actually taken place will not be put into the subjunctive under the influence of a negative in the principal clause.

3. When the principal clause contains a rhetorical question, e.g. *Andreas* ll. 1372-3

> Hwylc is þæs mihtig   ofer middangeard,
> þæt he þe alyse ...

'Who is there on earth so powerful that he can free you?' or '... powerful enough to be able to free you?' This of course means 'There is no-one ...'; cf. §165.3.

Causal Clauses

§176 The main causal conjunctions are the *for* formulae, *nū*, and *þæs* (*þe*). *Þe*, *þȳ*, and *þȳ þe*, are sometimes found.

When the true cause is given, the causal clause has an indicative verb. The subjunctive is regularly used for a rejected reason, e.g.

*Ne cwæþ he þæt na forþon þe him wære anig gemynd þearfendra manna,
ah he wæs gitsere* ... 'He said that, not because he cared at all about
needy men, but because he was a miser ...'

Clauses of Comparison

§177   1. Comparisons involving 'than' are expressed in OE by
þonne or (occasionally and only after a negative principal clause)
þon mā þe. There is a strong tendency for the *þonne* clause to have
the subjunctive when the principal clause is positive, e.g. *Ic Ælfric
munuc and mæssepreost, swa þeah waccre þonne swilcum hadum
gebyrige, wearþ asend* ... 'I Ælfric, monk and mass-priest, though
weaker than is fitting for such orders, was sent ...', and the indicative when the principal clause is negative, e.g. *Beowulf* ll. 247-9.
However, exceptions are not uncommon.

2. Comparisons involving 'as' may be expressed by
(a) *swā* 'as' or *swā swā* 'just as';
(b) *swā ... swā* 'so ... as';
(c) *swā* + superlative;
(d) *swylce* 'such as';
(e) *swylce ... swā* 'such ... as';
(f) *þæs (þe)*, e.g. *Beowulf* l. 1341 and (with a superlative)
    Beowulf l. 1350.
For further details, see the appropriate word in §168. The prevailing
mood in these clauses is the indicative.

3. Comparisons involving 'the ... the' are expressed by *þy ... þy*,
e.g. *Maldon* ll. 312-13. The verbs are in the indicative.

4. Comparisons involving hypothesis are expressed by *swā* or
swilce 'as if' followed by the subjunctive. When the time reference
is to the past, the preterite subjunctive is found in the 'as if' clause,
e.g. *Wanderer* l. 96 and *Finnsburh* l. 36. When it is to the present,
we find the present subjunctive in the 'as if' clause, e.g. *Christ*
ll. 179-181 and ll. 1376-7. The preterite subjunctive is not used of
the present as it is in OE type C Conditions (see §179.4) or in MnE
'He runs as if he were tired'; the MnE equivalent of the OE idiom
would be 'He runs as if he be tired'.

Clauses of Concession

§178   1. Simple concessive clauses are usually introduced by
þēah (þe) 'though'. The prevailing mood is the subjunctive, whether
the concession is one of fact or hypothesis.

Note

Sometimes, we have *þēah ... eall*, as in *Beowulf* l. 680 *þeah ic eal
mæge*. Here *eall* is an adverb, perhaps with the sense 'easily'. But

this probably represents a stage in the development of 'although';
see OED s.v. *all* C adv. II 10, and note that in such ME examples as
The Pardoner's Tale lines 371, 449, and 451 (line references to Skeat's
edition), *al* is still an adverb and the concession is expressed by the
word-order V.S.

2. Disjunctive concessions are expressed by *sam . . . sam* 'whether
. . . or'. In such clauses, the subjunctive is the rule, e.g. *sam hit sy
sumor sam winter* 'whether it is summer or winter'.

3. As in MnE, an element of concession is often present in indefinite adjective clauses (e.g. *Beowulf* ll. 942 ff. and ll. 142-3) or in
indefinite adverb clauses of place (e.g. *Genesis* ll. 2723 ff.) or time
(e.g. *Genesis* ll. 1832 ff.). On the possibility that there was a special
OE idiom expressing indefinite concession, see Klaeber's note on
Beowulf l. 968.

4. Concession can sometimes be expressed by putting the verb
first without any conjunction. The two most common types are
swelte ic, libbe ic 'whether I live or die' and *hycge swa he wille* 'let him
think as he will', 'no matter what he thinks'. The first type often
occurs in the form *wylle ic, nylle ic* 'willy-nilly'.

Clauses of Condition

§179 1. For purposes of our discussion, we may divide conditions into three types:

A. If you believe this, you are making a mistake.
   If you believed this, you made a mistake.
B. If you were to believe this, you would make a mistake.
   Here the implication is 'and you might'; the possibility remains.
C. If you believed this, you would be making a mistake.
   If you had believed this, you would have made a mistake.
   Here the implication is 'But you don't' or 'But you didn't'; the
   condition cannot be fulfilled.

In OE, conditions of all three types may be introduced by *ġif* or
(less commonly) *þær*, both meaning 'if'. Points which must be
specially noted are set out below.

2. Type A Conditions fall into two main groups—those in which
both clauses have the indicative, e.g. *Maldon* ll. 34-5 and ll. 36-41,
and those in which the verb of the principal clause is imperative or
expresses a wish in the subjunctive. In these sentences, the 'if' clause
usually has the subjunctive, e.g. *sec, gif þu dyrre* 'seek if you dare'.
This point is well-illustrated by the two almost parallel *ġif* clauses
in *Beowulf* ll. 445-453.

3. Type B Conditions are not common in OE. From those which

do occur, we can conclude that (as in MnE) the preterite subjunctive could be used in them.

Note

Occasional examples, e.g. *Christ* ll. 840ff., *Charms* 2 ll. 45ff., and *Riddles* 4 ll. 11-12, suggest that the present subjunctive may sometimes have been used in type B Conditions in OE; cf. §177.4. But there is difference of opinion about this and the matter is not yet completely investigated.

4. Type C Conditions regularly have the preterite subjunctive in both clauses, e.g. *ac hit wære to hrædlic, gif he ða on cild-cradole acweald wurde* . . . 'it would have been too early if He (Christ) had been killed in His cradle . . .' and perhaps (with *þær* and in dependent speech)

and þæt wiste eac   weroda Drihten,
þæt sceolde unc Adame   yfele gewurðan
ymb þæt heofonrice,   þær ic ahte minra handa geweald

'and the Lord of Hosts also knew that things would turn out badly between Adam and me about that heavenly kingdom, if I had control of my hands'.

Note

The fact that I say 'perhaps' here is important. In MnE we can distinguish unreality in the past, present, and future, by means of the verb alone, e.g.

If he had been here, it wouldn't have happened.
If he were here, it wouldn't be happening.
If he were coming, it wouldn't happen.

But (as is pointed out in more detail in §§195-198) the OE verb was not as flexible an instrument as the MnE verb. Hence an Anglo-Saxon had to use the preterite subjunctive in all these examples. In other words, he could say that a thing was unreal or impossible, but he was unable to say when it could not happen unless he used an adverb or some other device.

Thus both the OE examples cited in this section have the preterite subjunctive. But the first refers to something which did not happen in the past, while the second might refer to something which is impossible at the time when Satan spoke—the implication being 'if only I had control of my hands now, but I haven't'. But it could also be translated 'God knew that trouble would arise between Adam and me if I were to have control of my hands'.

This raises a further difficulty and explains the 'perhaps'. Does this interpretation mean that there was a possibility that Satan might have control of his hands (type B Condition) or that such a thing was impossible when God spoke? The issue here is complicated by questions of God's foreknowledge, though perhaps our own knowledge of the story enables us to dismiss the latter possibility. But enough has

been said to make it clear that the Anglo-Saxon 'rule' that 'unreality
is timeless' is not without its advantages.

A clearer example is *Beowulf* ll. 960-1, discussed in §198.

5. *Būtan* and *nymþe, nemne, nefne* both have two meanings—
'unless' and 'except that'. Meaning 'unless', both usually take the
subjunctive, e.g. *Beowulf* l. 966 and l. 1056. Meaning 'except that',
both usually take the indicative, e.g. *Beowulf* l. 1560 and l. 1353.

6. 'On condition that' may be expressed by *gif* or by the *wiþ*
formula (see §171).

7. Conditions expressed by the word-order V.S. without a conjunction—e.g. 'Had I plenty of money, I would be lying in the sun
in Bermuda'—occasionally occur in OE prose, e.g. *eaðe mihte þes
cwyde beon læwedum mannum bediglod, nære seo gastlice getacning* 'this
saying could easily be concealed from laymen were it not [for] its
spiritual meaning'. The only certain example in the poetry is
Genesis ll. 368-370; here it is arguable whether a line is missing or
whether the poet deliberately left the *þonne* clause unfinished to
obtain a dramatic effect.

8. On comparisons involving hypothesis, see §177.4.

Adverb Clauses Expressing Other Relationships

§180 The divisions outlined above are for convenience only and
are far from being watertight, for one relationship often involves
another. Thus, while clauses of time with *oþ* (*þæt*) often shade into
result, and *þæt* after verbs of motion can often be translated 'until',
other temporal clauses may contain elements of cause or of condition.
Similarly, indefinite adjective clauses are often the equivalent of
conditional clauses, e.g. *Beowulf* ll. 1387-8.

Note

This latter relationship is very clearly seen in some ME sentences
which contain an adjective clause which must be rendered by a conditional clause in MnE, e.g. Hall *Selections from Early Middle
English*, p. 54 l. 11 and l. 21 (cf. p. 54 l. 16) and *Sir Gawain and the
Green Knight* l. 1112.

Other Ways of Expressing Adverbial Relationships

§181 1. Parataxis; examples will be found in §§182-186.

2. Participles; see §204.

3. Infinitives; see §205.

4. Prepositional phrases, e.g. *mid* expressing condition *mid Godes
fultume* 'with God's help, if God helps us'; *þurh* expressing cause
þurh þæs cyninges bebod 'by command of the king'; and *þurh* expressing time *þurh swefn* 'in a dream, while he dreamt'.

vi PARATAXIS

Introduction

§182 The Anglo-Saxons were far from primitive. At the time of the Norman Conquest, Sir Arthur Bryant tells us in *The Story of England*, Britain had long led Western Europe in monastic learning, was famous for her craftsmen, and was the best administered and richest of all the western kingdoms. But old traditions are hard to kill and it is not always realized that her language too was far more developed for the expression of both prose and poetry than any other contemporary European vernacular and that authors using it sometimes rose to very great heights. Look for example at the poem *The Dream of the Rood* and at the magnificent passage beginning *Ne forseah Crist his geongan cempan* in Ælfric's Homily on the Nativity of the Innocents.

Some of the reasons for the belief that Old English was a primitive language have been discussed in §§148-152. Another is the frequent use of parataxis. Some writers, steeped in the periodic structure of Latin and Greek, seem unable or unwilling to believe that parataxis can be anything but a clumsy tool used by people who did not know any better. Certainly, S. O. Andrew (in *Syntax and Style in Old English*) does well to draw our attention to inconsistencies in the editorial punctuation of Old English texts. But he allows himself to be swayed too much by his conviction that good writing must necessarily be periodic. Today, when the long and complicated sentence is losing favour in English, we will perhaps be more in sympathy with the constructions described in the following paragraphs, more able to appreciate the effect they produced, and less likely to believe that the juxtaposition of two simple sentences was necessarily less dramatic or effective than one complex sentence. During his journey to the Underworld in search of Eurydice, Orpheus met the Parcae. *Ða ongon he biddan heora miltse; ða ongunnon hi wepan mid him*, the story continues. Here the word-order supports the view that the two sentences are independent (see §151), and suggests that the writer is giving equal prominence to the two ideas. The effect he was after can perhaps be achieved by the translation 'Then he asked for their pity and they wept with him'. At the end of the same story, the final disappearance of Eurydice is related thus: *Ða he forð on ðæt leoht com, ða beseah he hine under bæc wið ðæs wifes; ða losade hio him sona* 'When he came into the light, he looked back towards his wife. Straightway she disappeared from his sight'. Here a powerful dramatic effect would be lost if we took only one of the clauses with *þā* + V.S. as principal.

§183 The term 'parataxis', with its adjective 'paratactic', has been abandoned by some writers because of its ambiguity. Here it is used in a purely formal sense to mean a construction in which sentences are not formally subordinated one to the other. 'Asyndetic' and 'syndetic' mean respectively without and with conjunctions such as *ond* and *ac*. The term 'co-ordinating' (often used for the MnE equivalents 'and', 'but', and so on) is avoided here because in OE *ond* and *ac* are frequently followed by the order S. . . . V. (see §145), which is basically a subordinate order. The opposite of 'parataxis' is 'hypotaxis', which implies the use of one or more of the conjunctions discussed in §§154-180. Examples follow.

Hypotaxis: When I came, I saw. When I saw, I conquered.
Asyndetic Parataxis: I came. I saw. I conquered.
Syndetic Parataxis: I came and I saw and I conquered.

List of Conjunctions and Adverbs Commonly Used

§184   On word-order after these words, see §§144 and 145.

1. Those meaning 'and', 'both . . . and', etc. (traditionally called 'cumulative'):

> *and, ond* 'and' (see below);
> *ǣġhwæþer (ġe)* . . . *ġe* . . . *(ġe)* '(both) . . . and . . . (and)';
> *ǣġþer (ġe)* . . . *ġe* . . . *(ġe)* '(both) . . . and . . . (and)';
> *ēac* 'also, and'; *ġe* 'and'; *ġe* . . . *ġe, ǣġþer* . . . *and* 'both . . . and'.

The *ond* clause can of course imply more than mere continuity and is often the equivalent of an adverb clause. Thus *ofer Eastron gefor Æþered cyning; ond he ricsode V gear* could be translated 'During Easter Æthered died after ruling five years'. This of course often happens today, especially in conversation.

2. Those meaning 'but', 'however', etc. (traditionally called 'adversative'):

> *ac* 'but, on the contrary'; *furþum* 'also, even';
> *hūru* 'however, indeed', etc.;
> *hwæþere* 'however, yet'; *swāþēah* 'however, yet';
> *þēah* 'however, yet' (see also §178);
> *þēahhwæþere* 'however, yet'.

3. Those meaning 'either . . . or' (traditionally called 'alternative'):
> *hwilum* . . . *hwilum* 'at one time . . . at another time';
> *(ǣġþer) oþþe* . . . *oþþe*; *swā* . . . *swā*; *þe* . . . *þe*.

4. Those involving a negative:
> *nā, ne, nō* 'not';
> *(nāhwæðer ne)* . . . *ne* . . . *(ne)* 'neither . . . nor . . . (nor)';
> *nalles, nealles* 'not at all, not';

(*nāðor ne*) ... *ne* ... (*ne*) 'neither ... nor ... (nor)';
nǽfre 'never'; *næs* 'not' (a short form of *nalles*).

An example of 'not only ... but also' will be found in *na þæt an þæt he wolde mann beon for us, ðaða he God wæs, ac eac swylce he wolde beon þearfa for us, ðaða he rice wæs* 'not only was He willing to become man for us when He was God, but He was also willing to become poor for us when He was rich'.

The following points should be noted:

(*a*) The OE verb is normally negatived by *ne* immediately preceding it. But if the negative is stressed, as in *Wanderer* l. 96 and *Seafarer* l. 66, *nā* (=*ne* + *ā*) or *nō* (=*ne* + *ō*) is used. In *Phoenix* l. 72 the MS *no* should be emended to *ne* because the negative is unstressed.

(*b*) The arrangement seen in *Ne com se here—Ne* + V.S.—is common in negative principal clauses; see § 146.4.

(*c*) Contraction of the negative *ne* with a following word beginning with a vowel, *h*, or *w*, produces *nis* from *ne is*, *næfde* from *ne hæfde*, *noldon* from *ne woldon*, and so on.

(*d*) *Ne* not before a finite verb is a conjunction, e.g. *ne tunge ne handa* 'neither tongue nor hands', *ne leornian ne tæcan* 'neither to learn nor to teach'.

(*e*) *Nā* and *nō* are used to negative words other than finite verbs, e.g. *He wæs Godes bydel ond na God* 'He was God's messenger and not God'.

(*f*) One negative does not cancel out another, as it does in formal MnE. The OE use is similar to that seen in such non-standard sentences as 'I didn't do nothing to nobody'; cf. *on nanum men nyton nane are* '[they] show mercy to no-one'. This could be added to the list of things which make some people think of OE as a primitive language; see § 182.

(*g*) On a 'semi-subordinating' use of *ne*, see § 185.2.

5. Those meaning 'for' (traditionally called 'illative'). A recent article on MnE 'for' (*American Speech* 30 (1955), 151) states: 'The only practical conclusion is that the conjunction has two uses, subordinating and co-ordinating, and that punctuation is of no significance in identifying either'. In other words, MnE 'for' can sometimes be replaced by 'because'. In OE, the situation is even more complicated, for *forþon* can mean, not only 'for' and 'because', but also 'therefore'. No rule can be laid down for distinguishing these uses.

Parataxis without Conjunctions

§ 185 Two main types of asyndetic parataxis may be distinguished.

1. Here the two sentences are of equal status, as in the well-known

Veni. Vidi. Vici. Examples are especially common in the poetry, e.g. *Beowulf* ll. 1422-4 and *Maldon* ll. 301-6.

2. Examples of the second type occur in *Eadmund cyning awearp his wæpnu, wolde geæfenlæcan Cristes gebysnungum* and *þa comon þeofas eahta, woldon stelan þa maðmas*, where the clauses beginning with *wolde* and *woldon* respectively could be translated 'wishing to imitate Christ's example' and 'intending to steal the treasures'. Note

(*a*) These clauses do not themselves contain a grammatically-expressed subject.

(*b*) They are actually, though not formally, subordinate to the clause which precedes them; for this reason they are sometimes said to be in 'semi-subordination'.

(*c*) They explain the motive for the action of the principal clause and are the equivalent of an adverb clause of purpose or cause.

This idiom occurs with verbs other than *willan*, e.g. *he sæt on ðæm muntum, weop ond hearpode* which can conveniently be translated 'he sat on the mountains, weeping and harping'. Similar examples occur with an initial negative, e.g. *Beowulf* ll. 1441-2 'Beowulf arrayed himself in princely armour without (or 'not') worrying about his life'.

Some Special Idioms

§186   1. . . . *wæs gehāten* ' . . . was called' is frequently used independently of the rest of the sentence, e.g. *mid heora cyningum, Rædgota ond Eallerica wæron hatne* 'with their kings, [who] were called R. and E.' (notice the change from the dative to the nominative case) and *þa wæs sum consul, þæt we heretoha hataþ, Boetius wæs gehaten* 'there was a certain consul—we use the word *heretoha*—[who] was called B.'. Cf., with the verb 'to be' only, . . . *gefor Ælfred, wæs æt Baðum gerefa*, 'A., [who] was reeve at Bath, died'.

2. For '*swā* + negative + indicative', see §168 s.v. *swā* 2(*d*).

vii CONCORD

§187   The main rules of agreement in OE are set out below. They will present little difficulty to any reader with a knowledge of an inflected language.

1. Nouns, Pronouns and their modifiers

(*a*) They agree in number, gender, and case, e.g. *se Ælmihtiga Hælend* 'the Almighty Saviour', *ðæs eadigan apostoles* 'of the blessed apostle', and *and þe cwicne gebindaþ* 'and will bind you alive'.

Note

The masc. ending -*e* in nom. acc. pl. of adjectives is often used for fem. and neut., especially in later texts.

(b) The participle in a participial phrase usually shows similar agreement, e.g. *Hinguar and Hubba, ge-anlæhte þurh deofol* 'H. and H., united by the devil'. But it need not, e.g. *Abraham geseah þær anne ramm betwux þam bremelum be þam hornum gehæft* 'A. saw there a ram caught among the brambles by his horns'.

(c) *Gehāten* 'called' with a noun usually has the nominative irrespective of the case of the word with which it is in apposition, e.g. *into anre byrig, Gaza gehaten* 'into a city called Gaza'; cf. *for ðy hit man hæt Wislemuða* 'therefore we call (lit. 'one calls') it W.' where the nominative *Wislemūða* is the equivalent of the modern italics or inverted commas, and the second example in §186.1.

(d) After *wesan* and *weorþan* the participle often agrees with the subject, e.g. *hie wurdon ofslægene* 'they were slain' and *þe mid him ofslægene wæron* 'who were killed with them'. But it need not, e.g. *þa wurdon hiora wif swa sarige on hiora mode ond swa swiðlice gedrefed . . .* 'then their wives became so sorrowful and so greatly distressed in mind . . .' See further §§201-203.

(e) After *habban*, the participle may agree with the object or may remain uninflected; see §200.

2. Pronouns and their antecedents

(a) They agree in number and gender, e.g. *to þæm cyninge . . . he . . . his feores* 'to the king . . . he . . . for his life'; *anno flotan . . . oo* 'a pirate . . . he (lit. 'that')'; and *se hearpere . . . ðæs nama* 'the harper, whose name'.

(b) The main exceptions arise from the conflict between natural and grammatical gender, e.g. *ðæs hearperes wif* (neut.) *. . . hire sawle* 'the harper's wife . . . her soul' and *an swiðe ænlic wif, sio wæs haten Eurydice* 'a most excellent wife, who was called E.'. Similarly, in a passage from the Preface to the *Cura Pastoralis* we find *ðone wīsdōm* followed first by the grammatically right masculine *hine* and then by the neuter *hit* which seems appropriate to us. Thus there are already signs that the feeling for grammatical gender is weakening.

Note

Agreement in case between pronoun and antecedent is a matter of chance, not principle, despite Quirk and Wrenn *An Old English Grammar* §121(c). In the examples they cite, *rōde* and *hēo* do not agree in case and the relative *ðāra þe* would have to be replaced by the acc. pl. *þā* of the declined relative *se*, i.e. *ðāra* has the case of the principal clause; see §163.1.

(c) Special uses of *hit, þæt, hwæt*, and the like, in which these neuter pronouns are used without regard to the number and gender of the noun to which they refer, should be noted, e.g. *þæt wæron eall*

Finnas 'they were all Finns' and *Hwæt syndon ge . . .?* 'Who are you . . .?' See further §168 s.v. *þæs . . . þæt,* note 1.

3. Subject and Verb

(*a*) Subject and verb agree in number and person. Dual pronouns are followed by plural verbs.

(*b*) Collective nouns and indefinite pronouns cause much the same problems as they do today, e.g. *an mægð . . . hi magon cyle gewyrcan* 'a tribe . . . they can make cold' and *þonne rideð ælc, and hit motan habban* 'then each man rides, and [they] can have it'.

(*c*) With *ond þæs ymb XIIII niht gefeaht Æþered cyning ond Ælfred his broður,* where *gefeaht* is singular, cf. 'Here comes Tom, and Jack, and all the boys'.

(*d*) When the relative pronoun *þāra þe* means 'of those who', the verb of the adjective clause can be singular or plural.

viii The Uses of the Cases

These will not present much difficulty to those familiar with an inflected language. On the cases used after prepositions, see §§213-214.

Nominative

§188 The case of the subject, of the complement, and of address, e.g. *Gehyrst þu, sælida?* 'Do you hear, seaman?' See also §187.1(c).

Accusative

§189 1. The case of the direct object.

2. It also expresses duration of time, e.g. *ealne dæg* 'all day', and extent of space, e.g. *fleon fotes trym* 'to flee one foot's pace'.

Note

It is important to realize that already in OE the nominative and accusative are frequently the same. In the plural they are always the same except in the 1st and 2nd pers. pron. In the singular, many nouns have the same form in the nominative and accusative, and the distinction depends on the form of any demonstrative or possessive adjective, or on that of any adjective, which may qualify the noun. See further §140.

Genitive

§190 1. The case of possession, e.g. *Hæstenes wif* 'Hæsten's wife'.

2. The subjective genitive—*þæs cyninges bebod* 'the king's command', i.e. 'the king commanded'—differs in function from the objective genitive—*metodes ege* 'fear of the Lord', i.e. 'we fear the Lord'.

3. The genitive may describe or define, e.g. *swete hunig and wyn-sumes swæcces* 'honey sweet and of pleasant taste', *ðreora daga fæsten* 'a fast of three days', and *an lamb anes geares* 'a one-year-old lamb'.

4. The partitive genitive is common, e.g. *an hiora* 'one of them' and *þreora sum* 'one of three'. See also § 194.

5. Thc genitive is used adverbially, e.g. *dæges ond nihtes* 'by day and night', *micles to beald* 'much too bold', *upweardes* 'upwards', *þæs* 'therefore, so, after that'.

6. The genitive occurs after some adjectives, e.g. *þæs gefeohtes georn* 'eager for the fight', and after some verbs, e.g. *fanda min* 'try me' and *hie þæs fægnodon* 'they rejoiced at that'. Your glossary should give you this information when you need it.

Dative

§ 191 1. The case of the indirect object, e.g. *ond he hi him eft ageaf* 'and he afterwards gave them back to him'.

2. It may express possession, e.g. *him on heafod* 'on his head'.

3. It may express time, e.g. *hwilum* 'at times' and *ðære ylcan nihte* 'in the same night'.

4. The dative absolute is used in imitation of the Latin ablative absoluto, e.g. *gewunnenum sige* 'victory having been gained'.

5. The dative occurs after some adjectives, e.g. *ise gelicost* 'most like to ice', sometimes after comparatives, e.g. *sunnan beorhtra* 'brighter than thc sun', and after some verbs, e.g. *þæt he him miltsian sceolde* 'that he should have mercy on him'. Here too your glossary should help you.

Instrumental

§ 192 Where there is no special instrumental form (and some-times when there is), the dative serves.

1. The instrumental expresses means or manner, e.g. *þone ilcan we hataþ oþre naman æfensteorra* 'we call the same by another name —evening star', *fægere ende his lif betynde* 'closed his lifc with a fair end' (but cf. the dative in *geendode yflum deaþe* 'ended with an evil death'), and *hlutre mode* 'with a pure mind'.

2. It expresses accompaniment, e.g. *lytle werede* 'with a small band'.

3. It expresses time, e.g. *þy ilcan geare* 'in the same year'.

ix ARTICLES, PRONOUNS, AND NUMERALS

Articles and Pronouns

§ 193 1. There are no 'articles' as such in OE. Thc demonstrative *se* does duty for 'the' and 'that', the demonstrative *þes* means 'this',

e.g. *Her on þysum geare for se micla here, þe we gefyrn ymbe spræcon* ...
'In this year the great army which we spoke about before went ...'
Sometimes, however, *se* can be translated 'this', e.g. *anne æþeling se wæs Cyneheard haten—7 se Cyneheard wæs þæs Sigebryhtes broþur* 'a princeling who was called C. and this C. was the brother of the S. already mentioned'.

2. The demonstrative is frequently not used in OE where we would use it today, e.g. *wælstowe gewald* 'command of the battle-field', and, from the poetry (where its absence is even more common), *fram beaduwe* 'from the battle' and *Oddan bearn* 'the sons of Odda'. But the reverse is sometimes true, e.g. *sio lar* 'learning'.

3. In examples like *Æþered cyning* we have either absence of a demonstrative pronoun 'Æthered the King' or (more likely in view of *Iohannes se godspellere* 'John the Evangelist') a different arrangement of appositional elements 'King Æthered'. Hence *Æþelwulf aldormon* might be the equivalent of 'General Smith'.

4. The indefinite article is even rarer; thus we find *holtes on ende* 'at the edge of a wood', *to wæfersyne* 'as a spectacle', and *on beorg* 'onto a mountain'. *Ān* is sometimes used, e.g. *to anum treowe* 'to a tree' and *an wulf* 'a wolf'. But usually *ān* and *sum* mean something more, e.g. *an mægð* 'a certain tribe' and *sum mon* 'a certain man'. Sometimes these words have an even stronger sense, e.g. *þæt wæs an cyning* 'that was a peerless King', 'that wás a King', and *eower sum* 'a particular one among you', 'your leader'. In this sense, and as the numeral 'one', *ān* is strong. Meaning 'alone', it is usually weak, e.g. *he ana*, but may be strong, e.g. *ðone naman anne* 'the name alone'.

5. *Se* is also used as a relative pronoun; see §162.3. Sometimes, as in *Beowulf* l. 1296, it may be either demonstrative or relative. But the difficulty is of little practical consequence.

6. The third person pronoun is sometimes used ambiguously, so that we cannot readily tell to whom it is referring. A well-known series of examples is found in the story of Cynewulf and Cyneheard in the entry for 755 in the Parker MS of the Anglo-Saxon Chronicle. But this is rather the result of inexperience in handling the language than of defects in the language itself, for later in its development, OE managed to make the meaning clear with no more pronouns at its disposal. The same is, of course, true of MnE.

7. A pronoun subject is frequently not expressed. Often the subject not expressed is the same as that of the preceding clause. But the absence of a subject does not certify that it has not changed; see, e.g. *Maldon* ll. 17-21, where the subject changes twice in l. 20 without any pronoun. A pronoun object may be similarly unexpressed, e.g. the sentence quoted in §167.6. Sometimes, however, *se* is used instead of *hē* to make clear that a subject has changed,

e.g. *Maldon* ll. 150 and 227. This avoids the ambiguity which could arise from a repeated or an absent *hē*, e.g. *Maldon* l. 286 and *Beowulf* l. 57.

Numerals

§ 194 The cardinal numerals can be used

1. as adjectives agreeing with a noun, e.g. *þrim gearum ær he forþferde* 'three years before he died' and *mid XXXgum cyningum* 'with thirty kings';
2. as nouns followed by a partitive genitive, e.g. *to anre þara burga* 'to one of the cities' and *þritig cyninga* 'thirty kings'.

x Verbs

On the detailed uses of the indicative and subjunctive in subordinate clauses, see the discussions on the appropriate clause.

The Uses of the Present and Preterite Tenses

§ 195 As we have seen in § 89, the OE verb distinguished only two tenses in conjugation—the present and the preterite. Hence despite the fact that the beginnings of the MnE resolved tenses are found in OE (see below), the two simple tenses are often used to express complicated temporal relationships. This is one of the things which made Professor Tolkien once say in a lecture that most people read OE poetry much more quickly than did the Anglo-Saxon minstrel, reciting or reading aloud as he was to an audience which needed time to pick up the implications of what he was saying. And this would apply, not only to the subject-matter, especially to the hints and allusions which frequently had great significance, but also to the relationships between paratactic sentences such as those discussed in §§ 182-185 and to the actual relationship in time between two actions both of which were described by a simple tense of a verb. Thus it is important for us to understand what these simple tenses could imply.

§ 196 The present expresses, not only a continuing state as in *Wlitig is se wong* 'The plain is beautiful', and *ðeos woruld nealæcð þam ende* 'this world is drawing near to its end', but also the passing moment, the actual 'now' for which MnE often uses a continuous tense, e.g. *hwæt þis folc segeð* 'what this people are saying, say now'. It is also used for the future, e.g. *þas flotmenn cumaþ* 'these seamen will come', and (as in equivalent examples in MnE) for the future perfect, e.g. *seþe þæt gelæsteð, bið him lean gearo* 'a reward will be ready for him who does (shall have done) that', and (with a subjunctive *gefeohte* as explained in § 179.2) *gif hwa gefeohte on cyninges*

huse, sie he scyldig ealles his ierfes 'if anyone fight (shall have fought)
in the king's house, let him forfeit all his property'.

In the principal clause in the last sentence, the subjunctive *sie*
expresses a command and could be translated 'he shall forfeit'. The
present subjunctive can also express a wish, e.g. *abreoðe his angin*
'may his enterprise fail', or a prayer, e.g. *God þe sie milde* 'May God
be merciful to you'.

The only verb which has a special future form is the verb 'to be',
where *bið* and its forms are used for the future, e.g. *bið him lean gearo*
above, and for the statement of an eternal truth (a use sometimes
called 'gnomic'), e.g. *wyrd bið ful aræd* 'Fate is quite inexorable' and
þonne bið heofena rice gelic þæm tyn fæmnum 'Then the Kingdom of
Heaven is like unto ten virgins'. But *is* may do the same job, e.g.
Heofena rice is gelic þæm hiredes ealdre 'The Kingdom of Heaven is
like unto a man that is an householder'.

The historic present sometimes occurs.

§197   The preterite indicative is used

1. of a single completed act in the past;

2. of an act continuing in the past. Both of these are exemplified
in *soðlice þa ða men slepon, þa com his feonda sum* 'truly, while men
were sleeping, one of his enemies came';

3. for the perfect, e.g. *ic mid ealre heortan þe gewilnode* 'I have
wished for Thee with all my heart';

4. for the pluperfect, e.g. *sona swa hie comon* 'as soon as they had
come' and (with a strengthening *ær*) *and his swura wæs gehalod þe
ær wæs forslægen* 'and his neck, which had been cut through, was
healed'. (Cf. the use of *ærur* in *Dream of the Rood* l. 108.)

§198   The preterite subjunctive may refer to the past, e.g. *ond ge
wiðsocon þæt in Bethleme bearn cenned wære* 'and you denied that
a child was born in Bethlehem', or to the future-in-the-past, e.g.
the two sentences quoted at the end of §174.

It has already been pointed out in §179.4 that unreality is timeless in OE. An interestingly ambiguous example of this is seen in
Beowulf ll. 960-1

Uþe ic swiþor
þæt ðu hine selfne   geseon moste . . .!

Here Beowulf might be saying to Hrothgar either

'I could wish that you could see Grendel now'; in other words
'I wish that he hadn't got away'

or   'I could wish that you could have seen Grendel yesterday';
in other words 'I wish that you had been at the fight and had
seen how badly wounded he was'

or   'I could wish that you could see Grendel tomorrow'; in other
words 'I wish that we could find his body and so know that he
is dead'.

But the context strongly suggests the second.

The Resolved Tenses

Introduction

§199   This term is used to mean tenses made up from a participle
(present or past) or an infinitive together with the verb 'to be', the
verb 'to have', or one of the 'modal' verbs (see §206), e.g. MnE 'He
is coming', 'He is come', 'He has come', 'He will come'. The beginnings of these forms are seen in OE, with one important difference
which throws light on their origin. A MnE example will explain this.
In *Ephesians* 6:14, the Revised Version reads 'Stand therefore,
having girded your loins with truth'. If we parsed 'having girded',
we would perhaps call it the perfect participle of the verb 'to gird',
with 'your loins' its object; at any rate, we would say that it was
part of the verb 'to gird'. But the Authorized Version reads 'Stand
therefore having your loins girt about with truth'. Here 'your loins'
is the object of the participle 'having' and 'girt about with truth' is a
phrase describing 'your loins'; hence 'girt' is adjectival rather than
verbal. That this was its original function in such phrases in OE
becomes clear when we study the agreement of some of the examples
cited below; to make this point, it will be convenient if we take first
the ancestor of the MnE perfect tense with 'have'.

The Verb 'to have' as an Auxiliary

§200   Examples in which the participle is adjectival are *he us
hafað þæs leohtes bescyrede* 'he has us deprived of that light' (where
the present tense of *habban* is followed by *bescyrede* a past participle
acc. pl. strong, agreeing with *ūs*) and *ac hi hæfdon þa heora stemn
gesetenne and hiora mete genotudne* 'but then they had their term of
service finished and their food used up' (where a past tense of *habban*
is followed by two participles both of which are declined acc. sg.
masc. strong, agreeing with *stemn* and *mete*, the objects of *hæfdon*).
These are clearly the ancestors of the MnE perfect and pluperfect
respectively.

But examples also occur in which there is no such declining of the
past participle to agree with the object, e.g. *Eastengle hæfdon Ælfrede
cyninge aþas geseald* 'The East Anglians had oaths given to King
Alfred' and *Hæfde se cyning his fierd on tu tonumen* 'The King had
his army divided in two'; cf. §187.1(b). This was, of course, a
necessary stage in the development of the MnE perfect and pluper-

fect tenses. The modern arrangement in which the participle precedes the object instead of having final position is found in such
examples as *Nu ðu hæfst ongiten ða wanclan truwa þæs blindan lustes*
'Now you have realized the fickle loyalty of blind pleasure'.

The Verb 'to be' as an Auxiliary of Tense

§201   1. It is found with the present participle as the ancestor
of the MnE continuous tenses. But here too the participle was
originally adjectival rather than verbal. It should also be noted that
the OE combination is not the exact equivalent of the modern usage.
Often it means the same as the corresponding simple tense, e.g. *þa
wæs se cyning openlice andettende þam biscope* 'Then the king openly
confessed to the bishop', though it may give greater vividness. (This
construction is perhaps restricted to texts translated from Latin.) But
sometimes it implies that an action continued for some time, e.g. *ond
hie þa . . . feohtende wæron* 'and then they kept on fighting' and *ða
ða se apostol þas lare sprecende wæs* 'while the apostle was explaining
this teaching'. In these examples, it comes close to the modern use.
   2. The verb 'to be' is also found with the past participle forming
the perfect and pluperfect of intransitive verbs, e.g. *Swæ clæne hio
[=lar] wæs oðfeallenu on Angelcynne* 'So completely was learning
fallen away in England' (where the participle is declined nom. sg.
fem. strong, agreeing with the subject) and *hu sio lar Lædengeðiodes
ær ðissum afeallen wæs* 'how the learning of Latin was fallen away
before this' (where the participle is not declined). Here too the
participle was originally adjectival rather than verbal.

The Passive

§202   Only one OE verb had a synthetic passive, viz. *hātte* 'is
called', 'was called', e.g. *se munuc hatte Abbo* 'the monk was called A.'.
Otherwise the idea was expressed by the impersonal *man* 'one'
with the active voice, e.g. *Her mon mæg giet gesion hiora swæð* 'Here
one can still see their track', or by the verbs 'to be' or 'to become'
with the past participle, e.g. *to bysmore synd getawode þas earman
landleoda* 'the miserable people of this land are (have been) shame-
fully ill-treated', *Æfter þæm þe Romeburg getimbred wæs* 'After Rome
was (had been) built', and *æfter minum leofum þegnum þe on heora
bedde wurdon mid bearnum and wifum færlice ofslægene* 'after my
beloved thanes who became (have been) suddenly killed in their beds
with their wives and children'. The inflexions in the first and third
of these examples show that here too the participle is adjectival
rather than verbal. But again the participle was not always declined, e.g. *hie beoð ahafen from eorðan* 'they are raised from the

earth'. (Can we definitely say it is not declined in the example
about Rome?)

§203   The difference between the forms with *wesan* and those
with *weorðan* is not well-defined. The former sometimes seem to
emphasize the state arising from the action, e.g. *he eall wæs beset mid
heora scotungum* 'he was completely covered with their missiles' and
(showing the continuing state by the use of *bið*) *ne bið ðær nænig ealo
gebrowen* 'nor is any ale brewed there', and the latter the action
itself, e.g. *þær wearþ se cyning Bagsecg ofslægen* 'there King B. was
killed' (lit. 'became slain'). But this does not always hold; cf. e.g.
on þæm wæron eac þa men ofslægene 'on it too the men were slain'.
Such fluctuations are natural in a developing language. The fact
that the *weorðan* form of the idiom disappeared suggests that the
language found other ways of making the distinction when it was
necessary, e.g. *þær se cyning ofslægen læg* 'where the King lay slain';
it was, as J. M. Wattie points out, 'the only false start' in the
development of the MnE verb.

Other Uses of the Present and Past Participles

§204   1. Present and past participles are found as nouns, e.g.
brimliþendra 'of the seamen' and *He is se frumcenneda* 'He is the
first-born', and as adjectives, e.g. *þinne ancennedan sunu* 'your only
son'.

2. They also introduce phrases which may be the equivalent of
adjective clauses, e.g. the sentences quoted in §187.1(*b*), or which
may express various adverbial relationships, such as time, e.g. *þæt
man his hlaford of lande lifigendne drife* 'that one should drive his
lord from the land while he still lives', or cause, e.g. *me þearfendre*
'to me in my need'. (What sex is the last speaker?)

3. Together with a noun or a pronoun, a participle may be inflected in the dative case in imitation of a Latin ablative absolute;
see §191.4.

4. Sometimes the exact grammatical status of such a phrase is
not certain. Thus the first two words in *astrehtum handum to Gode
clypode* 'with outstretched hands called to God' are taken by some
as an absolute and by others as a dative of 'attendant circumstances'.
Perhaps they are both. At any rate, such ambiguities are merely
terminological.

The Uses of the Infinitives

§205   This section sets out the normal uses of the OE uninflected
and inflected infinitives. Exceptional uses of the one in the functions
here allotted to the other, however, do occur.

1. The uninflected infinitive is usual after the auxiliaries mentioned in §206 and after *uton* 'let us', *þurfan* 'need', and **durran* 'dare'. The infinitive of a verb of motion is frequently not expressed in such circumstances, e.g. *ær he in wille* 'before he will go in'.

As in MnE, there are circumstances in which either the infinitive without *tō* or a present participle can be used, e.g. *Ic geseah ða englas dreorige wepan and ða sceoccan blissigende on eowerum forwyrde* 'I saw the angels weep bitterly and the demons rejoicing at your destruction'.

On the accusative and infinitive, see §161.

2. The inflected infinitive with *tō* is common in the following functions:

(a) To express purpose, e.g. *an wulf wearð asend to bewerigenne þæt heafod* 'a wolf was sent to guard the head' and, with a passive sense, *bindað sceafmælum to forbærnenne* 'bind them in sheaves for burning, to be burnt'. But the simple infinitive also occurs, e.g. *ut eode ahyrian wyrhtan* 'went out to hire workers'.

(b) With the verb 'to be' to express necessity or obligation, e.g. *Is eac to witanne* 'It must also be noted'.

(c) To complete the sense of a verb, e.g. *and begunnon ða to wyrcenne* 'and then they began to work'. But cf. *ða ongan ic ða boc wendan on Englisc* 'then I began to translate the book into English', where the infinitive without *tō* occurs.

(d) To complete the sense of a noun, e.g. *anweald to ofsleanne and to edcucigenne* 'power to kill and to restore to life', orof an adjective, e.g. *wæron æþelingas ... fuse to farenne* 'the nobles were eager to depart'.

(e) As the subject, or as the complement, of a sentence, e.g. *to sittanne on mine swyðran healfe ... nys me inc to syllanne* 'to sit on my right hand is not mine to give'.

The 'Modal' Auxiliaries

Introduction

§206   Some forms of the OE verbs *cunnan, willan, *sculan, magan,* and **mōtan*, still survive as auxiliaries today, viz. 'can', 'will', 'would', 'shall', 'should', 'may', 'might', and 'must'. As in OE, they are followed by the infinitive without 'to'. Their semantic history is a complicated one and even today the uses of some, especially 'shall' and 'will' and 'should' and 'would', cause great confusion to very many foreign speakers of English. Readers of OE too will find difficulties with them, but of a different sort, for the range of meanings they had in OE was wider than it is now.

Magan

§207   In *eorðe mæg wið ealra wihta gehwilce* 'earth prevails against
every creature', *magan* means 'to prevail against' and has the full
force of an independent verb; cf. Hopkins's 'I can no more'. In *þæt
he ealle þa tid mihte ge sprecan ge gangan* 'so that all the time he
could speak and walk', it means 'to be able', while in *Luke* 16:2 *ne
miht þu leng tunscire bewitan* 'you can no longer hold the steward-
ship', it means 'to be permitted to'. In these senses, it expresses a
shade of meaning which the subjunctive of a simple verb could hardly
do. The same is true in *Dream of the Rood* ll. 37-38, where we have a
statement of fact 'I could have destroyed all his foes' and not of
possibility 'I might have destroyed all his foes'. But this last use—
the MnE one—does occur in OE. A striking example is found in
Andreas ll. 544 ff.

Nænig manna is . . .

ðætte areccan mæg   oððe rim wite . . .

'There is no man . . . [of such a sort] that he may relate or know the
number'. The proper mood in such clauses is the subjunctive (see
§175.2); hence *wite*. But parallel to it is *āreċċan mæġ* 'may relate,
may tell'.

Note

  K. R. Brooks, the latest editor of *Andreas*, follows Grein in
emending to *mæġe*. Though possible, this does not seem essential.

Thus *magan* has shades of meaning which cannot always be accur-
ately distinguished. Does *Genesis* ll. 436-7 mean 'what we can win
by our own strength' or 'what God will allow us to win'? Consider
too *ðu miht* in *Dream of the Rood* l. 78.

  When it means 'to be permitted to' *magan* is a rival of **mōtan* 'to
be allowed to'; cf. *Luke* 16:2 quoted above with *Matthew* 20:15 *ne
mot ic don þæt ic wylle?* where the Authorized Version has 'Is it not
lawful for me to do what I will?', and *Maldon* ll. 14 and 235 with
Maldon ll. 83 and 95.

  But in the sense of 'to be able to' it frequently comes close to
cunnan; cf. Cædmon's statement *Ne con ic noht singan* 'I do not
know how to sing anything' with the angel's reply *Hwæðre þu meaht
me singan*[1] 'Yet you can sing to me'. Here, as the Latin original
nescio cantare suggests, *cunnan* may have its full sense of 'to know
how to'. But it comes close to the modern sense of 'to be able to'.

---

[1] So some MSS. MS T lacks *me*; so some read *þu me aht singan* 'you must
sing to me'. But here (i) we might expect an infl. inf. after *aht*; (ii) that *aht* could
mean 'must' is to me uncertain.

Mōtan

§208   The preterite of *mōtan* 'to be allowed to' is *mōste*, the ancestor of MnE 'must'. In *Maldon* l. 30 the present tense *þū mōst* comes close to meaning 'you must'. But it may be a very formal and ceremonious extension of the permissive use, perhaps with ironical overtones: 'The Danes bid me say that they are graciously pleased to allow you to send tribute in exchange for protection'. The sense of 'to be allowed to, may' seems to be the prevailing one for *mōtan* in OE.

Cunnan

§209   For an example of *cunnan* 'to know how to' shading into 'to be able, can' (its MnE sense), see §207 above.

Sculan

§210   The most important function of *sculan* is to express necessity or obligation. Thus it must be translated 'must' in *Se byrdesta sceall gyldan* 'The wealthiest must pay', expressing a general obligation, and 'has had to' in *Wanderer* l. 3, where *sceolde* has no future reference at all. In *Maldon* l. 60 too, *sceal* means 'must', but here the reference is more clearly to one specific act which must take place in the future.

Whether *sculan* ever represents the simple future is a matter of some dispute. Cædmon's reply to the comment of the angel quoted at the end of §207 was *Hwæt sceal ic singan?* Some of you may be tempted to translate this 'What shall I sing?' But the Latin has *Quid debeo cantare?* which demands the translation 'What must I (ought I to) sing?' Here then *sculan* clearly does not represent a simple future. And on the whole it will be safer for you to assume that it always has an idea of obligation, except in examples like those discussed in the next two paragraphs. When Ælfric in his grammar equates *lecturus sum cras* with *ic sceal rædan tomerigen*, it might seem a clear case of 'I shall read tomorrow'. But it probably means 'I must read tomorrow', for elsewhere Ælfric equates *osculaturus* with *se ðe wyle oððe sceal cyssan*. This does not mean that *wyle* and *sceal* mean the same thing, but that *osculaturus* has two possible meanings for Ælfric—futurity 'He is going to kiss' (see §211) and obligation 'He has to kiss'. So the OE version of *Matthew* 20:10 *And þa þe þær ærest comon wendon þæt hi sceoldon mare onfon*, which represents the Latin *Venientes autem et primi, arbitrati sunt quod plus essent accepturi*, is perhaps best translated 'And those who had come there first thought that they ought to receive more'.

Sculan can also express what is customary, e.g. *And ealle þa hwile þæt lic bið inne, þær sceal beon gedrync and plega* 'And all the time the body is within, there shall be drinking and playing'.

In *ðæs nama sceolde bion Caron* 'whose name is said to be C.', *sceolde* shows that the reporter does not believe the statement or does not vouch for its truth. You will probably meet other examples of this.

Willan

§211 The original function of *willan* seems to have been the expression of wish or intention, e.g. *ic wille sellan* 'I wish to give', *þe þær beon noldon* 'who did not wish to be there', and *he wolde adræfan anne æþeling* 'he wished to expel a princeling'. In these (with the possible exception of the second), there is some future reference. How far *willan* had gone along the road to simple futurity is difficult to determine, but examples like *Hi willað eow to gafole garas syllan* 'They wish to (will) give you spears as tribute',

æghwylc gecwæð,
þæt him heardra nan   hrinan wolde

'everyone said that no hard thing would touch him', and *þa Darius geseah, þæt he oferwunnen beon wolde* 'When D. saw that he would be conquered' (note the passive infinitive), come pretty close to it.

Willan, like MnE 'will', is sometimes found 'expressing natural disposition to do something, and hence habitual action' (*Oxford English Dictionary* s.v. 'will' 8), e.g. *He wolde æfter uhtsange oftost hine gebiddan* 'He would most often pray after matins'.

On paratactic *wolde*, see §185.2 and cf. the *þæt* clause with *willan* in

Geseah ic þa frean mancynnes
efstan elne mycle   þæt he me wolde on gestigan

'I saw the Lord of mankind hasten with great zeal in His wish to climb on to me'.

Impersonal Verbs

§212 These are more common in OE than in MnE, but should not cause you much trouble if you notice that the subject 'it' is often not expressed, e.g. *me ðyncð betre* 'it seems better to me' and *hine nanes ðinges ne lyste* lit. 'it pleased him in respect of nothing'. But *hit* does appear, e.g. *hit gelamp* 'it happened'.

xi PREPOSITIONS

§213 The most important prepositions, with their meanings and the cases they govern, are set out below in alphabetical order. For their use in prepositional conjunctions, see §171.

Those marked with a dagger † govern both accusative and dative, the distinction usually being accusative of motion, e.g. *and heo hine in þæt mynster onfeng* 'and she received him into the monastery', and dative of rest, e.g. *on þam huse* 'in that house'. However, this distinction is not always observed.

Prepositions often follow the word they govern, e.g. *him to* 'against them' and *him biforan* 'before him'.

Sometimes words which often occur as prepositions are used without a noun or pronoun, e.g. *þa foron hie to* 'then they went thither' and *het þa in beran segn* 'then [he] ordered [them] to carry in the banner'. Here we have something very similar to the separable prefixes of modern German.

List of Prepositions

§214 (Note: Some prepositions may be followed by the dative or the instrumental. As there is no significance in this variation, the instrumental has not been included in the list.)

æfter		dat. (acc.) 'after, along, according to'
ær		dat. 'before'
æt		dat. 'at, from, by'
be		dat. 'by, along, alongside, about'
beforan		dat. 'before, in front of'
betwux		dat. acc. 'among, between'
binnan	†	'within, into'
bufan	†	'above, upon'
būtan		dat. acc. 'except, outside, without'
ēac		dat. 'besides, in addition to'
for		dat. 'before (of place), in front of, because of'
fram		dat. 'from, by (of agent)'
ġeond		acc. 'throughout'
in	†	'in, into'
innan	†	'in, within'
mid		dat. acc. 'among, with, by means of'
of		dat. 'from, of'
ofer	†	'above, over, on'
on	†	'in, into, on'
onġēan		dat. acc. 'against, towards'
oþ		acc. (dat.) 'up to, until'
tō		gen. 'at, for, to such an extent, so'
		dat. 'towards, to, at, near'
		dat. 'as', in the idiom seen in *to frofre* 'as a consolation' and *to menniscum men* 'as a human being' (acc. 'towards')

tō-ġēanes	dat.	'against, towards'
þurh	acc. (dat.)	'through, throughout, by means of'
under †		'under, beneath'
wiþ	acc. gen. dat.	'towards, opposite, against, along, in exchange for'
ymb(e)	acc. (dat.)	'after, about or concerning'

VI AN INTRODUCTION TO ANGLO-SAXON STUDIES

i Some Significant Dates

§215   If the Anglo-Saxon period is taken as beginning in 449 and ending in 1066, it lasted for 617 years. It may help you to put this in perspective if you realize that this is roughly the same period of time as that which separates the battle of Crécy from the present day, or, to put it in literary terms, the birth of Chaucer from the death of Dylan Thomas.

Note

Where possible, the dates in §216 are taken from *Handbook of British Chronology*, ed. F. M. Powicke and E. B. Fryde (London, Royal Historical Society, 2nd ed., 1961).

§216   See pp. 120-123.

ii History

§217   The Germanic settlements in Britain, which (recent archaeological finds suggest) may have begun at least half a century earlier than the traditional A.D. 449, did not result in the immediate subjugation of the whole island under one Germanic king. Indeed, there is much evidence to suggest a vigorous revival of British fortunes, culminating about the time of the victory of Mons Badonicus (c. 490-517), which led to a renewed British predominance in some western and south-midland areas formerly overrun by the invader. Only with the battles that the Chronicle associates with the West-Saxon leaders Ceawlin, Cuthwulf, Cutha, and Cuthwine, (especially Biedcanford 571 and Dyrham 577) was Saxon control re-established in the Chilterns and Cotswolds. Romano-British elements, of course, still survived extensively in the population of Anglo-Saxon England.

The invading English, therefore, lived in independent kingdoms —there were ten south of the Humber in 600—cut off from one another by geographical barriers and by hostile British. It is in such conditions of isolation that sound-changes flourish, and hence peculiarities which were originally individual or tribal and which would have been eliminated in a larger community flourished unchecked. Thus by c. 700, the date of the earliest linguistic records, the four dialects mentioned in §2—Northumbrian, Mercian, West-Saxon, and Kentish—can be distinguished in a language which at the time of the invasions appears to have been spoken in much the same way by all those who came to England.

The two hundred or so years after the English victory at the unidentified Biedcanford are not well-documented and the history of the period is often obscure. There was certainly much fighting between the various kingdoms, with now one, now another, temporarily 'top-dog' under some powerful warrior-king, though there was a period of comparative peace during the late seventh and the eighth centuries in which the Northern civilization which produced Bede, Alcuin, and the like, flourished. By 800, however, four great kingdoms survived—Northumbria, Mercia, Wessex, and East Anglia.

Then came the Danes. First they made what might be called 'smash-and-grab' raids in the summer, taking their booty back home with them. In 851 they are recorded as wintering on the Isle of Thanet. In 865 they ravaged Kent. In 867 they moved from East Anglia to York. Over the next few years there was intense activity. One by one, the kingdoms of Northumbria, East Anglia, and Mercia, ceased to exist as independent kingdoms and in 878 Wessex too was nearly extinguished, for in that year King Alfred was taking refuge in Æthelney 'with a small band' while the Danes plundered his kingdom. But Alfred was equal to the challenge. His grasp of the principles of war as revealed by a study of his campaigns against the Danes, and his activities in education, learning, and administration, over the next twenty years until his death in 899, are such that, for some people at any rate, his only rival for the title 'The greatest Englishman of all' is Sir Winston Churchill. The Anglo-Saxon Chronicle has two simple, but revealing, phrases in its account of this period. In 878, it says, the whole of Wessex surrendered to the Danes *buton pam cyninge Ælfrede* 'except King Alfred'. He escaped and rallied his forces. Men flocked to his banner *and his gefægene wærun* 'and were glad of him'.

By 880, then, only Wessex remained of the four kingdoms existing in 800. The subsequent years were a period of uneasy peace in which the Danes settled and ploughed and in which the boundaries of Danelaw were established. The arrival of another great army from France in 892 led to more bitter fighting in which the invaders were helped by those in Northumbria and East Anglia. But gradually Wessex, under Alfred and his successors, won back land from the settled Danes and reconciled them to English rule. In 954 the Scandinavian kingdom of York ceased to exist and the permanent unification of England as one kingdom began. As a result England was able to enjoy a period of comparative peace in the second half of the tenth century in which the great revival of Benedictine monasticism took place, and in which England began to achieve

§216

TABLE OF DATES

Date	Lay	Religious	Literary
449	Traditional date of coming of Angles, Saxons, and Jutes.		The legend of Arthur may rest on a British leader who resisted the invaders. *c.* 547 Gildas writes *De Excidio Britanniae.*
560-616	Æthelbert King of Kent.		
c. 563		St. Columba brings Celtic Christianity to Iona.	
597		St. Augustine brings Roman Christianity to Kent.	
616-632	Edwin King of Northumbria.		
627		Edwin converted to Christianity.	
632	Edwin killed by heathen King Penda of Mercia.		
?632-654	Penda King of Mercia.		
635		Aidan settles in Lindisfarne, bringing Celtic Christianity.	
635		King Cynegils of Wessex converted.	
641	Oswald King of Northumbria killed by Penda.		
650-670	The Sutton Hoo ship burial may have taken place during this period.		
664		Synod of Whitby establishes supremacy of Roman Christianity.	

Date	Political events	Church & learning	Literary
664		St. Chad becomes bishop of York.	Cædmon uses Germanic alliterative verse for religious subjects during this period.
657-680		Hild Abbess of Whitby.	
680			Approximate earliest date for composition of *Beowulf*.
c. 678		English missions to the continent begin.	
c. 700			Date of first linguistic records.
709		Death of Aldhelm, Bishop of Sherborne.	
731			Bede completes *Historia Ecclesiastica Gentis Anglorum.*
735		Death of Beda. Birth of Alcuin.	
757-796	Offa King of Mercia.		
782		Alcuin settles at Charlemagne's court.	
793	Viking raids begin.	Sacking of Lindisfarne.	
800	Four great kingdoms remain —Northumbria, Mercia, East Anglia, Wessex.		
780-850			*fl.* 796 Nennius, author or reviser of *Historia Britonum.* Cynewulf probably flourishes some time in this period.
804		Death of Alcuin.	
851	Danes first winter in England.		
865	Great Danish Army lands in East Anglia.		

TABLE OF DATES (cont.)

Date	Lay	Religious	Literary
867	Battle of York. End of Northumbria as a political power.		
870	King Edmund of East Anglia killed by Danes. East Anglia overrun.		
871	Alfred becomes King of Wessex.		
874	Danes settle in Yorkshire.		
877	Danes settle in East Mercia.		
880	Guthrum and his men settle in East Anglia. Only Wessex remains of the four Kingdoms.		
?886	Boundaries of Danelaw agreed with Guthrum. Alfred occupies London.		The period of the Alfredian translations and the beginning of the Anglo-Saxon Chronicle.
892	Further Danish invasion.		
896	Alfred builds a fleet.		
899	Death of King Alfred.		
899-954	The creation of the English Kingdom.		
c. 909		Birth of Dunstan.	
937	Battle of Brunanburh.		Poem commemorates the battle.
954	The extinction of the Scandinavian kingdom of York.		
959-975	Edgar reigns.		

960	Dunstan Archbishop of Canterbury. The period of the Monastic Revival.	
c. 971		The Blickling Homilies.
978 or 979	Murder of King Edward.	
950-1000		Approximate dates of the poetry codices—Junius MS, Vercelli Book, Exeter Book, and Beowulf MS.
978 or 979 -1016	Ethelred the Unready reigns.	
988	Death of Dunstan.	
991	Battle of Maldon	Poem commemorates the battle.
990-992		Ælfric's Catholic Homilies.
993-998		Ælfric's Lives of the Saints.
1003-1023	Wulfstan Archbishop of York.	
c. 1014		Sermo Lupi ad Anglos.
1005- c. 1025	Ælfric Abbot of Eynsham.	
1013	Sweyn acknowledged as King of England.	
1014	Sweyn dies.	
1016	Edmund Ironside dies.	
1016-1042	Canute and his sons reign.	
1042-1066	Edward the Confessor.	
1066	Harold King	
	Battle of Stamford Bridge	
	Battle of Hastings	
	William I King	

nationhood—a short passage in *The Battle of Maldon* (ll. 51-54) may perhaps contain the beginnings of a sense of patriotism. Nevertheless, in the Laws of Canute we still find a threefold division into Wessex, Mercia, and Danelaw, which reflects the divisions of the earlier period.

The subsequent history of Anglo-Saxon England is well-known— the reigns of Ethelred the Unready, of the Danish dynasty, and of Edward the Confessor, were followed by Harold's victory at Stamford Bridge and his defeat at Hastings.

§218   The fortunes of Christianity fluctuated in Anglo-Saxon England, and students of its literature must grasp the implications of this fact, which are discussed in §§243-245. The Christianity of Roman Britain was not accepted by the pagan invaders, who brought with them the Germanic heroic code, which was in many ways no ignoble way of life. St. Columba and his followers brought Celtic Christianity to the north, while St. Augustine and his followers from Rome spread their teaching from the south until in 664 the Synod of Whitby established the supremacy of Rome. But heathenism was never very far away. King Edwin of Northumbria was killed by the pagan Penda of Mercia in 632. The Sutton Hoo ship burial, with its mixture of pagan and Christian grave-goods, probably took place in the second half of the seventh century. Throughout the Anglo-Saxon period, preachers inveighed against paganism. Alcuin asked his famous question 'What has Ingeld to do with Christ?' in 797, in a letter condemning the recitation of heathen poetry to monks. The invading Danes brought their paganism with them. Both King Alfred and King Ethelred stood sponsor at the baptism of some of their foes, and in 1012, during the lifetime of Ælfric and Wulfstan, Ælfeah Archbishop of Canterbury was murdered by drunken Danes. It is therefore possible that any Christian poet writing in Old English between 680 and 850, when most of the extant poetry was probably written, could have been a convert from paganism or the son of a pagan. If he was not either of these, he lived in a society where the battle between the pagan Germanic religions and Christianity had not been finally resolved. The mixture of Christian and pagan grave-goods in the ship-cenotaph at Sutton Hoo is paralleled by the mixture of Christian and pagan ideas in much of the poetry.

iii ARCHAEOLOGY

Introduction

§219   The belief that Anglo-Saxon civilization was decadent before the Norman Conquest dies hard, despite recent attempts to refute it. But it is without foundation. By 1066, English missionaries had preached Christianity in Scandinavia and, despite two centuries of Danish attacks, political unity had been achieved. The idea of nationhood had developed among her people; in its account of the dispute between Earl Godwine and Edward the Confessor over Count Eustace, the Chronicle observes that 'it was hateful to almost all of them to fight against men of their own race, for there were very few on either side who were worth much, apart from Englishmen. Moreover, they did not wish to put this country at the mercy of foreigners by fighting each other' (MS D, 1052). Despite the wars and rumours of wars of this period, England in 1066 possessed (in R. W. Chambers's words)

a civilization based upon Alfred's English prose as the national official and literary language. English jewellery, metal-work, tapestry and carving were famed throughout Western Europe. English illumination was unrivalled, and so national that the merest novice can identify the work of the Winchester school. Even in stone-carving, those who are competent to judge speak of the superiority of the native English carver over his Norman supplanter. In building upon a large scale England was behind Normandy. But what little is left to us of Eleventh Century Anglo Saxon architecture shows an astonishing variety. Its mark is 'greater cosmopolitanism, as compared to the more competent, but equally more restricted and traditional architecture of the Normans'.

Unfortunately, space does not permit a full treatment of these points; all that can be done is to provide you with the means of testing for yourself the truth of R. W. Chambers's vividly-expressed view that it seems as if 'Eleventh-Century England was getting into the Fifteenth; as if England was escaping from the Dark Ages without passing through the later Middle Ages at all'. A short Bibliography is given first. This is followed by a list of topics accompanied by brief comments and references to the books cited.

Note

The quotations given above are from R. W. Chambers *On the Continuity of English Prose from Alfred to More and his School* (Early English Text Society).

List of Abbreviated Titles

§220 For convenience, each book is given a brief title which is used in the sections which follow.

The Anglo-Saxons

D. M. Wilson *The Anglo-Saxons* (London, 1960)

A-S England
    P. Hunter Blair *An Introduction to Anglo-Saxon England*
    (Cambridge, 1956)
Note
    These two may profitably be consulted on most of the topics dis-
    cussed below. Both contain useful Bibliographies. See also § 258.

Archaeology
    Mediaeval Archaeology I, 1957

Architecture
    E. A. Fisher *An Introduction to Anglo-Saxon Architecture and
    Sculpture* (Faber and Faber, 1959)

Beowulf Introduction
    R. W. Chambers *Beowulf An Introduction with a Supplement by
    C. L. Wrenn* (3rd ed., Cambridge, 1959)

Everyday Life
    M. and C. H. B. Quennell *Everyday Life in Anglo-Saxon, Viking
    and Norman Times* (Batsford, 1926 or later)

How They Lived
    W. O. Hassall *How They Lived 55 B.C.-1485* (Basil Blackwell,
    1962)

Jewellery
    R. Jessup *Anglo-Saxon Jewellery* (Faber and Faber, 1950)

Bayeux Tapestry
    Reproductions of this will be found in
    E. Maclagan *The Bayeux Tapestry* (King Penguin, 1949)
    Douglas and Greenaway *English Historical Documents Volume II
    1042-1189* (Eyre and Spottiswoode, 1953)
    F. Stenton and others *The Bayeux Tapestry* (London, 1957)

Weapons and Warfare

§ **221** See *The Anglo-Saxons*, chapter IV.
    It may be of interest to note here how archaeological finds prove
the accuracy of the *Beowulf* poet's descriptions of swords, coats-of-
mail, helmets, and the like. Thus his mention of a helmet with
chain-mail is confirmed by discoveries of helmets with chain-mail to
protect the neck and cheeks of the wearer, while the helmet described in ll. 1030-1034 can be identified as a Romanesque helmet
with a solid comb and not the ribbed helmet seen in the Bayeux
Tapestry. See further *Archaeology*, pp. 57-67.
    Other points worthy of study are the Danish strategy in the last
decade of the ninth century and Alfred's methods of countering it,

and the careful way in which the young Beowulf leads his 'platoon' during his journey to Denmark and his stay there. When reading *The Battle of Maldon* you should ask whether Byrhtnoth's decision to let the Danes cross the causeway unmolested was tactically right or the result of *ofermod* (a characteristic attributed only to Byrhtnoth and Satan). (It can scarcely be a misguided expression of the English sense of 'fair play'.)

Life and Dress

§222   Some knowledge of how the Anglo-Saxons dressed, lived, ate, and drank, will help you to realize more clearly that the writers and scribes whose work you read, and the warriors, priests, statesmen, and others, whose lives you study, were human beings like yourself, subject to weariness and pain, and prey to the same emotions as you are. This knowledge can be acquired from *The Anglo-Saxons*, chapter III, or from *Everyday Life*, which give a reconstruction of life in Anglo-Saxon times. *How They Lived* deals more with mediaeval times, but gives interesting information on some points. The Bayeux Tapestry can be studied with profit. Works in Anglo-Saxon which throw light on the more personal and intimate sides of life include the *Leechdoms*, the *Charms*, and the *Riddles*. Ælfric's *Colloquy* (ed. G. N. Garmonsway, 2nd ed., Methuen, 1947) gives a picture of the life and activities of the middle and lower classes of whom we hear little elsewhere. But now and then those who are on the watch will catch momentary glimpses. Thus in the Chronicle for 897 (Parker MS), we find the names of three Frisian sailors killed in a sea-battle. The death of these men, who had been teaching the Anglo-Saxons the art of sea-fighting, is given poignancy by a few lines from the *Maxims* or *Gnomes* of the Exeter Book:

> Welcome is her beloved to the Frisian wife when the ship lies at anchor. His ship has returned and her husband, her own breadwinner, is at home. She welcomes him in, washes his sea-stained garments, gives him new clothes, and grants him on his return what his love demands.

Here are three Frisians whose garments will need no washing and who will be looked for in vain.

Architecture and Buildings

§223   Monochrome plates I and II in *Jewellery* illustrate timber huts and buildings. *Everyday Life* discusses timber huts and halls with illustrations, and provides as figure 1 an imaginary reconstruction in colour of an Anglo-Saxon Hall. See also *The Anglo-Saxons*, chapter III.

Aerial photographs taken in 1949 led to excavations at Old Yeavering, Northumberland, which revealed an Anglo-Saxon township. A large timber fort dated from the second half of the sixth century. A township outside the fort appeared to have developed in the seventh century. It included a massive timber hall with other smaller halls (one of which may have been a pagan temple later converted to Christian use) and a large timber grandstand for outdoor meetings. The large hall was replaced by an even more ambitious one and the grandstand was enlarged in the reign of King Edwin. The whole township was then destroyed by fire, probably by Cadwallon after Edwin's death in 632. The township was then rebuilt, still in timber, in what may have been Celtic style, and a Christian church was built around which there grew a large cemetery. This township too was destroyed by fire—perhaps by Penda in 651. The great hall, two smaller halls, and the church, were rebuilt. But towards the end of the seventh century, Yeavering was abandoned in favour of a new site called Melmin, a few miles away.

At Cheddar in Somerset, another Saxon royal residence was excavated in 1960-2. In King Alfred's time, it consisted of a two-storey hall and three smaller buildings, the largest of which was probably a *bur*; see *Beowulf* ll. 140 and 1310. Later kings carried out additions and reconstructions.

The discoveries at Yeavering throw light on the hall in *Beowulf* (see *Archaeology*, pp. 68-77) and help to fill out the picture given by the poet. Those at Cheddar may serve to illustrate two interesting stories in the Chronicle—the death of King Cynewulf (Parker MS, 755 and 784) and the escape of Archbishop Dunstan, who was left standing alone on a beam when the upper floor of a hall collapsed at Calne, Wiltshire (Laud MS, 978).

The excavations at Yeavering are discussed in *Archaeology*, pp. 148-9, those at Yeavering and Cheddar in *The History of the King's Works*, ed. H. M. Colvin, Volume I (London, 1963), pp. 1-6. I have leaned heavily on these, and acknowledge my debt to them.

§224 As far as we know, stone was used only for churches. *Architecture* contains a useful introduction to the study of Anglo-Saxon churches and crypts, with plans, photographs, and a bibliography. There are a large number of Saxon churches worth visiting. One which for some reason particularly stands out in my mind is that of St. Peter at Bradwell-iuxta-Mare in Essex, which is built mostly of masonry from the nearby Roman fort. A visit to this, to the site of the battle of Maldon on a farm on the R. Blackwater, and to the new nuclear power-station, would make quite an interesting day!

However, wood was used for churches when stone was not readily available. The church at Greenstead, Essex, where (tradition relates) the body of King Edmund of East Anglia rested in 1013 on its way from London to Bury St. Edmunds, is a surviving example of the kind, though its timbers may not date back to Anglo-Saxon times.

Sculpture and Carving

§225 *Architecture* gives an interesting introduction, with illustrations, to works in stone. Survivals include crosses such as those at Ruthwell and Bewcastle, sundials like that at Kirkdale, sepulchral slabs, fonts, and figures like the angels in the Church of St. Lawrence at Bradford-on-Avon. The different types of ornamentation show influences from different countries and civilizations—Mediterranean, Northern, and even Eastern.

The carved oak coffin of St. Cuthbert (late seventh-century) and the Franks Casket of whalebone carved with historical and legendary scenes framed with runes (early eighth-century) survive to show that Anglo-Saxon artists worked in media other than stone.

Jewellery and Metal-Work

§226 A fascinating and well-illustrated account which tells where the jewels can be seen will be found in *Jewellery*. The author writes:

> Side by side with its interest for the archaeologist and the historian, Anglo-Saxon jewellery has a foremost appeal to the artist and the craftsman of today, who find in a contemplation of its design and technique the exercise of something more than a bare academic interest. To the practising jeweller especially its excellence needs no commendation, and to him it has often yielded an inspiration far from that of unalloyed sentiment.

To test the truth of this claim, those in a position to do so should view what Anglo-Saxon jewellery they can, especially the Kingston Brooch and the jewels of the Sutton Hoo Treasure in the British Museum and the Alfred and Minster Lovell Jewels in the Ashmolean Museum, Oxford. Most of these are shown in colour in *Jewellery*. Other well-known treasures include the Pectoral Cross of St. Cuthbert (in the Cathedral Library, Durham), finger-rings which belonged to King Æthelwulf and to Queen Æthelswith, King Alfred's sister (both in the British Museum), and necklaces of amethyst, gold, or other material.

By viewing these beautiful objects, we are able to see that the love of beauty and craftsmanship we observe in *Beowulf* is no mere artistic pose, but an accurate reflection of the attitude of the people of his time. Like so many of their descendants, they could combine fierceness in battle with love of the beautiful.

GOE K

Embroidery

§227 'The tapestries' sings the *Beowulf* poet, 'shone gold-embroidered along the walls, many wondrous sights for those among men who gaze upon such things'. Unfortunately, none of these survive. The only remains of Anglo-Saxon embroidery of any consequence are the early tenth-century vestments now among the relics of St. Cuthbert at Durham, which were made to the order of Queen Ælfflæd, King Æthelstan's queen.

Strictly speaking, as Sir Eric Maclagan points out, the Bayeux Tapestry is 'no tapestry at all, the design being embroidered upon the material and not woven into it'. It is very possible that it was made in England within twenty years of the Conquest by English needlewomen working to the order of Bishop Odo of Bayeux.

Coins

§228 See *Anglo-Saxon Coins. Historical Studies presented to Sir Frank Stenton*, ed. R. H. M. Dolley (Methuen, 1961).

Manuscripts and Runic Inscriptions

§229 On illuminations and decorations, see *The Anglo-Saxons*, pp. 146 ff. and 156 ff.

On the contents and whereabouts of manuscripts, see
     N. R. Ker *Catalogue of Manuscripts containing Anglo-Saxon* (Clarendon Press, 1957).

On handwriting, see (in addition to the above)
     N. Denholm-Young *Handwriting in England and Wales* (2nd ed., Cardiff, 1964).

On runes, see
     R. W. V. Elliott *Runes* (Manchester, 1959).

The Sutton Hoo Ship-Burial

§230 In 1939, the excavation of a barrow at Sutton Hoo, Suffolk, revealed the ship-cenotaph of an East Anglian King. The British Museum *The Sutton Hoo Ship-Burial. A Provisional Guide* gives a detailed account of the finds. Their importance for students of *Beowulf* has been discussed by Professor Wrenn in *Beowulf Introduction*, pp. 508-523. He summarizes his conclusions thus:

> The Sutton Hoo discoveries, then, have furnished new evidence bearing on the date and genesis of *Beowulf*, clearing away obstacles to the early dating of the poem and affording a possible explanation of why so much Scandinavian subject-matter should

appear in an English poem. They have further clarified the blend of Christian and pagan elements in a yet homogeneous work. They have shown that the highly aesthetic approach to treasures in gold and gems and craftsmanship, which appears in *Beowulf* at first sight to be anachronistic, is paralleled at Sutton Hoo: that that joy in such treasures and the power to appreciate them which seemed a sophistication in *Beowulf* shared by its poet with his audience, had already been demonstrated by the craftsmen of East Anglian Rendlesham in the ship-burial of Sutton Hoo. Much light too has been thrown by comparison of the Sutton Hoo objects on the nature of some of the weapons and armour mentioned in *Beowulf*, as well as on the type of harp which must have accompanied its recitation.

A later article on the same subject by the same author will be found in *Mélanges de Linguistique et de Philologie* (Fernand Mossé in Memoriam) (Paris, 1959). It is reproduced in *An Anthology of Beowulf Criticism*, ed. by Lewis E. Nicholson (University of Notre Dame Press, 1963). On Music and Harps, see this and C. L. Wrenn 'Two Anglo-Saxon Harps', *Comparative Literature* 14 (1962), 118-128.

iv LANGUAGE

See first Preliminary Remarks on the Language (§§1-4).

Changes in English

§ 231   It has already been pointed out in § 140 that Old English was in process of changing from an inflected to an uninflected language. It has also been shown in the discussions on syntax that the distinction between subject and object—originally made by the contrast between nominative and accusative endings—was increasingly brought out by word-order and that prepositions more and more took over the function of the oblique cases as the inflexional endings became reduced. These changes in accidence and syntax, and in the pronunciation of unstressed vowels, affected the English language far more fundamentally than the later changes in spelling and in the pronunciation of vowels in stressed syllables.

The primitive Germanic languages developed a stress accent on the first syllable of words in place of the shifting stress of the original IE language which is seen, for example, in classical Greek and which has already been mentioned in §§ 90 and 105-106. As a result, differences in the pronunciation of unstressed syllables which had been important for making distinctions of meaning gradually disappeared. An important example in the endings of verbs has already been mentioned in § 113.3, and there are occasional spellings which suggest that the nom. pl. ending -*as* and the gen. sg. ending -*es* of strong masc. and neut. nouns were not always clearly distinguished in late OE.

Before the case endings finally disappeared, we can see the same job being done twice. In *he ofsloh ge þone cyning ge ða cwene* 'he slew both the king and the queen', we see subject and object distinguished by word-order and case-ending. In *mid ealre þære fierde* 'with the whole army', a preposition is followed by an oblique case. This stage was necessary before one of the two devices doing the same job could disappear. But once they existed together, the disappearance of one of them was almost certain, for few human beings like doing the same job twice. The increasing use of, and finally complete reliance on, word-order and prepositions made possible the ultimate disappearance of noun inflexions, apart from the genitive ending -*s* and the distinction between singular and plural. Similarly, new ways were found of distinguishing tense and mood in the verb; see the article by J. M. Wattie mentioned in §256.

The Danish Invasions

§232   The Danish invasions and settlements hastened this process, and perhaps caused it to be more complete than it might otherwise have been. OHG (the ancestor of Modern German) and OE were very similar in their grammatical structure. Yet today, while German has many inflexions and retains the three word-orders S.V., V.S., and S. . . . V., and other typically Germanic grammatical devices such as the distinction between strong and weak forms of the adjective, English has dispensed with them. Why? The Norman Conquest used to be blamed. As we shall see below, it was certainly not without effect here, although its influence on the language was felt more powerfully elsewhere. But the language of the invading Danes was, like Old English, a Germanic language. The roots of many words were similar, but the inflexional endings differed. When a Dane married an Anglo-Saxon woman, it must have been very confusing for their offspring to hear the one say *segls, segli*, where the other said *segles, segle*, or to find that one said *nema nemir nemi* for the present subjunctive singular forms of the verb 'to take' while the other used *nime* for all persons. Some confusion of endings was inevitable as a result of the fixing of the main stress (already mentioned in §231) in all Germanic languages, but this confusion must have been greater in bi-lingual communities of Danes and Anglo-Saxons.

The Norman Conquest

§233   Since King Ethelred had married a Norman wife in 1002, the influence of French began before the Conquest. But with the Conquest, and its subsequent use as the language of the court and of administration, Norman French became more important. Certain developments already under way in English may have been reinforced by similar tendencies in Norman French and also in Central French, which began to influence English after the accession of the Angevin Henry II in 1154. These are the standardization of word-order as S.V.O. and the loss of inflexions, which resulted in the development of the simple case system of Modern English. The commencement of parallel trends is attested in continental French of the twelfth century, although their completion was long drawn out and varied from region to region. Again, the fact that many French words had plurals in -*s* must have helped the native -*s* ending of *stanas* to oust its rival, the -*n* ending of *naman*, and to become the plural ending of Modern English nouns. But perhaps the most important influences of French were on vocabulary (see §234), on spelling, and on English prose. The French scribes abandoned the conservative English spelling, which often made distinctions which no longer existed, and introduced their own system. As a result it appears that sound-changes which had occurred gradually over the centuries had happened all at once. A similar situation might arise today if English were to be respelt phonetically by Russian scribes who used their own alphabet with the addition of a few English letters. After the Conquest, English prose gradually ceased to be used for official purposes and for history, but was still used for sermons and other religious works. Further reading on this topic is suggested in §259.

Vocabulary

§234 The vocabulary of OE was basically Germanic and the language was less hospitable to borrowings than it is today, frequently preferring to make its own compounds rather than admit foreign words; see §137. But some were admitted. Up to the time of the Norman Conquest, the following groups can be distinguished:

1. Latin
   (a) words borrowed in Pr. Gmc. times;
   (b) pre-650 borrowings in Britain;
   (c) post-650 borrowings in Britain.
2. Greek
   (a) direct borrowings, mostly by the Goths;
   (b) borrowings through Latin.
3. Celtic.
4. Scandinavian.
5. French.

References to books which deal with this subject will be found in §261. If you do study them, you will find it interesting to note how the words borrowed from the different languages reflect the relationships which existed between the two peoples concerned and so throw light on the history of the period.

Some Questions

§235   If, while studying OE, you consciously note the differences between OE and MnE, you will make your task easier and more interesting. Questions you might like to answer with the help of one of the histories of the language mentioned in §253 are:

1. Where did the -s plural of MnE come from? Did French have any influence here? (This has already been touched on in §233.)

2. Where did the -s of the MnE genitive singular come from?

3. How did 'of' become a sign of possession, as in 'The mast of the ship'?

4. When did -eth disappear as the ending of 3rd sg. pres. ind.?

5. Why do we find in Chaucer the ending -en for the pres. ind. pl. when OE has -að? Where did this -en ending come from?

v   LITERATURE

Introduction

§236   As has been pointed out in §218, the Germanic tribes who settled in England in the fifth century brought with them the Germanic heroic code. What we learn of it from Old English literature generally confirms the observations of Tacitus in his *Germania*. The salient points are these. The Germanic warrior was a member of a *comitatus*, a warrior-band. Life was a struggle against insuperable odds, against the inevitable doom decreed by a meaningless fate—*Wyrd*, which originally meant 'what happens'. There is no evidence in their literature that the pagan Anglo-Saxons believed in a life after death like that of Valhalla, the hall in Scandinavian mythology reserved for dead heroes, though there are references to the worship of heathen gods such as Woden, and the practice of burying coins, weapons, and other goods, with the dead, suggests a belief in some kind of after-life where they could be used. It is, however, a different kind of immortality which is stressed in their literature. This was *lof*, which was won by bravery in battle and consisted of glory among men, the praise of those still living. The poet's last word about the hero Beowulf in the poem which now bears his name is *lofgeornost* 'most eager for fame'. Two comments from the same poem throw light on this concept:

Swa sceal man don,
þonne he æt guðe gegan þenceð
longsumne lof; na ymb his lif cearað

'So must a man do when he thinks to win enduring fame in battle;
he will show no concern for his life' and

Wyrd oft nereð
unfægne eorl, þonne his ellen deah!

'Fate often spares an undoomed man when his courage is good'.

§ 237 A warrior brought up in this tradition would show a reck-
less disregard for his life. Whether he was doomed or not, courage
was best, for the brave man could win *lof* while the coward might
die before his time. This is the spirit which inspired the code of the
comitatus. While his lord lived, the warrior owed him loyalty unto
death. If his lord were killed, the warrior had to avenge him or die
in the attempt. The lord in his turn had the duty of protecting his
warriors. He had to be a great fighter to attract men, a man of noble
character and a generous giver of feasts and treasures to hold them.
So we read in *The Battle of Finnsburh*

Ne gefrægn ic næfre wurþlicor æt wera hilde
sixtig sigebeorna sel gebæran,
ne nefre swanas hwitne medo sel forgyldan
ðonne Hnæfe guldan his hægstealdas

'I have never heard it said that sixty conquering warriors bore themselves better or more worthily in mortal combat, or that any retainers
repaid the shining mead better than Hnæf's retainers repaid him'.

The whole code receives one of its last and finest expressions in
The Battle of Maldon, especially in the oft-quoted lines spoken by
the old warrior Byrhtwold

Hige sceal þe heardra, heorte þe cenre,
mod sceal þe mare, þe ure mægen lytlað

'Courage must be the firmer, heart the bolder, spirit the greater, the
more our strength wanes' (or 'our force diminishes'). Here we see
a noble manifestation of 'man's unconquerable mind'.

§ 238 Sometimes a conflict arose between loyalty to *comitatus*
and loyalty to kin. The annal for 755 in the Parker MS of the
Chronicle tells us of warriors who, in reply to offers of safe-conduct
and money from kinsmen in a hostile force, said 'that no kinsman
was dearer to them than their lord, and they would never follow his
slayer'. This seems to have been the proper attitude. But, as Miss
Whitelock points out, the fact that the Laws of Alfred allow a man
to fight in defence of a wronged kinsman only if it did not involve

fighting against his lord suggests that the claims of kin sometimes overrode the duty to a lord.

§239 A woman given in marriage as a *freoðuwebbe* 'a peace-weaver' to patch up a blood feud was often involved in such a conflict between loyalty to her lord, her husband, on the one hand, and to her family on the other. Freawaru was in this position, Hildeburh may have been; both feature in *Beowulf*. Sigemund's sister Signy was also involved in such a conflict of loyalties, although in her case the feud arose after the marriage. Thus the 'eternal triangle 'of Anglo-Saxon literature is based on loyalty rather than on sexual love (though such poems as *The Wife's Lament* and *The Husband's Message* show that such love existed—if we need any assuring on the point). No woman inspired the hero Beowulf, as far as we know. The great love of heroic literature is that of man for man in the noblest sense, the loyalty of warrior to warrior and of warrior to lord. This is not peculiar to the Anglo-Saxons. In the *Chanson de Roland*, Roland's betrothed Aude receives passing mention—even that is perhaps unusual—but Roland's great love is for Oliver. Just before his last battle, Roland cries to Oliver:

> For his liege lord a man ought to suffer all hardship and endure great heat and great cold and give both his body and his blood. Lay on with thy lance, and I will smite with Durendal, my good sword which the King gave me. If I die here, may he to whom it shall fall say 'This was the sword of a goodly vassal'.

Again, in his book *Island of the Dragon's Blood*, Douglas Botting tells the story of a sixteenth-century battle between the Portuguese and Arabs on the island of Socotra. The Portuguese leader, Tristan da Cunha, offered the Arabs terms. The story goes on:

> But the Arabs replied that they were much obliged to the worthy chief captain for wishing to spare their lives but that, in telling them of their captain's death, he had given them a sufficient reason for declining to receive the favour, for the Fartaquins [Mahri Arabs] were not accustomed to return alive to their land and leave their captain dead on the field, especially as he was the son of their King. Therefore he might do as he pleased for they were not going to yield.

But it is important to grasp that this loyalty is fundamental to much Old English poetry. Of course, the time was not far distant when the interest of writers switched from the 'heroic' love of man for man to the 'romantic' love of man for woman. C. S. Lewis characterizes the change which then came over European literature as a revolution compared to which 'the Renaissance is a mere ripple on the surface of literature'.

§240 Among the members of the *comitatus*, there was an insistence on decorum and etiquette—*cupe he duguðe peaw* 'he knew the usages of noble warriors' observes the *Beowulf* poet at one point— a respect for well-tried weapons, a love of precious jewels and beautiful things, joy in ships and in warriors marching, in horse races and beer, and in feasting and music in the hall. There was too a pride in being a well-governed people. The hall was an oasis of comradeship, order, warmth, and happiness, in sharp contrast to the threatening and chaotic world of discomfort and danger which lay outside. Old English poetry is not made up entirely of gloomy moments. Sometimes there is laughter and mirth.

§241 But there is also a great awareness of the transitoriness of life—*þis læne lif* 'this transitory life' sings the poet. Some critics of Old English literature sometimes talk as if this were an idea peculiar to Germanic or Anglo-Saxon paganism. But other peoples have grasped the idea that life is transitory. Numerous passages could be cited from Latin and Greek authors. Rider Haggard quotes a Zulu saying that life is 'as the breath of oxen in winter, as the quick star that runs along the sky, as the little shadow that loses itself at sunset'. A famous passage in *The Wisdom of Solomon*, chapter V, compares the passing of the things of this earth to the passage of a shadow, of a ship in the waves, and of a bird or an arrow through the air. In *James*, chapter IV, we read that life is 'a vapour that appeareth for a little time, and then vanisheth away'. You should therefore view with suspicion any comment on such poems as *The Wanderer* and *The Seafarer* which draws unreal distinctions between pagan and Christian elements as a result of failure to realize that the transience of life is a perpetual human theme peculiar to no civilization, age, or culture.

This theme of transience receives frequent expression in Old English poetry. Two fine examples are the famous lines at the end of *The Wanderer* and a passage from the less known *Solomon and Saturn*:

> Lytle hwile leaf beoð grene;
> ðonne hie eft fealewiað, feallað on eorðan
> and forweorniað, weorðað to duste

'For a little while the leaves are green. Then they turn yellow, fall to the earth and perish, turning to dust'. But while the theme is universal, the response is often different. In both *The Wanderer* and *The Dream of the Rood*, the passing of friends is lamented. But whereas in *The Wanderer* the thought provokes the famous response

'Where are they now?', the dreamer who has gazed upon the Cross affirms triumphantly that they live now in Heaven with the King of Glory.

§242 The transitoriness of all joys was brought home with special force to the man without a lord, always a figure of misery in Old English literature. He may have survived his lord because he was a coward who ran away from battle, like the sons of Odda in *The Battle of Maldon*, or by the fortune of war which decreed that he was badly wounded, but not killed, like the two survivors of the fights in the already-mentioned annal for 755. He may even have betrayed his lord, like Ceolwulf, the foolish king's thane who ruled Mercia as a Danish puppet for a few years after 874. Because of this uncertainty, a lordless man was suspect wherever he went. We can perhaps to some extent conceive his misery if we ponder the state of mind of people who find themselves in one of the following situations today—a trade-unionist expelled from his union and unable to earn money by his only skill; an army officer or an administrator suddenly expelled without compensation from a former colonial territory where he had made his career; a citizen of the West deserting to the East (or vice versa) for ideological reasons; a discharged convict unable to get a job; or a lonely refugee from behind the Iron Curtain who has left dear ones behind him and now exists without hope in a camp for 'displaced persons'.

§243 What joy and hope the coming of Christianity in the sixth century must have brought to such a man! And not to him alone, but also to those safely within a *comitatus*. For even they had little, if any, belief in a personal after-life, and no awareness of what Professor Southern has called 'the personal and secret tie between man and God'. Surrounded by few of the material comforts we take for granted today, liable to sudden attack and without any real hope for the future, they too must have found in Christianity the peace which passeth understanding. Doubtless, it was still true that

> Forðon sceall gar wesan
> monig morgenceald   mundum bewunden,
> hæfen on handa,   nalles hearpan sweg
> wigend weccean,   ac se wonna hrefn

'For many a spear, cold with the chill of morning, must be grasped with the palms, lifted by the hand. No sound of harp shall wake the warriors, but the dark raven'. But now the warriors could lie down under the protection of the Almighty and could rise with the name of Christ upon their lips.

§244 To be sure, conversion was neither universal nor immediate. But those who experienced it must have been a strange blend of

pagan and Christian, combining as they did the fierce courage and
pride of paganism with the new hope derived from Christianity—a
blend strikingly seen on the Benty Grange helmet which bears both
the pagan boar and the Christian Cross. Something of the same (but
perhaps in reverse) must, one imagines, be part of the make-up of
those middle-aged and elderly Russians of today who were brought
up Christians but who have consciously or unconsciously been influenced by the teachings of Marx. In 1961 Mr. Khrushchev was
reported as saying that the Soviet Union possessed a 100-megaton
bomb 'which, God grant it, we may never have to explode'. Whether
this invocation of God was deliberately cynical, the accidental result
of thought-habits formed in youth, or proof that he really is a
Christian at heart, one cannot say. But the fact that he could call
on God will help us to understand why the *Beowulf* poet could say
in the same poem both

> Wyrd oft nereð
> unfægne eorl, þonne his ellen deah!

'Fate often spares an undoomed man, when his courage is good' and

> Swa mæg unfæge   eaðe gedigan
> wean ond wræcsið   se ðe Waldendes
> hyldo gehealdeþ!

'Thus may an undoomed man whom the grace of the Almighty
protects easily survive misery and banishment'.

From this it follows that a poem which contains distinctly pagan
and distinctly Christian ideas (as opposed to one which deals with
themes common to both, such as the transience of life) need not be
a Christian reworking of a pagan poem. Its author may have been
a converted pagan, or, like thousands of middle-aged Russians today,
a man who, because he had lived with survivors of a past civilization,
could grasp its values imaginatively and appreciate them even while
he himself belonged to a new age.[1]

§245   We have heard recently of Roman Catholic missionaries
in Africa singing the Mass to the rhythms of a Congo war-chant and
of the weaving of native songs and dances into the same church's
baptismal ceremony in New Guinea. Missionaries in Anglo-Saxon
England similarly 'baptized' pagan institutions, methods, and concepts. The Yeavering excavations give evidence of a pagan temple
converted to Christian use. Bede's account of the poet Cædmon
tells how, between 657 and 680, Cædmon sang his famous *Hymn* and
so used heroic alliterative verse for Christian purposes—a develop-

[1] But see D. Whitelock *The Audience of Beowulf* (Oxford, 1951), esp.
pp. 22-28, and now also Appendix B to this *Guide*.

ment of great importance for Old English literature. And in *The Seafarer* and other poems, we find the pagan idea of *lof* Christianized —it now consists of praise on earth and life in Heaven and is to be won by fighting against the Devil and by doing good.

If we bear all this in mind, the incongruities to which our attention is so often drawn by critics of Old English poetry will trouble us less. After all, we can today 'thank our lucky stars' and say 'By Jove!' without believing that the stars really influence our lives or that Jupiter will protect us in battle. Similarly, if we find that our own interpretation of *Beowulf* commits us to the view that its author was a passionate believer in Christianity, we need not be deterred by the fact that he speaks of the power of *wyrd*.

§246   These problems loom large in Old English literature because we know very little about the genesis of most poems. *Cædmon's Hymn* is attributed to Cædmon and four poems—*Fates of the Apostles, Elene, Juliana*, and *Christ II*—bear Cynewulf's 'signature' in runes. But this does not give us much help, for Cynewulf is little more than a name. The unfortunate fact is that we just do not know for whom, by whom, when, where, or with what aim, most of the poems were written. This inevitably creates difficulties for us when we try to elucidate them and may lead us to criticize a poem for not having a structure which appeals to us or for not being the poem we think it ought to be.

Poetry

§247   In *An Introduction to Old English Metre*, Alan Bliss makes three points which need stressing here. The first is that 'OE poetry is not at all primitive; on the contrary, it is very highly artificial and sophisticated'. The second is that 'the vocabulary of OE poetry differs widely from that of prose'. The third is that 'OE poetry varies from most other types of poetry in that the metrical patterns are . . . selected from among the patterns which occur most commonly in natural speech'. The metrical unit is the half-line. Two half-lines alliterating together form the alliterative line which survived into ME and had a glorious flowering in the fourteenth century with such works as *Sir Gawain and the Green Knight* and *Piers Plowman*.

§248   Apart from *The Metres of Boethius* and the Metrical Version of the Psalms found in the Paris Psalter, the bulk of Old English poetry is to be found in four manuscripts, all of which date approximately from the second half of the tenth century. They are the Junius MS, the Vercelli Book, the Exeter Book, and the *Beowulf* MS. Further description of these MSS here would be superfluous, but you may find it interesting to answer the following questions:

Why was the Junius MS so-called? And why did some people call it the Cædmon MS? Has it any connexion with Milton? How did the Vercelli Book become associated with Italy? Why is the *Beowulf* MS known as Cotton Vitellius A.xv? What happened to it in 1731? Where can the Exeter Book be seen? How did it get there?

There are, of course, poems which are not found in these four MSS. They have been collected in a volume known as *The Anglo-Saxon Minor Poems*, which is referred to in § 264.

§ 249 The extant poems can be roughly classified according to subject matter.

1. Poems treating heroic subjects
Beowulf. Deor. The Battle of Finnsburh. Waldere. Widsith.

2. Historic Poems
The Battle of Brunanburh. The Battle of Maldon.

3. Biblical Paraphrases and Reworkings of Biblical Subjects
The Metrical Psalms. The poems of the Junius MS; note especially *Genesis B* and *Exodus. Christ. Judith.*

4. Lives of the Saints
Andreas. Elene. Guthlac. Juliana.

5. Other Religious Poems
Note especially *The Dream of the Rood* and the allegorical poems —*The Phoenix, The Panther,* and *The Whale.*

6. Short Elegies and Lyrics
The Wife's Lament. The Husband's Message. The Ruin. The Wanderer. The Seafarer. Wulf and Eadwacer. Deor might be included here as well as under 1 above.

7. Riddles and Gnomic Verse

8. Miscellaneous
Charms. The Runic Poem. The Riming Poem.

Note

Four poems—*The Fates of the Apostles, Elene, Christ II,* and *Juliana*—contain Cynewulf's 'signature' in runes.

Prose

§ 250 As has already been pointed out in § 182, English prose was far from being a primitive vehicle of expression at the time of the Norman Conquest. You will be able to watch it developing in the Chronicle and elsewhere. One interesting question you may try to answer for yourself is 'Whose prose do you prefer—that of Alfred or Ælfric?'

§251 Old English prose may be said to fall into the seven main divisions set out below.

1. The Anglo-Saxon Chronicle

The surviving MSS—lettered A to H—are discussed in *The Anglo-Saxon Chronicle*, ed. Dorothy Whitelock (Eyre and Spottiswoode, 1961), pp. xi-xviii. MS E (The Laud Chronicle) continues until the death of Stephen in 1154. This is, to all intents and purposes, the end of historical writing in English prose until the fifteenth century.

Miss Whitelock observes that 'the confident attribution of the work to Alfred's instigation cannot be upheld'.

2. The Translations of Alfred and his Circle

King Alfred explained his educational policy in his famous Preface to the *Cura Pastoralis*. This is perhaps the first of his translations. He also translated the *Historia adversus Paganos* of Orosius, in which he incorporated the story of the voyages of Ohthere and Wulfstan, the *De Consolatione Philosophiae* of Boethius, and the *Soliloquia* of St. Augustine. He is also responsible for a legal code.

Bishop Wærferth of Worcester translated the *Dialogues* of Gregory the Great at Alfred's request. The OE version of Bede's *Ecclesiastical History* has long been attributed to Alfred. Miss Whitelock, in her British Academy Lecture in 1962, finds no evidence for this, but says that it remains a probability that the work was undertaken at Alfred's instigation.

3. Homiletic Writings

The most important of these are

(*a*) *The Blickling Homilies*, 971.

(*b*) Ælfric's *Catholic Homilies*, 990-2, and *Lives of the Saints*, 993-8.

(*c*) *The Homilies* of Wulfstan, who died in 1023.

4. Other Religious Prose

This includes translations of portions of both the Old and New Testaments, and a version of the Benedictine Office.

5. Prose Fiction

Here we find the story of *Apollonius of Tyre*, *Alexander's Letter to Aristotle*, and *The Wonders of the East*. Renwick and Orton point out that these show 'that long before the Conquest the Anglo-Saxons found entertainment in the exotic romanticism of the East'.

6. Scientific and Medical Writings

7. Laws, Charters, and Wills

VII SELECT BIBLIOGRAPHY

A separate Bibliography is provided for each chapter of the book; details of the arrangement will be found in the Contents.

For convenience of reference, each section of the Bibliography has been given its own number and the section-numbers of the discussions to which the books relate have been placed in brackets after each heading in the Bibliography.

GENERAL

§252 A most useful guide is

> W. L. Renwick and H. Orton *The Beginnings of English Literature to Skelton 1509* (The Cresset Press, 2nd ed., 1952).

This contains an introduction to the literature of Old (and Middle) English, a bibliography of each text, with a note about its contents and any points of critical importance, and an Index.

A helpful review of studies up to 1958 will be found in

> D. Whitelock *Changing Currents in Anglo-Saxon Studies. An Inaugural Lecture* (Cambridge, 1958).

For more recent bibliographical information, see the books by S. B. Greenfield, E. G. Stanley, and C. L. Wrenn, cited in §263.

I PRELIMINARY REMARKS ON THE LANGUAGE (§§1-4)

§253 An excellent Introduction to Old English will be found in §§1-22 of A. Campbell's *Old English Grammar* (Clarendon Press, 1959, reprinted with corrections 1962).

On the history of the English language generally, the following books will answer most questions you are likely to ask:

> Simeon Potter *Our Language* (Penguin, 1950)
> C. L. Wrenn *The English Language* (Methuen, 1949)
> A. C. Baugh *A History of the English Language* (Routledge and Kegan Paul, 1951)
> G. L. Brook *A History of the English Language* (Andre Deutsch, 1958).

One of the first two, which are both designed for the general reader as well as for the student, could be read in full. The other two, in the initial stages, are perhaps more suited for reference.

You should not need a dictionary initially, as your reader or primer will almost certainly supply a glossary. When you do, you will find that there are two short dictionaries:

> H. Sweet *The Student's Dictionary of Anglo-Saxon* (Oxford, 1897)
> J. R. Clark Hall *A Concise Anglo-Saxon Dictionary* (4th ed., with Supplement by H. D. Meritt, Cambridge, 1960).

The most complete dictionary is that known as *Bosworth-Toller*. It is published by the Oxford University Press, and consists of a Dictionary and a Supplement. The original Dictionary was very deficient in the letters A-G. Here, in particular, you will have to consult both Dictionary and Supplement.

Some have found

> J. F. Madden and F. P. Magoun Jr. *A Grouped Frequency Word-List of Anglo-Saxon Poetry* (The Harvard Old English Series, 1967)

a very helpful guide to learning vocabulary. This lists the words which occur in OE poetry, starting with those which are used most frequently. Most of the first 300 words at least are very common in prose texts.

II   ORTHOGRAPHY AND PRONUNCIATION (§§5-9) AND III   INFLEXIONS (§§10-135)

§254   Although A. Campbell's *Old English Grammar* (Clarendon Press, 1959) is too detailed for you to use by itself in your first few months, it may be safely consulted when you are in difficulty. By looking at the Contents (pp. vii-xi) or the Index, you will be able to find full paradigms, lists of examples of strong verbs or anything else you want, and lucid explanations of any difficulty you may encounter.

IV   WORD FORMATION (§§136-138)

§255   Very helpful discussions and lists will be found in chapter IV of Quirk and Wrenn's *An Old English Grammar* and in pp. 39-43 of N. Davis's *Sweet's Anglo-Saxon Primer*, which are mentioned in §256.

V   SYNTAX (§§139-214)

§256   There is really no book on Old English Syntax similar to Campbell's *Old English Grammar*. There are plenty of monographs, but many of them are in German and most of those in English are too complicated for the beginner. One which may prove useful is J. M. Wattie's article called 'Tense' in *Essays and Studies* XVI (1930); this deals with the topics discussed in §§195-211.

Short but helpful treatments of the syntax will be found in:

N. Davis *Sweet's Anglo-Saxon Primer* (Clarendon Press, 1953 or later)

P. S. Ardern *First Readings in Old English* (N.Z.U.P., 1948)

R. Quirk and C. L. Wrenn *An Old English Grammar* (Methuen, 1955 or later)

G. L. Brook *An Introduction to Old English* (Manchester University Press, 1955).

VI INTRODUCTION TO ANGLO-SAXON STUDIES (§§215-251)

These lists do not necessarily include works referred to in the book by Renwick and Orton mentioned in §252.

History (§§215-218)

§257 The following are recommended:

P. Hunter Blair *An Introduction to Anglo-Saxon England* (Cambridge University Press, 1956)

P. Hunter Blair *Roman Britain and Early England 55 BC-AD 871* (Nelson, 1963)

F. M. Stenton *Anglo-Saxon England* (2nd ed., Oxford, 1947)

Dorothy Whitelock (ed.) *English Historical Documents* Volume I c. 500-1042 (London, 1955).

Archaeology (§§219-230)

§258 See §220, the section in which each topic is discussed, and

T. D. Kendrick *Anglo-Saxon Art to 900* (London, 1938)

T. D. Kendrick *Late Saxon and Viking Art* (London, 1949)

H. M. Taylor and Joan Taylor *Anglo-Saxon Architecture* (2 vols., Cambridge, 1965).

Language (§§231-235)
History of English Prose

§259 On the topics mentioned in §233, see

R. W. Chambers *On the Continuity of English Prose from Alfred to More and his School* (E.E.T.S.).[1]

Some of the points he raises are discussed in

N. Davis 'Styles in English Prose of the Late Middle and Early Modern Period' in *Les Congrès et Colloques de l'Université de Liège*, Volume 21 (1961), pp. 165-184.

[1] But his suggestion (p. lxxxvi) that the line between OE and ME can be drawn between the Peterborough annals for 1131 and 1132 is not now accepted; see *The Peterborough Chronicle 1070-1154*, ed. Cecily Clark (Oxford, 1958) p. xl.

See also

R. M. Wilson 'English and French in England 1100-1300', *History* 28 (1943), 37-60.

Vocabulary

Word Formation

See §255.

Changes of Meaning

§260 This is a difficult subject. Chapter VII of Simeon Potter's *Modern Linguistics* (Andre Deutsch, 1957) is a useful and helpful introduction. See §4.

Borrowings

§261 See

M. S. Serjeantson *A History of Foreign Words in English* (Routledge and Kegan Paul, 1935)

J. A. Sheard *The Words We Use* (Andre Deutsch, 1954).

Literature (§§236-251)

Topics raised in §§ 236-246

§262 On the transition from Epic to Romance, see

R. W. Southern *The Making of the Middle Ages* (Hutchinson, 1953), chapter V.

On the heroic way of, and attitude to, life, see

D. Whitelock *The Beginnings of English Society* (Penguin, 1952)

J. R. R. Tolkien *Beowulf. The Monsters and the Critics* (British Academy Lecture, 1936)

D. Whitelock *The Audience of Beowulf* (Oxford, 1951).

General Criticism

§263 W. P. Ker *Medieval English Literature* (O.U.P., 1912) can still be recommended, though its views on *Beowulf* are now generally out of favour. On this topic, see

A. G. Brodeur *The Art of Beowulf* (California, 1959).

On the poetry, see

C. W. Kennedy *The Earliest English Poetry* (O.U.P., 1943).

For an introduction to the prose, see pp. lvii ff. of

R. W. Chambers *On the Continuity of English Prose* (E.E.T.S.).

Recent studies of Old English literature include:
Stanley B. Greenfield *A Critical History of Old English Literature*
(London, 1966)
E. G. Stanley (ed.) *Continuations and Beginnings* (London, 1966)
C. L. Wrenn *A Study of Old English Literature* (London, 1967).

Poetry Texts

§264 Since the Renwick and Orton bibliography (see §252)
appeared in 1952, *The Anglo-Saxon Poetic Records*, published by
Columbia University Press and Routledge and Kegan Paul, have
been completed. The volumes are

I   Junius MS
II   Vercelli Book
III Exeter Book
IV   Beowulf and Judith
V   The Paris Psalter and the Meters of Boethius
VI   Anglo-Saxon Minor Poems.

Other editions of poems to appear since then include

Beowulf with the Finnesburg Fragment edited by C. L. Wrenn
(Harrap, 1953)
Three Old English Elegies edited by R. F. Leslie (Manchester,
1961)
Andreas and The Fates of the Apostles edited by K. R. Brooks
(Oxford, 1961)
Juliana edited by Rosemary Woolf (Methuen, 1955)
Cynewulf's Elene edited by P. O. E. Gradon (Methuen, 1958)
The Seafarer edited by I. L. Gordon (Methuen, 1960)
The Phoenix edited by N. F. Blake (Manchester, 1964).

Appreciation of the Poetry

§265 See §137 and

Alan Bliss 'v. The Appreciation of Old English Poetry' in *An
Introduction to Old English Metre* (Basil Blackwell, 1962)

C. L. Wrenn '7. Verse-Technique' in *Beowulf with the Finnesburg
Fragment* (Harrap, 1953)

H. C. Wyld 'Diction and Imagery in Anglo-Saxon Poetry',
Essays and Studies XI (1925), 49-91

D. C. Collins 'Kenning in Anglo-Saxon Poetry', *Essays and
Studies* 12 (1959), 1-17

Randolph Quirk 'Poetic language and Old English metre' in
Early English and Norse Studies presented to Hugh Smith
(London, 1963)

L. D. Lerner 'Colour Words in Anglo-Saxon', *Modern Language
Review* 46 (1951), 246-249.

I have discussed some of the difficulties hinted at in §246 at
greater length, with particular reference to *Beowulf*, in an article in
Neophilologus 1963, pp. 126-138.

The Use of Oral Formulae

§266   See §137 and

F. P. Magoun Jr. 'Oral-Formulaic Character of Anglo-Saxon
Narrative Poetry', *Speculum* 28 (1953), 446-467

S. B. Greenfield 'The Formulaic Expression of the Theme of
"Exile" in Anglo-Saxon Poetry', *Speculum* 30 (1955),
200-206

A. Bonjour '*Beowulf* and The Beasts of Battle', *Publications of
the Modern Language Association of America* 72 (1957),
563-573

H. L. Rogers 'The Crypto-Psychological Character of the Oral
Formula', *English Studies* 47 (1966), 89-102.

Note

One needs to beware of the notion sometimes advanced that
formulaic poetry is necessarily 'oral' and that all poems must be
either strictly 'oral' or strictly 'literary'. Lettered or 'literary' poets
certainly carried on the techniques of their 'oral' predecessors, and
there seems no real reason why one man should not combine the two
techniques.

Metre

§267   A helpful discussion on OE metre, which explains it in
terms of MnE examples, is that by J. R. R. Tolkien, to be found in
C. L. Wrenn's revision of J. R. Clark Hall's translation of *Beowulf*,
(George Allen and Unwin, 1940). Metre is discussed at pp. xxviii-
xliii. C. L. Wrenn discusses metre briefly in his edition of *Beowulf
with the Finnesburg Fragment* (Harrap, 1953), pp. 77-80. Another
helpful explanation is that which once appeared in Henry Sweet's
Anglo-Saxon Reader, but has been omitted from the Tenth and later
editions.

For a fuller account, you can turn to *An Introduction to Old English
Metre* by Alan Bliss, published by Basil Blackwell, Oxford, 1962.
Do not overlook Appendix II Practical Scansion.

In the early stages you may find the following mnemonic helpful.

It refers to the six types of half-line in the Sievers system as described by Professor Tolkien. In the doggerel (a University of Melbourne *macédoine*), each half-line conforms metrically to the basic pattern of one of the types and alliterates on the stressed syllables with the letter by which that type is known.

A.	Anna angry	´ × ´ ×	falling-falling
B.	And Byrhtnoth bold	× ´ × ´	rising-rising
C.	In keen conflict	× ´ ´ ×	clashing
Da.	Ding down foemen	´ ´ ` ×	falling by stages
Db.	Deal death to all	´ ´ × `	broken fall
E.	Each one with edge	´ ` × ´	fall and rise

I am indebted to a New Zealand friend for this series of half-lines from Old English poetry which illustrate the five types with the correct initial consonant:

A.	*ān æfter ānum*	(*Beowulf* 2461)
B.	*wæs þæt beorhte bold*	(*Beowulf* 997)
C.	*of carcerne*	(*Andreas* 57)
Da.	*deorc dēapscua*	(*Beowulf* 160)
Db.	*dēop dēada wǣġ*	(*Maxims* I. 78, MS)
E.	*egsode eorl*	(*Beowulf* 6, MS).

Prose Texts

§268   Editions and translations of most of the prose texts are available. For details you should consult your reader and the book by Renwick and Orton mentioned in §252. Important works which have appeared since the latter was published include:

The *Anglo-Saxon Chronicle* translated by G. N. Garmonsway (Everyman's Library 624)

The *Anglo-Saxon Chronicle. A Revised Translation* edited by D. Whitelock (Eyre and Spottiswoode, 1961)

The *Old English Apollonius of Tyre* edited by P. Goolden (Oxford, 1958)

The *Homilies of Wulfstan* edited by **Dorothy** Bethurum (Oxford, 1957)

The *Benedictine Office* edited by James Ure (Edinburgh, 1957)

Homilies of Ælfric A Supplementary Collection edited by John C. Pope (Early English Text Society, 1967).

Appendix A STRONG VERBS

This Appendix, which contains some of the more common strong verbs, is intended to illustrate §§90-109 and 131-134.

As is pointed out in §92, the 3rd pers. sg. pres. ind. is not part of the gradation series. For this reason, these forms are printed in italics in this Appendix.

You will find here further examples of the simplification of endings referred to in §112.2; note

drīehþ < *drēogan*   (class II)
cwiþþ < *cweþan*   (class V)

and   *wierþ* < *weorþan*   (class III).

From *bindan* (class III) we find 2nd and 3rd pers. sg. pres. ind. *bintst* and *bint*.

Verbs in which Verner's Law forms occur (see §§105-107) are marked †.

Verbs without Verner's Law forms where they might be expected (see §108) are marked ‡.

When the forms of a verb rhyme with those of the verb before it in the list, I have left the principal parts for you to fill in.[1]

The Appendix is not a complete list of Old English strong verbs. You may find it useful to note down in the appropriate place any new verbs you come across in your reading.

APPENDIX A.1   CLASS I

Inf.	3rd Sg. Pres. Ind.	1st Pret.	2nd Pret.	Past Ptc.
bītan 'bite'	*bītt*	bāt	biton	biten
flītan 'contend'				
slītan 'tear'				
wītan 'blame'				
ġewītan 'go'				
wlītan 'behold'				
wrītan 'write'				
bīdan 'await'	*bītt*	bād	bidon	biden

---

[1] The principle of 'rhyme association' is an important one. Thus most verbs borrowed into English are made weak. But the French borrowing 'strive' became strong through association with verbs like 'drive'. Similarly the Old English weak verb 'wear' became strong through association with the strong verbs 'bear' and 'tear'.

Inf.	3rd Sg. Pres. Ind.	1ſt Pret.	2nd Pret.	Past Ptc.
glīdan 'glide'				
rīdan 'ride'				
slīdan 'slide'				
blīcan 'shine'	*blīcþ*	blāc	blicon	blicen
swīcan 'fail'				
drīfan 'drive'	*drīfþ*	drāf	drifon	drifen
belīfan 'remain'				
grīpan 'seize'	*grīpþ*	grāp	gripon	gripen
hrīnan 'touch'	*hrīnþ*	hrān	hrinon	hrinen
scīnan 'shine'				
stīgan 'ascend'	*stīġþ, stīhþ*	stāg¹	stigon	stigen
hnīgan 'bow to'				
† līþan 'go'	*līþþ*	lāþ	lidon	liden
† scrīþan 'go'				see §108.
† snīþan 'cut'				
‡ mīþan 'conceal'	*mīþþ*	māþ	miþon	miþen
‡ rīsan 'rise'	*rīst*	rās	rison	risen

Contracted Verbs (see §103.3)

† lēon 'lend'	*līehþ*	lāh	ligon	ligen
† tēon 'accuse'				
† þēon 'prosper'²				
† wrēon 'cover'				

Note

The following weak verbs are found with ī in the infinitive:
ċīdan 'chide', *cwīþan* 'lament', *ġedīgan* 'survive', and *līxan* 'gleam'.

APPENDIX A.2   CLASS II

Inf.	3rd Sg. Pres. Ind.	1st Pret.	2nd Pret.	Past Ptc.
bēodan 'offer'	*bīett*	bēad	budon	boden
brēotan 'break'	*brīett*	brēat	bruton	broten
flēotan 'float'				
ġēotan 'pour'				
scēotan 'shoot'				

¹ The form *stāh* sometimes occurs as a result of unvoicing of *g*.
² Historically a verb of class III. See A. Campbell *Old English Grammar* §739.

	3rd Sg.			
Inf.	*Pres. Ind.*	*1st Pret.*	*2nd Pret.*	*Past Ptc.*
† ċēosan 'choose'	*ċīest*	ċēas	curon	coren
† drēosan 'fall'				
† frēosan 'freeze'				
† hrēosan 'fall'				
† lēosan 'lose'				
crēopan 'creep'	*crīepþ*	crēap	crupon	cropen
drēogan 'endure'	*drīehþ*	drēag	drugon	drogen
flēogan 'fly'				
lēogan 'tell lies'				
hrēowan 'rue'	*hrīewþ*	hrēaw	hruwon	hrowen
† sēoþan 'boil'	*sīeþþ*	sēaþ	sudon	soden
brūcan 'enjoy'	*brȳcþ*	brēac	brucon	brocen
lūcan 'lock'				
būgan 'bow'	*bȳhþ*	bēag	bugon	bogen
dūfan 'dive'	*dȳfþ*	dēaf	dufon	dofen
scūfan 'shove'				

Contracted Verbs (see § 103.4)

† flēon 'flee'	*flīehþ*	flēah	flugon	flogen
† tēon 'draw'				

Note

The following weak verbs are found with *ēo* in the infinitive:
frēogan 'love', *nēosan* (*nēosian*) 'seek out', and *sēowan* (*sēowian*)
'sew'.

APPENDIX A.3   CLASS III

	3rd Sg.			
Inf.	*Pres. Ind.*	*1st Pret.*	*2nd Pret.*	*Past Ptc.*
(a) see § 95.				
breġdan 'pull'[1]	*britt*[2]	bræġd	brugdon	brogden
streġdan 'strew'				
berstan 'burst'[3]	*birst*	bærst	burston	borsten
(b) see §§ 96-98.				
beorgan 'protect'	*bierhþ*	bearg	burgon	borgen

[1] This verb has been taken as the basic paradigm of class III (see § 95) to
make explanation easier. Originally it belonged elsewhere; see A. Campbell
Old English Grammar § 736 (b).
[2] Regular forms of 3rd sg. pres. ind. are not recorded.
[3] See § 95 f.n. 1.

Inf.	3rd Sg. Pres. Ind.	1st Pret.	2nd Pret.	Past Ptc.
ċeorfan 'cut'	ċierfþ	ċearf	curfon	corfen
hweorfan 'go'				
sweorcan 'grow dark'	swierċþ	swearc	swurcon	sworcen
weorpan 'throw'	wierpþ	wearp	wurpon	worpen
† weorþan 'become'	wierþ	wearþ	wurdon	worden
feohtan 'fight'	fieht	feaht	fuhton	fohten
† fēolan 'press on'[1]		fealh	fulgon	folgen

(c) See §§96-97 and 99.

delfan 'dig'	dilfþ	dealf	dulfon	dolfen
helpan 'help'	hilpþ	healp	hulpon	holpen
belgan 'be angry'	bilhþ	bealg	bulgon	bolgen
swelgan 'swallow'				
meltan 'melt'	milt	mealt	multon	molten
sweltan 'die'				

(d) See §100.

ġieldan 'pay'	ġielt	ġeald	guldon	golden
ġiellan 'yell'	ġielþ	ġeal	gullon	gollen
ġielpan 'boast'	ġielpþ	ġealp	gulpon	golpen

(e) See §101.

grimman 'rage'	grimþ	gramm	grummon	grummen
swimman 'swim'				
ġelimpan 'happen'	ġelimpþ	ġelamp	ġelumpon	ġelumpen
bindan 'bind'	bint	band	bundon	bunden
findan 'find'[2]				
grindan 'grind'				
windan 'wind'				
drincan 'drink'	drincþ	dranc	druncon	druncen
scrincan 'shrink'				
swincan 'toil'				
onġinnan 'begin'	onġinþ	ongann	ongunnon	ongunnen
winnan 'fight'				
singan 'sing'	singþ	sang	sungon	sungen
springan 'spring'				
swingan 'flog'				
þringan 'crowd'				
wringan 'wring'				

[1] See §133.2. Regular forms of 3rd sg. pres. ind. do not seem to be recorded.

[2] In the 1st pret. funde is found alongside fand; see §109.

| | | 3rd Sg. | | | |
Inf.		Pres. Ind.	1st Pret.	2nd Pret.	Past Ptc.
birnan 'burn'[1]		birnþ	barn	burnon	burnen
irnan 'run'[1]					

(e) Exceptional

frignan 'ask'	friġneþ	fræġn	frugnon	frugnen
murnan 'mourn'	myrnþ	mearn	murnon	

Note

The following verbs are weak:
hringan 'ring' and *ġeþingan* 'determine'.
On *bringan* see §123.2.

APPENDIX A.4   CLASS IV
                  (See §94 f.n. 1)

| | 3rd Sg. | | | |
Inf.	Pres. Ind.	1st Pret.	2nd Pret.	Past Ptc.
beran 'bear'	birþ	bær	bǣron	boren
teran 'tear'				
brecan 'break'	bricþ	bræc	brǣcon	brocen
cwelan 'die'	cwilþ	cwæl	cwǣlon	cwolen
helan 'hide'				
stelan 'steal'				
scieran 'cut'[2]	scierþ	scear	scēaron	scoren
niman 'take'[3]	nimþ	nam, nōm	nōmon, nāmon	numen
cuman 'come'[3]	cymþ	cōm	cōmon	cumen

APPENDIX A.5   CLASS V
                  (See §94 f.n. 2)

| | 3rd Sg. | | | |
Inf.	Pres. Ind.	1st Pret.	2nd Pret.	Past Ptc.
† cweþan 'say'	cwiþþ	cwæþ	cwǣdon	cweden
etan 'eat'	itt	ǣt[4]	ǣton	eten
fretan 'devour'				
metan 'measure'	met[5]	mæt	mǣton	meten
‡ ġenesan 'survive'	ġeneseþ[5]	ġenæs	ġenǣson	ġenesen

---

[1] Originally *brinnan, rinnan*. But metathesis occurred; see §95 f.n. 1.
[2] See §103.1.   [3] See §§103.2 and 109.
[4] See §109.   [5] Regular forms are not recorded.

	3rd Sg.			
Inf.	*Pres. Ind.*	*1st Pret.*	*2nd Pret.*	*Past Ptc.*
sprecan 'speak'	*spricþ*	spræc	sprǣcon	sprecen
specan 'speak'				
wrecan 'avenge'				
tredan 'tread'	*tritt*	træd	trǣdon	treden
wefan 'weave'	*wifþ*	wæf	wǣfon	wefen
ġiefan 'give'[1]	*ġiefþ*	ġeaf	ġeafon	ġiofon
onġietan 'perceive'[1]	*onġiet*	onġeat	onġēaton	onġieten

Weak Presents (see §116)

biddan 'ask'	*bitt*	bæd	bǣdon	beden
licgan 'lie'	*liġeþ, līþ*	læġ	lǣgon	leġen
† þicgan 'partake'	*þiġeþ*	þeah[2]	þǣgon	þeġen
sittan 'sit'	*sitt*	sæt	sǣton	seten

Contracted Verb (see §103.3)

† sēon 'see'	*siehþ*	seah[2]	sāwon	sewen

APPENDIX A.6   CLASS VI

	3rd Sg.			
Inf.	*Pres. Ind.*	*1st Pret.*	*2nd Pret.*	*Past Ptc.*
dragan 'draw'	*dræhþ*	drōg	drōgon	dragen
faran 'go'	*færþ*	fōr	fōron	faren
galan 'sing'	*gælþ*	gōl	gōlon	galen
hladan 'load'	*hladeþ*[3]	hlōd	hlōdon	hladen
wadan 'go'	*wadeþ*[3]			
sacan 'quarrel'	*sæcþ*	sōc	sōcon	sacen
scacan 'shake'				
standan 'stand'[4]	*stent*	stōd	stōdon	standen

Weak Presents (see §116)

hebban 'lift'	*hefeþ*	hōf	hōfon	hafen
swerian 'swear'	*swereþ*	swōr	swōron	sworen
scieppan 'create'[5]	*sciepþ*	scōp	scōpon	scapen

Contracted Verbs (see §§103.3 and 108)

† lēan 'blame'	*liehþ*	lōh, lōg[6]	lōgon	lagen
† slēan 'strike'				slagen, slǣgen

[1] See §103.1.   [2] See §97.
[3] Regular forms do not seem to be recorded.
[4] See §94 f.n. 3.   [5] See §103.1.
[6] See §108.

APPENDIX A.7   CLASS VII
(See § 104)

Inf.	3rd Sg. Pres. Ind.	1st Pret.	2nd Pret.	Past Ptc.
(a)				
bannan 'summon'	benþ	bēonn	bēonnon	bannen
spannan 'span'				
blāwan 'blow'	blǣwþ	blēow	blēowon	blāwen
cnāwan 'know'				
māwan 'mow'				
sāwan 'sow'				
flōwan 'flow'	flēwþ	flēow	flēowon	flōwen
grōwan 'grow'				
rōwan 'row'				
spōwan 'succeed'				
fealdan 'fold'	fielt	fēold	fēoldon	fealden
healdan 'hold'				
wealdan 'rule'				
feallan 'fall'	fielþ	fēoll	fēollon	feallen
weallan 'boil'				
weaxan 'grow'	wiext	wēox	wēoxon	weaxen
bēatan 'beat'	bīett	bēot	bēoton	bēaten
hēawan 'hew'	hīewþ	hēow	hēowon	hēawen
hlēapan 'leap'	hlīepþ	hlēop	hlēopon	hlēapen
	Weak Present (see § 116)			
wēpan 'weep'	wēpeþ	wēop	wēopon	wōpen
(b)				
hātan 'call'	hǣtt	hēt	hēton	hāten
ondrǣdan 'fear'	ondrǣtt	ondrēd	ondrēdon	ondrǣden
rǣdan 'advise'[1]				
lǣtan 'let'	lǣtt	lēt	lēton	lǣten
slǣpan 'sleep'	slǣpþ	slēp	slēpon	slǣpen
	Contracted Verbs (see § 108)			
† fōn 'seize'	fēhþ	fēng	fēngon	fangen
† hōn 'hang'				

[1] A weak preterite rǣdde is also found.

Appendix B CHRISTIAN INFLUENCE IN OLD ENGLISH LITERATURE

A Supplementary Note

A reviewer of this book as it originally appeared observed that my treatment of Anglo-Saxon imaginative writing, while describing 'the well-known combination of respect for fierceness in battle with love for intricacy in craftsmanship that does indeed inform the poetry in which the heroes under heaven, eager for fame, wished to be commemorated' was

far less informative precisely about that other important strand in Anglo-Saxon thinking: the complex and subtle influence exerted by Christian notions, images and patterns of thought on whatever pagan substrate we can still reliably discern. A generalized allusion to the 'comforts' of the Christian message, and a string of modern analogies, do not provide a counterweight to the heavy emphasis placed on the pagan attitude to life.

Christian subject-matter figures prominently in any listing of Anglo-Saxon vernacular writings, and Christian attitudes permeate even *Beowulf* itself. The *matière chrétienne* is moreover only the dominant, idea-giving element in that whole complex of Mediterranean culture to which Anglo-Saxon writers, singers and speakers gained access. Its importance rests less on its quantity that [sic] on its centrality and seminal rôle.

The aesthetic appeal of the sweetly and decorously conducted heroic life, leading to its Pyrrhic *Endsieg*, was to prove insufficient compared with the ethical and intellectual strength derived from Classical philosophy and Christian doctrine (and even from dogma) —from, in Pickering's neatly drawn contrast, Boethius or Augustine. The sense of history and the appreciation for the exemplary life could turn to the Bible and the lives of the saints. The special interest of Anglo-Saxon literature is not only that it preserved much of the spirit and still more of the aesthetic forms of the pagan past, but also that it witnessed, and shows in a paradigmatic way, the impact of Latin and Christian forms of thought and expression in the very presence of the living body of pagan civilisation, from the viewpoint of a people islanding themselves off, in time and space, from the springs of that civilization.[1]

[1] L. Seiffert in *English Philological Studies* 10 (1967), 62-64.

I acknowledge the validity of the criticism that there was a lack of balance and agree that the influence of Christianity on the literature should have had more attention than passing references to monastic learning and the Benedictine Revival and brief lists of religious writings in verse and prose.[1] It is certainly true that most Old English prose and much of the poetry shows a deep knowledge of Christian doctrine, a firm belief in the Christian message, and the influence of Christian ways of thinking.

But where the literature is not overtly Christian, I find it difficult to be sure of the 'centrality and seminal rôle' of Christian matter and Mediterranean culture. So, while admitting the 'impact of Latin and Christian forms of thought and expression' on much Old English literature, I remain unsure of the extent to which 'Christian attitudes permeate even *Beowulf* itself'. As I hope to show elsewhere, I believe that, while the view that *Beowulf* is deeply Christian is defensible, it is not demonstrable.[2] Nor am I sure that I understand the point of the word 'even'. Quite apart from poems such as *The Ruin, Wulf,* and *The Wife's Lament,* in which there are no Christian references, it would not be hard to find poems which are less 'permeated' by Christianity than *Beowulf* is. Examples include *Deor, The Husband's Message, The Battle of Brunanburh,* and perhaps *The Battle of Maldon* (where, despite the presence of indisputably Christian references, the tone is strongly 'heroic').

[1] This influence has now been well analysed by Geoffrey Shepherd in his article 'Scriptural Poetry' in *Continuations and Beginnings* (see § 263). But it seems to me possible that on p. 3 he may have over-emphasized the influence of Christian literacy in claiming that 'the marvel is that among Anglo-Saxons generally the adaptation [of western and latinised Christian literacy] was so nearly total'. The Church was (I suppose) in control of the production and preservation of documents. Hence it seems to me arguable that the fact that 'we are almost completely ignorant of what it was like to be a pagan Anglo-Saxon of the sixth century' does not necessarily imply a similar ignorance on the part of later Anglo-Saxon warriors and peasants. We have clear evidence that stories were orally transmitted. The same could be true of pagan legends and beliefs.

[2] In my Introduction to Kevin Crossley-Holland's translation of *Beowulf,* to be published in the autumn of 1968 by Macmillan (London), and Farrar, Straus and Giroux (New York).

INDEX OF SUBJECTS

The references are to the numbered sections. The abbreviations n. and f.n. stand for 'Note' and 'Footnote' respectively.

You may find it useful to remember that §§252-268 comprise the Bibliography, and to note the entries 'sound-changes', 'spelling variations', and 'technical terms explained'.

This Index does not give references to what are merely passing mentions of persons, poems, places, or things.

absence of subject or object, 168 n. 1
  s.v. *þæs ... þæt*, 193.7
absolute, see 'dative absolute'
accusative and infinitive, 155, 161
accusative case, 189
adjective clauses, 159, 162-165 (for details, see Contents), 168 n. 1 s.v. *þæs*
  ... þæt, 178.3, 180, 187.3(d), 204.2
adjectives:
  weak declension, 63, 65; strong
  declension, 63, 66-67; their uses,
  64; dissyllabic adjectives, 68-69;
  adjectives with *æ* in the stem, 70;
  those ending in *-o*, *-u*, 71; those
  ending in *-h*, 72; those ending in *-e*
  73; comparison, 74-76
adverb clauses, 166-180 (for details,
  see Contents)
adverbial relationships expressed in
  other ways, 180-181, 184.1, 190.5,
  191.3, 192, 204.2, 205.2
adverbs, formation and comparison,
  135
agreement, see 'concord'
Alcuin, 217, 218
Alfred, King, 139, 148, 172, 217, 218,
  221, 251
analogy, 44, 60.2, 70, 108-109
analysis, exercise in, 172
Anglo-Saxons not primitive, 182
anticipation, 148
apposition, 187.1 (c), 193.3
archaeology, 219-230 (for details, see
  Contents), 258
architecture, 219, 220, 223-224
articles, 193

æ/a fluctuation, 35-36, 70, 103.3 f.n.
Ælfric, 150, 222, 251

Bayeux Tapestry, 220, 221, 222, 227
Bede, 153, 168 s.v. *þonne* 2, 217
Beowulf, 221, 223, 226, 230, 244, 245,
  248, 249, 263, 264, 265
bibliography, 252-268
borrowing of words, 234, 261
breaking, 96-99, 100 n., 103.3, 114 n.,
  123.1, 133.2
buildings, 223-224
Byrhtnoth, 221

carving, 219, 225
cases:
  those found in OE, 11, 140; concord, 187; uses of, 188-192, 213-
  214; distinctions disappearing,
  189 n., 231-233
causal clauses, 176
Cædmon, 153, 168 s.v. *þonne* 2, 245-
  246, 248
changes in English, 140, 231-233, 235,
  253
changes of meaning, 4, 260
Cheddar, 223
Christianity, 217, 218, 219, 243-245,
  and Appendix B
clause order, 142
coins, 228, 236
collective nouns, 187.3
comitatus, 236 ff.
comparison:
  of adjectives, 74-76; of adverbs,
  135; clauses of, 177
complement, 188, 205.2
compound words, 6, 12, 41, 136, 137
concession, clauses of, 146.5, 173, 178
concord, 12, 162, 187
condition, clauses of, 146.5, 177.4,
  179, 180

conjunctions:
introducing adverb clauses, 167-171; introducing noun clauses, 154 ff.; parataxis, 184
consecutive clauses, see 'result, clauses of'
consonants, 9, 117 n.
contracted verbs, 103.3-103.6, 107-108, 114
contraction of *ne*, 184.4
correlation, 150-153, 169
Cynewulf, 246, 249 n.

Danish invasions, 217, 218, 221, 232
dates, table of, 215-216
dative absolute, 191.4, 204
dative case, 191
dependent desires, 154, 155-156
dependent exclamations, 154
dependent questions, 154, 157-160
dependent statements, 154, 155-156
derived paradigms, see 'How to Use this Guide'
dialects, 2-3, 217
dictionaries, 253
differences between Old and Modern English, see 'Modern English'
diphthongs, 8
dissyllables, 26, 41-44, 68-69
doubling of consonants, 117 n.
Dream of the Rood, The, 241
dress, 222
dual number, 11, 89.3, 187.3

embroidery, 219, 227
English, changes in, see 'changes in English'
Epic to Romance, 239, 262

final clauses, see 'purpose, clauses of'
formulae, oral, see 'oral formulae'
future, 196, 210, 211
future-in-the-past, 174

gender, 11-13, 136 n. 1, 187. See also the note in 'How to Use this Guide'
genitive case, 190
Germanic heroic code, 218, 236 ff., 262
Germanic languages, 1, 105-107
gradation, 90 ff., 136
Grimm's Law, 105-107

h lost, 37-39, 72, 103.3, 103.4, 114 n.
heavy groups, splitting of, 149
heroic code, 218, 236 ff., 262

history, 217-218, 257
hypotaxis, 183
hypothesis in comparisons, 177.4

i-mutation, 52-57, 92, 112.1, 116, 117 n., 123, 128 n., 135, 136
impersonal verbs, 212
Indo-European language(s), 1, 90, 105-106, 140
infinitive, accusative and, 161
infinitives, uses of, 205
inflexions, 10-135 (for details, see Contents), 140, 231-233, 254. On 'Learning the Inflexions', see 'How to Use this Guide'
instrumental case, 192

jewellery, 219, 226

kennings, 137, 265
key paradigms, see 'How to Use this Guide'

Latin originals, 139, 150
length marks, see 'How to Use this Guide'
levelling, 108-109
life and dress, 222
literature, 236-251, 252, 262-268, and Appendix B
lordless man, 242
loss of *h*, 37-39, 72, 103.3, 103.4, 114 n.

manuscripts, 219, 229
meaning, changes of, see 'changes of meaning'
medial vowels, 26, 41-44, 68-69
metal-work, 219, 226
metre, 39 n., 247, 267
'modal' auxiliaries, 206-211
Modern English, differences between it and Old English, 5-9, 108-109, 139-153, 155, 159-160, 166, 199, 231-233, 235, 253. See also 'Learning the Vocabulary' in 'How to Use this Guide'
moods:
those found in OE, 89.2; in noun clauses, 156, 160; in adjective clauses, 165; in adverb clauses, 173-179; syntax, 195-211 (for details, see Contents)
music, 230

n lost before *h*, 123.2
nasals, influence of, 101, 103.2
negatives, 165.2, 175.2, 184.4

nominative case, 187.1, 188
'normalizing', 3
Norman Conquest, 182, 219, 232, 233, 250
noun clauses, 154-161 (for details, see Contents), 163.6
nouns:
  endings, 13; weak nouns, 22-25; strong nouns, 33-62 (for details, see Contents. But note those with æ in stem, 36; those ending in -h, 37-39, and in -o, -u, 40; dissyllabic nouns, 41-44); concord, 187; collective, 187.3; participles as nouns 204.1
number, 11, 89.3, 187
numerals, 82-86, 194

object, absence of, 193.7
object, position of, 143-147
Old English:
  defined, 1; dialects, 2, 3; not a primitive language, 148-152, 182, 184.4 (f), 247, 250. For how it differs from Modern English, see 'Modern English'
oral formulae, 137, 266
orthography, 5, 254

palatal diphthongization (p.d.), 100 103.1
paradigms, key, derived, and other, see 'How to Use this Guide'
parataxis, 182-186 (for details, see Contents)
parsing, see 'How to Use this Guide'
participles:
  declension, 111, 116; concord, 187; uses 199-204, 205.1
passive voice, 89.5, 202-203
person, 18, 21, 89.4
place, clauses of, 173, 178.3
poetry, 247-249, 263, 264-267
prefixes, 6, 138, 213
prepositions, 140, 163.3, 213-214, 231
prepositional conjunctions (formulae), 169-171
prepositional phrases, 169, 181.4
principal clause, influence on mood of subordinate clause, 156, 165, 173, 174, 175, 177, 179.2
pronoun object, position of, 144.2
pronouns:
  declension, 15-21; uses, 15, 162-164, 193; personal pronouns in relative

combinations, 162.2, 163.2; concord, 187
pronunciation, 6-9, 231, 254
prose, 139, 150, 172, 182, 219, 233, 250-251, 259, 263, 268
purpose, clauses of, 175

questions, 146, 154, 157-160. See also 'rhetorical questions'

recapitulation, 148
reduplicating verbs, 93
relative pronouns, see 'adjective clauses'
resolved tenses, 199 ff.
result, clauses of, 168 n. 1 s.v. þæs ... þæt, 175
rhetorical questions, 157, 165.3, 175.3
runic inscriptions, 229

sculpture, 219, 225
Seafarer, The, 241
semantics, 4, 260
semi-subordination, 185.2
separable prefixes, 213
short cuts to learning:
  (Note: You should familiarize yourself with the Abbreviations and Symbols, pp. xv-xvi, and read the section on 'How to Use this Guide')
  pronouns, 19; weak nouns, 22; strong nouns, 33-34, 47, 58, 61; adjectives, 65, 66; nouns, adjectives, and pronouns, 77-80; strong verbs, 90 ff., 112-113; weak verbs, 117, 118-119, 125; all verbs, 131-134
sound-changes (laws):
  general, 35, 217; affecting dissyllables, 41-44 (nouns), 68-69 (adjectives); æ/a fluctuation, 35-36, 70, 103.3 f.n.; breaking, 96-99, 100 n., 103.3, 114 n., 123.1, 133.2; doubling of consonants, 117 n.; gradation, 90 ff., 136; Grimm's Law, 105-107; i-mutation, 52-57, 92, 112.1, 116, 117 n., 123, 128 n., 135, 136; influence of nasals, 101, 103.2; loss of h, 37-39, 72, 103.3, 103.4, 114 n.; loss of n before h, 123.2; palatal diphthongization, 100, 103.1; syncopation or reduction of endings, 112.2; u>o, 123.3; Verner's Law, 105-108, 113.4, 136. See also 'spelling variations'

spelling, 5, 233
spelling variations:
  an/on, 3, 101, 103.2; *æ/a*, 35-36,
  70; *ea/e*, 3; *ie/y/e/i*, 3, 8; *o/u/w*, 40,
  71; *-on/-en*, 113.3; *y/o*, 123.3
splitting of heavy groups, 149
stress, 6, 41, 90, 105-106, 231
subject:
  absence of, 168 n. 1 s.v. *þæs* ...
  þæt, 193.7; concord, 187
suffixes, 13, 136, 138
Sutton Hoo, 218, 230
syllables, 26-27
syntax, 139-214 (for details, see Contents), 231-233, 256. See also
  'Understanding the Syntax' in
  'How to Use this Guide'

table of dates, 215-216
tapestry, 219, 227. See also 'Bayeux
  Tapestry'
technical terms explained:
  (Note: See also 'short cuts to learning' and 'sound-changes')
  sounds, 7-9, 26-32, 35, 117 n.; inflexions, 10-12, 87-89, 174, 199;
  syntax, 143 and f.n., 154, 162, 165
  f.n., 166, 167, 169, 174, 183, 199;
  parsing, see 'How to Use this
  Guide'
tenses:
  present and preterite, 89.1; syntax,
  195-211 (for details, see Contents)
time, clauses of, 174, 178.3, 180
transitoriness of life, 241 ff.

unreality timeless in OE, 179.4 n., 198

verbs:
  general, 14, 131-134; strong, 87-
  114 (for details, see Contents);
  weak, 87, 93, 115-126 (for details,
  see Contents); reduplicating, 93;
  contracted, 103.3-103.6, 107-108,
  114; weak presents, 103.6, 116,
  133.1; others, 127-129; preterite-
  present, 130; concord, 187; syntax,
  195-211 (for details, see Contents);
  impersonal, 212
Verner's Law, 105-108, 113.4, 136
vocabulary:
  changes of meaning, 4, 260; word
  formation, 136-138 (for details, see
  Contents), 255; borrowings, 234,
  261; of poetry, 247, 265-266; dictionaries, 253. See also 'Learning
  the Vocabulary' in 'How to Use
  this Guide' and 'compound words'
voice, 89.5
vowels, 7, 26-32. See also 'medial
  vowels'

Wanderer, The, 241
warfare, 221
weak presents, 103.6, 116, 133.1
weapons, 221, 236
word formation, 136-138 (for details,
  see Contents), 255
word-order, 140, 143-147, 150-153,
  178.4, 179.7, 182, 231-233
Wulfstan, 218, 251

Yeavering, 223, 245

INDEX OF WORDS

The references are to the numbered sections.
The letters LV mean that the word in question will be found in 'Learning the Vocabulary' in the section 'How to Use this Guide'.
The abbreviations n. and f.n. stand for 'Note' and 'Footnote' respectively.

æ follows a, þ follows t.
ċ is to be found under c, ġ under g, and ð under þ.
ġe- is ignored, so that ġemunan appears under m.

Nouns, adjectives, and pronouns, will be found under the nominative singular, and verbs under the infinitive. Verbs discussed in Appendix A only are excluded.

You may find it useful to remember that lists of conjunctions used in adverb clauses are given in §168 (non-prepositional) and §171 (prepositional).

ā- and its compounds, 138
ac, 144, 145, 183, 184.2
āc, LV, 58
āgan, 130
-an, -on and its compounds, 138
ān, 82, 83, 193.4
āna, 83
and, ond, 183, 184.1
anda, 3
andswarian, 124, 132.1
ār, LV
ār-weorþ, 137
āþ, 35
-aþ, -oþ and its compounds, 138

æfter, 171, 174, 214
æġ, 34
æġ- and its compounds, 138
æġhwæþer, 184.1
æġþer, 184.1 and .3
æ-lāreowas, 137
ælmes-ġeorn, 137
ǣr, 152 n., 168, 171, 174, 197.4, 214
ǣr-dæġ, 137
ǣr-gōd, 137
æt, 214

bannan, 116 f.n., 133.5
bār, LV
bāt, LV
bæc, 26
bæþ-weġ, 137
bǣr, 136
be, 214
be- and its compounds, 138
bearo, -u, 40
ġebed, 41

beforan, 214
bēġen, 84
bēodan, 110-113, 134, 136
bēon, 127, 196, 201-203
beorht-nes, 138
beran, 93, 136
berstan, 93
betwix, betwux, 171, 214
betwux-āleġed-nes, 137
(ġe-)bīdan, 6, 9, 112.2, 134
biddan, 9, 112.2, 116, 134
bindan, 6, 91
binnan, 214
bītan, 112.2, 134
blanden-feax, 137
blind, 63
blīþe, 73
blīþe-mōd, 137
blōd, 136
blōdiġ, 136
bōc, 58
boga, 9
-bora, 136
brād, LV
brecan, 94 f.n. 1
breġdan, 93, 95, 99, 102
brenġan, 122, 123.2
bringan, 123.2, 133.5
brōþor, 60, 106
brūcan, 93
brȳd, 49
būan, 134
bufan, 214
būtan, būton, 168, 179.5, 214
bycgan, 122, 123.3
bysiġ, 26

163

ćeaster, 50
ćeorfan, 100 n.
ćēosan, 107 and f.n., 112.2, 136
ćild, LV, 34
ćild-isć, 138
cnapa, 9
cnāwan, 104
cniht, 26
cnyssan, 116
comitatus, 236 ff.
cræft, 26
crēopan, 91, 92, 93
cuman, 103.2, 109
cunnan, 130, 206, 207, 209
cwellan, 122, 123.1
cwēn, 49
cweþan, 156
cwic, 81
cyning, 41
cynn, 106
cyre, 107 f.n., 136
cȳþan, 156

dǣd, LV, 49
dæġ, 36
dēma, 136
dēman, LV, 116
Dene, 46
dēor, 4
dohtor, 60
dōm, LV, 35, 136
-dōm and its compounds, 13, 138
dōm-ġeorn, 137
dōn, 128
dragan, 9
drǣdan, 104
drīfan, 3, 113.2
drinc, 136
drincan, 95, 101, 102, 136
*dūgan, 130
*durran, 130, 205.1
duru, 61, 62

ēac, 184.1, 214
ēage, 24
eahta, 82
eahtoþa, 82
eald, 3, 75
eallunga, 135
eall-wealda, 137
ecg, LV, 9
eft-sīþ, 137
eġes-full, 137
-els and its compounds, 13

-en and its compounds, 138
-end and its compounds, 13, 138
ende, 45
engel, 26, 41, 42, 44, 50, 68
Engla-lond, 137
eoh, 38
eorl, 4, 7
-ere and its compounds, 13, 138
etan, 109
-ettan and its compounds, 138
ēþel, 26

fāh, 72
faran, 91, 93
fæder, 60, 106
færeld, 41
fæt, LV, 36
ġefēa, 25
feallan, 104, 116 f.n., 133.5
feld, 61, 62
feoh, 38, 39, 79
feoh-lēas, 138
feohtan, 95, 98, 102
fēolan, 133.2
fēond, 59
feorr, 135
fēorþa, 82
fēower, 82
fēowertiġ, 86
fīf, 82
fīfta, 82
fīftiġ, 86
findan, 109
fisc, 106
fisc-ere, 138
flōd-weġ, 137
flot-weġ, 137
folc-lagu, 137
fōn, 103.5, 107, 108
for, 158, 169-170, 171, 176, 184.5, 214
for- and its compounds, 6, 138
for-bēodan, 136
ford, 61, 62
fore-set-nes, 137
forma, 82
forþ-ġeorn, 137
fōt, LV, 58
fram, 214
fremman, 116 (paradigm), 117, 119, 125, 126, 133.5
frēond, 59
frēond-scipe, 138
frēosan, LV
freoðuwebbe, 239

Fres-lond, 137
fugol, 4, 44
-full, 138
furþum, 168 s.v. þā, 184.2
fyllan, 116

gadrian, 124
gān, 128
gāt, 58
ġe, 184.1
ġe- and its compounds, 6, 138
ġē, see þū
ġearo, -u, 71
ġeond, 137, 214
ġeong, 75
ġiefan, LV, 103.1
ġiefu, 12, 34, 47 (paradigm), 61, 62
  66 n. 2, 67, 68, 79
ġieldan, 95, 100, 102
ġiellan, LV
ġif, 151, 152 n., 160, 168, 179
ġit, see þū
glæd, 70, 74
gnæt, 9
god, 35
god-spel, 137
gōd, 65, 67, 71, 76
gōs, 58
guma, 3

habban, 126, 187.1, 200
-hād and its compounds, 13, 138
hāl, 136
hāliġ, LV, 68
hām, LV
hand, 34, 48, 61, 62
hār, LV
hāt, LV
hātan, 89, 93, 186.1, 187.1, 202
hǣlan, 136
hǣleþ, 44
hē, hit, hēo, 18, 27, 162.2 and n., 163.2,
  193.6
hēafod, 9, 41, 42, 44, 50, 68
hēah, 72, 75
hēah-clif, 41, 137
hēah-ġerēfa, 137
hēah-þungen, 137
healdan, 8, 93
heall, 8
hebban, 116
hell-waran, 137
helpan, 95, 99, 102
Hengest, 41
hēo, see hē

hēr, 152 n
here, 45, 46
hīe, 81
hīeran, 3, 116, 117, 119, 125
hit, 148, 154, 187.2. See also hē
hlāf, LV, 9
hleahtor-smiþ, 137
hof, 35
hōn, 103.5, 107, 108
hran-rād, 137
hraþe, 135
hrædlīċe, 135
hrēow-ċeariġ, 137
hrēowiġ-mōd, 137
hringan, 133.5
hron-fisc, 41
hū, 158
hūru, 184.2
hūs, LV, 35
hwā, 20, 158, 164
hwanon, 158
hwæl-weġ, 137
hwǣr, 158, 164
hwæt, 20, 158, 187.2
hwæþer (þe), 160
hwæþere, hwæþre, 152 n., 184.2
hwelċ, 158
hwider, 158
hwīlum, 184.3
hwonne, 151, 158, 159 n. 2, 168, 174
hycgan, 126

iċ, wit, wē, 21, 162 n.
ielde, 46
ieldu, 51
iermþu, 51
-iġ and its compounds, 138
in, 214
-ing and its compounds, 13, 138
-ing, -ung and its compounds, 13, 138
innan, 214
inn-faru, 137
in(n)-gang, 41, 137
-isc, 138
īsern, 41

-lāc and its compounds, 13
lang, 75
lange, 135
lār, 34, 48 (paradigm), 49, 50, 58, 61,
  62, 67, 68
lār-hūs, 137
-lǣċan and its compounds, 138
lǣdan, 133.3
lǣtan, 104, 133.3

-lēas, 138
lēode, 46
lēof, 74
libban, 126
-lić and its compounds, 138
līf, LV
limpan, 27
-ling and its compounds, 13
lōcian, 124
lof, 236 ff.
lufian, 93, 124, 125, 132.1
lūs, 58
lȳt, 135
lȳtel, 76

magan, 130, 206, 207
man, 202
mann, 12, 58, 59
mearh, 39
mere-wēriġ, 137
mētan, 121
metod, 26, 41, 43
mićel, 26, 69, 76
mićle, 135
mid, 171, 174, 181, 214
miht, LV
mīn, 63
mis-, 138
mis-dǣd, 138
mīþan, 108
mōdor, 60
mōnaþ, 44
moniġ, 69
morgen, 6
*mōtan, 130, 206, 208
ġemunan, 130
mūs, 58

nā, 184.4
nāhwæðer, 184.4
nalles, nealles, 184.4
nama, 3, 22
nāðor, 184.4
nǣfre, 184.4
næs, 184.4
ne, 135, 144.1, 146, 175.1, 184.4, 185.2
nefne, nemne, nymþe, 168, 179.5
nerian, 116, 117, 119, 124, 125
-nes(s), -nis, -nys and its compounds,
   13, 138
nigon, 82
nigoþa, 82
niht-waco, 137
niman, 103.2, 109
nō, 184.4

norþ, 135
norþan, 135
nō ðȳ ǣr, 168
nū, LV, 152 n., 168, 176

of, 214
ofer, 137, 214
ofer- and its compounds, 6
ofer-mæġen, 138
ofermōd, 221
oft, 9, 135
on, 137, 214
-on, -an and its compounds, 138
ond, and, 139, 144, 145, 184.1
onda, 3
onġēan, 214
open, 136
openian, 136
or- and its compounds, 138
oþ, oð, 168, 171, 174, 214
ōþer, 63, 82, 83
oþþæt, 171, 174, 180
oþþe, 171, 174, 184.3

pæþ, 9

rǣdan, LV
-rǣden and its compounds, 13, 138
rǣran, 107 f.n.
reććan, 122
rīce, 45, 46
rīsan, 9, 107 f.n., 108

salu-pād, 137
sam . . . sam, 168, 178
sāwol, 50, 68
sǣ-weall, 6, 136
scēap, scēp, 3
scieppan, 103.1
scieran, 103.1
scīnan, 3, 93, 112.1
scip, LV, 9, 12, 34 (paradigm), 35, 36,
   41, 42, 43, 45, 48, 61, 66 n. 2, 67, 68
scip-rāp, 137
-scipe and its compounds, 13, 138
scōh, 37
scop, 137
scrīþan, 108
scrūd, 136
scrȳdan, 136
*sculan, 130, 206, 210
se, 15, 16, 162-164, 193
searo, -u, 40
Seaxe, 46
sēćan, 122, 123

secgan, 126
seġl-rād, 137
sellan, 4, 122
sendan, 116, 121
seofon, 82
seofoþa, 82
sēon, 3, 103.3, 107, 114
se þe, 162.4, 163 n. 1
soþo, 162.4, 163 n. 1
se'þe, 163.1, 163 n. 1 and 2, 187.3 (d)
siex, 82
siexta, 82
sittan, 9
siþþan, 152 n., 168, 174
slēan, 103.3, 108 and f.n.
snīþan, 107
spannan, 133.5
specan, 109
spere, 45
stān, 12, 27, 33 (paradigm), 34, 35, 36,
    39, 40, 41, 42, 43, 45, 58, 59, 62,
    66 n. 2
standan, 94 f.n. 3
stede, 45, 46
stelan, 134
storm-sæ, 137
strang, 75
streċċan, 122
streġdan, 95
sum, 193.4
-sum and its compounds, 138
sundor-halgan, 137
sunne, 23
sunu, 34, 48, 61
swā, 152 n., 168, 177, 184.3, 186.2
swā hraþe swā, 168
swā hwā swā, 164
swā hwǣr swā, 164, 168, 173
swā hwæt swā, 164
swā hwider swā, 173
swā lange swā, 168, 174
swan-rād, 137
swā oft swā, 168
(swā) sōna swā, 168
swā swā, 168, 177
swā . . . swā (swā), 168, 177
swā þæt, 167, 168, 175
swā . . . þæt, 167, 168, 175
swā þēah, 184.2
swā wīde swā, 168
swelċe, swilċe, swylċe, 168, 177
swelċe . . . swā, 177
sweord-bora, 136
sweostor, 12, 60

swerian, 116, 132.1
swimman, 116 f.n., 133.5
swīþe, 135
synn, LV
synn-full, 137, 138
tǣċan, 121.4, 122 f.n.
tēon, 103.4
tēoþa, 82
tīen, 82
til, 65, 66, 73
timbrian, 6, 124
tō, 158, 167, 168 n. 2 s.v. þæs . . . þæt,
    171, 175, 205.2, 214
ō- and its compounds, 138
tōġēanes, 214
tōþ, 58, 106
tredan, 93, 109
trēow, 9
tungol-cræft, 137
twēġen, 82, 84
twēntiġ, 86
þā, 81, 151, 163.1, 168, 169, 174, 182
þā . . . ærest, 168
þā . . . furþum, 168
þā hwīle þe, 167, 168, 174
þanon, 152 n., 168, 173
þās, 81
þā þā, 151
þæs . . . þæt, 167, 168, 175
þæs (þe), 163.5, 167, 168, 174, 176, 177
þæs . . . þo, 168
þǣr, 9, 152, 168, 173, 179
þæt, 148, 154, 155, 156, 163.5, 167,
    168 and n. 1 s.v. þæs . . . þæt, 175,
    180, 187.2
þæt/þe variations, 168 n. 1 s.v.
    þæs . . . þæt, 169
þætte, 155, 175
þe, 151, 162-164, 167, 168 and n. 1
    s.v. þæs . . . þæt, 169, 176, 184.3
þēah . . . eall, 178
þēahhwæþere, 184.2
þēah (þe), þēh (þe), 152 n., 168, 178,
    184.2
þenċan, 122, 123.2
þenden, 168, 174
þerscan, 95
þes, 15, 17, 193
þe/þæt variations, 168 n. 1 s.v.
    þæs . . . þæt, 169
þider (þe), 150, 151, 152, 168, 173
þīn, 63
ġeþingan, 133.5

-þ(o), -þ(u) *and its compounds*, 13, 138
þon mā þe, 168, 177
þonne, 151, 152 *and* n., 168, 174, 177, 179
þridda, 82
þrīe, 82, 85
Þrī-nes, 137
þrītiġ, 86
þū, ġit, ġē, 21, 162 n.
þurfan, 130, 205.1
þurh, 181, 214
þȳ lǣs (þe), 167, 168, 175
þynċan, 122, 123.2
þȳ (þe), 168, 176
þȳ ... þȳ, 167, 177

un- *and its compounds*, 138
under, 214
-ung *and its compounds*, 13, 138
unnan, 130
ūt-gān, 138
uton, 205.1

wan- *and its compounds*, 138
wæter, 44
wē, *see* iċ
weald, 61, 62
wealh, 39
weallan, 133.5
weaxan, 104
wefan, 109
wel, 135
wel-þungen, 137
wel-willende, 137
weorpan, 95, 98, 102

weorþan, 187.1, 202-203
wēpan, 104.1, 116, 133.1
wer, 26, 35
werod, 41, 43, 44
wesan, 187.1, 202-203
wīd-cūþ, 137
wīd-sǣ, 137
wīf, 12, 35
wīfmann, 12
willan, 129 (*paradigm*), 185.2, 205.1. 206, 210, 211
wīn-druncen, 137
wine, 45, 46
winnan, 116 f.n., 133.5
wīs-dōm, 138
wīs-hycgende, 137
wit, *see* iċ
witan, 130
wīte, 45
wiþ, 171, 179.6, 214
word, 34 (*paradigm*), 35, 40, 41, 43, 48, 61, 67, 68
wrēon, 103.3, 107
ġewrit, 41
wrītan, 9
wudu, 61
wulf-hēafod-trēo, 137
wyrċan, 122, 123.3
wyrd, 236

yfel, 26, 69, 76
yfle, 135
ymb- *and its compounds*, 138
ymb(e), 214
ȳþ-hengest, 137